"A 'Must Read' for Everyone..."

In the 1300s one of the greatest horrors of human suffering was the Bubonic Plague, or "Black Death," which took the lives of 30 million people — approximately 25 percent of Europe. The Surgeon General has said that AIDS will make the Black Death look like a Sunday school picnic.

△ △ △

Al Haffner has written a truly powerful challenge to sexual attitudes today. His findings on sex as addiction, the seductiveness of pornography, the threat of AIDS, the emotional holocaust of abortion, are "must read" for everyone, but especially singles.

Josh McDowell
Bestselling Author and Speaker

The awakening of the individual conscience is accomplished by this vital and most relevant work of Al Haffner. All who read this scholarly, yet practical approach to America's greatest dilemma will be challenged to purity and will become knowledgeable as to the "high cost of free love."

D. B. Reeves, Pastor
Past president, Pastors' Conference
Southern Baptist Convention, California

The High Cost of Free Love

Al Haffner

Here's Life Publishers

First printing, February 1989
Second printing, June 1989

Published by
HERE'S LIFE PUBLISHERS, INC.
P. O. Box 1576
San Bernardino, CA 92402

Library of Congress Cataloging-in-Publication Data

Haffner, Al.
   The high cost of free love.
   Includes bibliographical references.
   1. Sexual ethics.   2. Sex (Psychology).   3. Sex—Religious aspects—
Christianity.   4. Sex customs.   I. Title.
HQ31.H225   1989   306.7   88-32038
ISBN 0-89840-244-1

Unless otherwise indicated, Scripture quotations are from *The New American Standard Bible,* © The Lockman Foundation 1960, 1962, 1963, 1968, 1971, 1972, 1975, 1977.

Scripture quotations designated KJV are from the *King James Version.*

For More Information, Write:
L.I.F.E.—P.O. Box A399, Sydney South 2000, Australia
Campus Crusade for Christ of Canada—Box 300, Vancouver, B.C., V6C 2X3, Canada
Campus Crusade for Christ—Pearl Assurance House, 4 Temple Row, Birmingham, B2 5HG, England
Lay Institute for Evangelism—P.O. Box 8786, Auckland 3, New Zealand
Campus Crusade for Christ—P.O. Box 240, Colombo Court Post Office, Singapore 9117
Great Commission Movement of Nigeria—P.O. Box 500, Jos, Plateau State Nigeria, West Africa
Campus Crusade for Christ International—Arrowhead Springs, San Bernardino, CA 92414, U.S.A.

Contents

Dedication

To
Crosby, Bronson and Jonathon
May you learn from others' mistakes,
and become wise in life
by being wise in the truth
of God.

Acknowledgments

There are two women
who deserve particular recognition
for their contributions to this work.

The first is Ingrid Bengis,
author of a book I quote a number of times:
Combat in the Erogenous Zone.
Her lucid insights and ruthless honesty into the human,
particularly female, condition in the arena of love and sex
were dramatically important to my own thinking.
I thank her for her striking candor
and salute her in her pursuit of truth.

The second woman is Mar'Sue,
who made the time possible for me to
complete the formulation of this work,
and who constantly encouraged me and cheered me on
throughout the process.
I am honored to be able to call her my wife.

A Personal Word From the Author

"Do you want to?" she asked. "Have you done it before?"

"Sure," I lied. We were sitting in the back seat of a borrowed car on a dark Saturday night. We had already been there for some time.

"Then let's hurry—I promised my mom I'd be home before midnight," she said as she took off the rest of her clothes.

We were both fifteen years old.

When it was over, I got out of the car and walked to the edge of the mountain cliff. I looked up into the clear night at the millions of stars, and had no idea what had just begun in my life.

This book is about power, the power of sex to make the things we value the most—love, relationships, and life—crumble in our hands.

On that simple yet dramatic night began the things I talk about in *The High Cost of Free Love:* addiction, patterning, the bonding—and the tearing when something precious is over . . .

I gave my life to Jesus Christ years later and things smoothed out considerably. I married a terrific woman, we had some terrific kids, and all would have been fine, except . .

Only the married can know the times of unbearable, unbelievable pressure that can come upon the marriage union. When it all crashed in on us, we snapped in different ways. Why? Because she was a virgin before we were married; I wasn't.

After the separation, I buried my pain in multiple relationships. I had never used drugs or alcohol as a teen or college student, so I didn't turn to those—sex was the drug I chose to dull the cutting edge of my anguish. And in my wife's mind, probably, my involvements precluded any possibility of reconciliation.

All this caused me to look more closely at the role sex was designed to play in interpersonal relationships, and I discovered how its power turns on us when we use it outside its intended context. *The High Cost of Free Love* is the result of that deep desire to know.

I will not presume
to speak of anything
except what Christ
has accomplished
through me.

Romans 15:18

Introduction

The sexual revolution has come to full bloom. Its roots in the '60s, its stalk and branches spreading and reaching to the limits in the '70s, the bud has now blossomed in the '80s. What once was hushed has become commonplace; what once was condemned as immoral is now accepted as normal. The idyllic flower of sexual freedom waves proudly like a banner throughout the western world as if it were some self-evident truth heretofore held unnaturally at bay.

A closer look, however, reveals something quite different. What appears to be the natural beauty of personal expression is actually an empty façade of cultural concession. The flower of peace and love that symbolized the sexual revolution of unrestrained licentiousness is actually a garish tattoo stitched onto pink flesh. Its bloom is and always has been artificial, but now, in its third decade, it oozes blood and pus. Those who have bought its lie are hollow and lonely, and even dying. That flower is just as dead as the day it was cut into that flesh.

Confusion abounds over sexual need, sexual freedom, and sexual consequences. There is the fantasy of free sex, which is proclaimed both brazenly and subtly on television, in films, and in the general culture. In contrast there is the acerbic reality, which is found on nightly news programs, in medical files, and within the shattered chambers of the broken hearted. Revealed are the sobering and painful consequences to "free" love. Is it possible for these two opposite factions to continue to coexist?

In an age of pluralistic ideologies, is it possible to say something about this subject which is not only ultimately true, but also is consistent philosophically, physiologically, and humanly? For what it is worth, such is the aim of this work.

Every position needs a polemic. This is a polemic for sexual abstinance for singles. It is a story etched in blood as both the wounded and the victorious stumble back from the battle of pain and temptation. These truths have been hammered out on the front lines of the war, yet they are the very weapons that can rebuild an exciting life of strength and purity which can be particularly satisfying. These thirteen truths beat with identical life; they are not just thirteen cold stones lined up in a row.

I believe you are in for an adventure. Life is an adventure, learning is an adventure, and learning to live can be the most profitable adventure of all. Benjamin Franklin said, "Experience teaches a costly school, but a fool will learn in no other." That school need not be yours, however. You can learn the high cost of free love before you have to pay the price yourself.

1

Psychology of the Heart

"I always thought of myself as a good kid with decent morals. I just wanted freedom and tried to achieve what I thought would be maximum pleasure.

"I became painfully disappointed when I found guilt instead of freedom, pain instead of love, suffering instead of pleasure, and distance instead of closeness."

A teenager.[1]

Sheila was sitting opposite me at the Student Union Restaurant on the Houston University campus. She had dreamy, caramel skin and big green eyes—the *Vogue* ideal. Suddenly, startlingly, she tore off the crust covering her inner thoughts and said, "I cannot feel. I don't know if I'm in love, or if I'll ever be in love. I don't think I would recognize it if I were. I just am . . . numb."

Sheila was currently living with her boyfriend, whom she seemed to care little for. She was at a burnout stage in relating to the opposite sex, with little idea of where to turn next, and her trail of intimacies had left her little in touch with herself. Her deadened state was setting her up for an encounter with some mystical Eastern guru, or some off-the-wall cultic barnstormer, or a fling with lesbianism. Sheila's plight is not uncommon.

"Love is in the air," the song says, yet that statement barely hints at the cauldron of sensuality that envelops our culture. Love and sex rhythmically beat through all of us and we swirl in the vibrations of the heated tempo. But little is said of the down side of intimacy, the aftermath, the wreckage. Sheila's smashed heart is an example of the flotsam found after the storm of passion has come and gone.

Some people are aware that outright hedonism is bad for the character. Yet even that evaluation is rendered dubious when proponents of "free love," like sex therapist Dr. Ruth Westheimer, traverse the campuses of America with a "sex for all and all for sex" philosophy. They enliven age-old immorality with humor and piquant justification. The hard truth, however, is that the emotional and psychological scars from busted relationships are in some ways worse than the flagrancy of the promiscuity. But this fact is little recognized in our culture if actions are any indication. For instance, according to the National Center for Health Statistics, based on a 1982 survey of 7,069 women, fully 80% had intercourse before marriage. Mirra Komarovsky, in her study, "Women in College: Shaping New Feminine Identities," points out that there is approval of sex within friendship and commitment. Expresses one coed from the study:

> It is generally assumed that women at this college will have some sexual experiences in their four years here. Ideally, what is desired is a relationship based on friendship and love, though not necessarily involving commitment to marriage. One-night stands, and sleeping around are dis–approved of.[2]

Another 20–year–old from the University of Miami, Florida, said similarly, "Whether or not you're a virgin doesn't matter, as long as you don't sleep around. If you have one boyfriend, everyone considers you a good girl."[3]

What Statistics Say

Professors D. Sherwin and Sherry Corbett, sociologists at Miami University, Oxford, Ohio, did a longitudinal study that spanned 21 years and involved 3,000 students. Their findings corroborate the above: Virginity among college women dropped from 75 percent in 1963 to an all-time low of 38 percent in 1978; currently it is at 43 percent. The upturn, according to the researchers, is because girls during the '70s were imitating traditionally carefree masculine attitudes toward premarital sex. Virginity among male students, conversely, has shown a steady downward trend from 1963, when it was 40 percent, to 34 percent in 1978, to its current low of 28 percent.[4]

These college figures are reflected in the general populace as well. A Gallup Poll of teenagers 13-18, taken in 1981, states that

62 percent of non-church-going youth and 52 percent of church-attending youths did not think premarital sex to be wrong.

The slant of the questions in these surveys deals with the morality, or right versus wrong, of premarital sex. And it is a short hop from saying it is not morally wrong to saying it is okay. After all, if it is not morally wrong, then it is not wrong at all, right? Wrong. Morals aside, premarital sex is damaging and costly in four areas: psychologically, emotionally, physically, and spiritually.

Psychic and Emotional Realities

In the arena of sex, there are psychic and emotional realities that go beyond exhilaration and the fleeting sensation of sexual ecstacy. These subliminal factors are plugged into the sex organs. There is no sexual encounter without their interplay. In marriage, these factors serve as a constructive, cementing role binding two people together. It is the all–important mortar that binds all the other factors of the relationship. Outside of marriage these same factors are the fires that consume, leaving the soul a barren husk, charred and scarred. As the leaving of each intimate relationship tears like the uprooting of a tree, we are more on guard, more sealed off from inner giving, from the deep letting go that is so refreshing in the unsoiled state. Such was Sheila's plight.

Is this religious hype? Just more rain–on–my–parade boo-hooing from the cosmic killjoy crowd? Too many nonreligious writers and researchers are making the same observations and drawing the same conclusions. Says Jess Lair of *I Ain't Much, Baby, but I'm All I've Got* fame:

> When I started teaching in college, I saw that quite a few of my students would have sex with each other, when what they really needed was closeness and wholeness. But there wasn't one in a hundred who could admit to their honest feelings about themselves and the other person. It seemed like everyone was doing the wrong thing to the wrong person for the wrong reason. I just shook my head at all the madness, and thought if I didn't laugh, I'd cry.[5]

The Death of Intimacy

Sound melodramatic? Those who deal daily with fractured lives after the demise of intimacy think not. Second only to auto accidents, suicide is the most common cause of death among college students. To help deal with the crises, many colleges now have set up peer counseling centers with 24–hour hotlines manned by volunteers. The overseers of these suicide hotlines, of which the one at Stanford, California, is typical, say that the predominant problem students face is the ending of a relationship. For most it is the first time they have really gotten involved deeply, and the sense of loss and emptiness can seem unbearable.

One who escaped the suicide trap to tell about it spoke of her relationship with a fellow medical student 15 years earlier:

> It was after we had spent the day in bed making love and singing Beatles' songs that he told me, "This is it."
>
> I didn't know what he was talking about so I asked, "This is what?"
>
> He replied, "I'm not going to see you any more."

This woman recalled that her emotional pain was so bad that she said, "I thought I'd die. It took me four years to get over that humiliation, and even now as I speak, I still want to knock his teeth out."[6] Her bitterness is indicative of the painfully long and rocky road to recovery from a sexually intimate union.

This same study states that preoccupation with one's ex-lover and plaguing thoughts of revenge were reported by well over half the respondents. Many referred to the lingering aftermath as "haunting."

Why are these negative repercussions of love rarely spoken of? There seems to be a conspiracy of silence, with the result that each individual believes himself to be encountering something unique, something uncommon to the rest of the human race. Many cite the media as the messenger of misrepresentation. Robin Norwood, family therapist, says of media romanticism:

> Television portrays seductive relationships as though they were reality, when they lack all the ingredients for stability or real emotional and caring intimacy. There is no trust, no security—just all this drama.[7]

Our society, often our friends, and certainly literature, television and films conspire like hidden vampires to suck the life's blood from our understanding. They prevent us from confronting the mournful backside of sexual intimacy. In the story we see the handsome, the beautiful, the charismatic walk away from the intensity of sexual encounter as from a refreshing shower.

James Bond and his feline fillies are the classic mode of this caricature of life. On television, which panders incessantly to our sexual appetite, 81 percent of all allusions to sexual intercourse occur between unmarried people.[8] In their carefree gaiety, the protagonists propound a lie: all the joys with none of the heart-rending, soul-shattering bitterness and pain. Who's kidding who?

We can quickly become cynical, seeing cupid as a culprit in disguise, a henchman bearing flowers thought to be for celebration, when in reality they are for the inevitable funeral.

Myths and Half-truths

As our insides disintegrate at the demise of an affair, we may become bewildered because we have been subsisting on a diet of myths and half-truths. When things don't go right, we assume that the problem is our weakness, not the empty beliefs we have been ingesting or the lifestyle we have been living. *Aren't we doing what everybody is doing?* we reason. *Aren't we saying what everybody is saying? Isn't everyone else coping okay?*

Perhaps not. We all have a different-sized ball of twine. Some just take longer to come unraveled. Let's look at some of the myths which so often hold sway over us:

1. Sex is purely a physical need, a physical activity, which is unrelated to the past, bears no ramifications into the future, and has no negative implications for the present.

2. Others aren't going through what I am going through. They have it all together; I don't. Others don't experience pangs of self-doubt. They don't castigate themselves for their weaknesses and failings, and they aren't lonely. I am lonely and I am not okay, and sex is a viable vehicle for bracing up my faltering self-image.

3. It is possible to be sexually active with impunity, without a residual consequence. Since sex is just a physical craving, it does not touch my inner self.

4. Our immediate choices do not bear results into the future. Life is a continuum of unrelated spots, not a cause/effect flow of actions and reactions that impugn our naked reality with irrevocable consequences.

5. When things go wrong, as when relationships fall apart, or we cannot seem to get into a meaningful relationship without it self–destructing, we blame our inability to cope, and not the practices of our lives. It is as if, when we eat sugar and get cavities, we blame the poor quality of our teeth rather than the sugar.

6. Society, culture, and my immediate environment are not

determining my decisions. I am making them independent of any extraneous influences.

The Nature of Women and Men

These myths perpetuate a fog in which it is difficult to see how sexual entanglements confound our lives. But because of the way sex operates—indeed, the way it was designed to operate—its devastating power reverberates throughout one's emotions, mind and spirit, and even the body. How this happens is dealt with from different angles and at different levels throughout this book. But first, a look at the nature of women and men. In the film, "The Breakfast Club," the leading lady was heard to say:

> It's a double-edged sword, isn't it?
> If you say you haven't, you're a prude;
>   if you say you have, you're a slut.
> If you did, you wish you hadn't;
>   if you didn't, you wish you had.

The thoughts and ideas we are dealing with pertain to both men and women. Nevertheless, in some ways the impact of sexual license hits women hardest. Before getting into the rationale behind this, however, a brief review of the perspective on women in Christianity might be helpful.

That the feminist movement views Christianity as a perpetrator of historical prejudices and archaic injustices is indeed an unfortunate misunderstanding. Says Ruth Simpson, author of *From the Closet to the Courts:*

> The church is a major oppressor of all women . . . There is a growing awareness among women in the feminist movement that the church has been a key force in maintaining the laws responsible for the oppressed condition of women.[9]

Jesus' Approach

Granted, Hebrew culture per se, out of which Christianity sprang, was essentially no different from its pagan neighbors in assigning women a place somewhere down around cattle and furniture, though the Scriptures of Old Testament times are hardly supportive of that view. But Jesus Christ came on the scene as truly radical, much more so than we in current western culture can appreciate. Jesus unselfconsciously treated women as ordinary human beings. The most striking thing about the role of women in the life and teaching of Jesus is simply that they were there. The presence of women among the followers of Jesus, as attested throughout the gospels, and His serious teaching of them was without precedent.

In Matthew 12:50, Jesus said, "Whoever does the will of My Father who is in heaven, he is My brother and My sister and My mother." This "whoever" set Him apart from other rabbis, for he was including women as equals among all His disciples.

The thought of that day was not only that women were inferior to men in every way, but also that they were incapable of learning religious truth. Those who attempted to teach women were reproved severely, and it was believed that, if women were taught theological truth, they would become irresponsible to their homes and families, and would even become infertile.[10] The *Talmud,* the traditional writings of Jewish rabbis, stated: "It would be better if the words of the law were burned than that they should be given to a woman."

Jesus Christ, a revolutionary in this realm as well, confronted and defied these untruthful traditions at every turn. In John 4, His disciples were shocked, for instance, that He would actually talk with a woman in public, let alone teach her. The fact that she was a contaminated Samaritan, and wholly immoral, compounded their incredulousness. Yet Jesus spoke to her of some of the most profound theological truths recorded anywhere in the New Testament, with no condescension.

Luke 10:38-42 tells of Mary playing the role of disciple and sitting at Jesus' feet to hear Him teach, while her sister Martha banged away in the kitchen. Not only did Jesus commend Mary for her choice, but He also defended her, emphasizing, "[It] shall not be taken away from her." Dinner could wait.

Most significant, perhaps is the fact that Jesus chose women to be the first to observe and to herald the greatest event in human history, the resurrection. Is it any wonder, then, that women were first at the cradle and last at the cross? They had never known a man like this man. A prophet and teacher who did not nag at them, nor cheapen them with empty flattery. He had no ax to grind, no uneasy male dignity to defend. He was neither patronizing, nor condescending; no one would ever conclude from His teaching or parables that there was anything "funny" about women's nature.

From this brief background we can see that Jesus Christ, and by extension, both the Christian faith and God the Father, are positive on women. Woman's role as submissive to man's (to her husband predominantly) is not any more a condemnation of her as inferior than is Jesus' own self-proclaimed submission to His Father in heaven.

Satan's Attitude

Contrary to God's attitude toward women is Satan's attitude. Many are familiar with the results of the fall and the ensuing "curses" laid down by God. There is much talk of the enmity between the woman's seed (a reference to Jesus Christ in ultimate fulfillment) and Satan's seed in Genesis 3:15: "I will put enmity between you [Satan] and the woman, and between your seed and her seed; he shall bruise you on the head [an allusion to Christ wielding an ultimately fatal blow to Satan], and you shall bruise him on the heel [i.e., Satan will harass Jesus and, by extension, His people]." But little is said about the first part of the verse: "I will put enmity between you [Satan] and the woman!"

Although Satan desires the demise of all of us, his hatred of women is blistering and ferocious. Women having spent most of history as second-class citizens at best, their having been maligned, ripped off, raped, and in general treated unfairly and unjustly, are all testimony to this fact. And not surprisingly, women have the most to lose from premarital sex. From the trauma of emotional and psychological scars and the deadness of a hardened heart to unwanted pregnancy, the stigma of having an incurable disease, and the horror of having had an abortion . . . all of it is worse for the woman. And Satan conspires moment by moment so as many women as possible will be blinded to reality and swept into the vortex.

Differing Views

The woman is by nature a relater and a responder, and was designed to participate in sex with her whole being. For her, sex is an aspect of that relating on all levels, and it impacts all areas of her life. If her first sexual experience is within a committed, contractual, life-long love affair, her need for love and security is met and her potential for sexual fulfillment and psychological wholeness can be fully realized.

The man functions quite differently, and social anthropologist Dr. David Givens highlights this difference in his description of the local bar scene:

The crowd arrived to compete for standing room in which to see and be seen. I found myself thinking how different this courting scene must appear to women than it does to men. Viewed through feminine eyes, the Casual Zone is inhabited by people with whom to evolve emotional ties; through masculine eyes, it seems populated with bodies, faces, and figures, with whom to "have sex" first, and a relationship if it comes to that, second. These could be two species mingling in this crowd.[11]

Women and Sex

Dr. Givens goes on to note, particularly of women: "Casual affairs so tax a person's energy and self-esteem that few [women] pursue recreational sex for long periods of time. They lose respect, both for themselves and for their partners."

But this emotional pain is not usually experienced during the relationship. It comes at the end. Reality hits like a sledgehammer and she feels like an object; she doesn't feel known for *who* she is, and the psyche is repulsed at such a realization. One disheartened victim of the "casual zone" compares the feeling to "dry ice tearing off a layer of skin."[12] Because for the woman sex is interwoven within the whole relationship, a "casual" experience can cut her deeper and harden her harder than is generally true for the man.

We can argue for equal pay, equal working conditions, equal vote, equality before God, and dozens of other ways women are equal to men, but somewhere the distinction between equality and sameness has been blurred. Increasingly, women are failing to realize they have a lot more to lose than their dignity when they jump into the sack with some joker who claims he loves them. The wisdom of experience speaks from the other side through the gritted teeth of grief:

> None of my friends and none of their friends, no matter how many interests or commitments they have to the world of action and ideas, are capable of sailing off into the airy brightness of a concluded love affair. Certainly I am not. Inevitably there are consequences both internal and external. If bodies are being killed all over the world because of politics rather than love, spirits are being smashed right next door, in apartment houses and shacks and on the street because of love.[13]

Men and Sex

As different as men and women are, the men do not escape unscathed from the consequences of exercising their sexuality within dating. It can seem that they do, because it is said that a woman "gives sex," whereas a man "scores." The idea of loss does not normally attach itself to the man. Of course, he can be hurt by the fallout of a decimated affair, but the spiritual parameters of intimacy are where the cuts run deepest for him.

In Ephesians 5:25 men are admonished to "love your wives, just as Christ also loved the church." Although the how and wherefore of this command is difficult to grasp, believing that one can be sexually active, eating the fruit of another's vineyard, yet at some future point enter into a divinely ordained marriage and fulfill this great admonition without a slip, slights both reason and reality. In the course of courting, the man plays the dating game, taking and taking. When he finally commits, he discovers he doesn't have what it takes to go the distance for real love. His inner strength has been spent. The growing divorce rate, as it parallels the increasing sexual freedom of our culture, testifies to this.

The simple yet crushing truth is that a man can lose his capacity to love purely, wholly, and selflessly. That which the woman needs the most—to be loved, deeply and singularly—he cannot do. How and why this happens is part of the mystery of sex. Suffice it to say that to lose the ability to love and then miss this noble calling is indeed a high price to pay for transient pleasure. In the words of the poet Abrahams:

> Some men died by shrapnel,
> Some men went down in flames,
> But most men perished inch by inch,
> Playing little games.
> "The Night They Burned Shang Hi"

Bonding

There is a phenomenon in music in which a certain note, played on a brass instrument at a certain volume, brings forth not only its own sound, but also a harmonic. It is almost an illusion, but it is there. I knew a trombonist who could play a note, hum the third at the same time, and the harmonic fifth would sound also, as if by magic.

In sex there is a similar harmonic effect. The dynamics of the physical communion produce a transcendental oneness, a floating, mingling union with the rushing current of the passion. The pleasure transpires on one plane while on another this sense of euphoria floats the mind and emotions in a warm hue that bonds the two into one. That which was believed to be an end in itself becomes a doorway to a great beyond.

The power of sex is not in its ability to thrill but in its ability to bond. The bonding power lasts, and that is the power that wreaks such devastation when used out of context. God purposed that, in marriage, the two people are to be bonded forever through the sexual union. To use that bonding power outside the intended life-long state is like trying to empower a car with a jet engine from a 747. The car, the street, the surrounding houses, and the people involved all get chewed up in the process. Nothing wrong with jet engines and nothing wrong with cars; the two just were not designed for each other. Likewise, nothing wrong with sex and nothing wrong with dating. But put sex into dating and you get flying shrapnel.

In addition to the bonding power of all sexual relationships, the first encounter creates its own set of dynamics. Testimonies indicate that it is not just one among many, but that it stands apart. Sally's words typify the experience of many women:

> I remember the time, the day, the place, and what I as wearing. I remember what he said, what he did, and what I felt. I have probably forgotten most of the days of the last eleven years since then, but I'll never forget that moment. I was sixteen; he was much older. I was desperately in love with him at the time, though because of our age differences he didn't come around much. As for the experience itself, I was pretty much disappointed—no, I was very disappointed. The relationship went on after that night, but it sort of faded in and out.

> What amazed me was the impact that that event, and therefore he, had on me. By the time I was out of high school I had slept with maybe fifteen or so guys, but often when I would wake up in the morning he would be the one on my mind.

> Even years later when I was halfway across the country going to college I would look up from a bench in the Quad or in the cafeteria with the sure sense that he was coming; he was going to appear any minute, walking toward me. Not that I missed him as a person. I was not still in love with him. But there was just this sense, this anticipation. Then it would pass, and I could feel a dull thud in my guts, and even though I could not explain it, I knew that an important part of me was lost forever.

Patterning

Sexual intimacy can be destructive because throughout an intimate relationship an identity is woven as two blend into one.

Then it ends. The fabric of the unity is ripped apart, and the myth of idyllic love floats off into oblivion. When this happens repeatedly, patterning begins to take place. The forming of patterns is almost unavoidable because actions and choices are not isolated in some time warp, but grow like small seeds dropped into the ground. Knowing where actions will lead is like looking at a road map to see where a turn in the road will take you. Patterns, like roads, take you only one direction.

Through sexual involvement one becomes accustomed to relating sexually. One looks to the balm of sex to soothe the fractured innards as the pursuit for the "right" person continues. In his article, "Love in the Casual Zone," David Givens reports on his interview with one swinger: "Jane uses sex as a physical trial-by-sex way of testing a partner's potential compatablity. The problem is, no one passes. She's had nine partners in the last three months."[14] Nevertheless, he reports, Jane is looking for someone "really right." The heat, the passion, the deep satisfaction of sexual fulfillment is hoped to be rounded out with this new relationship. Not being sexual is rarely considered; who can go backward in any aspect of life, much less this aspect? Compared with the zing of sex, a celibate relationship can seem flat and two dimensional, like melted vanilla ice cream.

Addiction

According to Dr. John Money, professor of medical psychology at John Hopkins University Medical School, "The idea that sex is as addicting as drugs is relatively new to science."[15] The fact that sex has an addictive hook is certainly not new, however, to the folks in the fast lane. Like any addiction, it evolves in us slowly. By comparison, David Crosby, of the musical group "Crosby, Stills, and Nash," commented after a series of arrests for drugs, "I didn't set out twenty years ago to be addicted to cocaine. Nobody wants to be a drug addict; it just sort of crept up on me." Sexual addiction, like drug addiction develops slowly, but can grip just as tightly.

It is no news that much of the pressure within dating is exerted by these two forces, patterning and addiction. This goes beyond just liking sex, or doing what comes naturally when possessed by "love" as Hollywood would have us believe. In a common scenario, the guy wants sex (regardless of whatever words may so glibly fall out of his mouth) because he got it from the last girl (patterning) and because he *needs* it . . . he is addicted. Many women have been brainwashed into believing that a guy needs it because he is male. This is not really accurate. He needs it because he is addicted. If he were a virgin, he would not "need" it, but now he needs it *because* this girl is not his first—she is somewhere down the line in his string of intimacies. She needs to realize that she is not responsible to meet the needs of his addiction, and the chance that this string of intimacies will stop here, with her, is remote.

This is why many parents are justifiably anxious if their daughter dates someone considerably older than herself. The chances are great that he is much more sexually experienced, and leading her down that path is no big deal to him. It is nothing new. Unfortunately, the parents don't share that concern with their daughter; they just bite their fingernails in private, and she is left to encounter the man's advances with no prior warning.

It should also be noted that women are as susceptible to sexual addiction as men, and some hassle guys the same way.

The "I'll-try-anything-once" Deception

Sexual lawlessness is one of the strongest addictions of all because it springs from our biological make-up and emotional need. Consequently, the approach, "I'll try anything once," is a deception that ignores the addictive aspect of sin, the addictive aspect of our own nature, and the addictive aspect of sex. We do not try something once, to turn from it necessarily just because we don't like it. There is not a person who thought his first cigarette tasted terrific, yet millions are addicted. They kept at it for one reason or another until it did taste good. People of junior high and high school age are particularly susceptible to the try-it-and-see philosophy, though none of us ever really outgrows it. The pressure, both subtle and overt, can be deafening.

Partying is a general go-along-for-the-ride sort of thing that quickly can become an endless, self-destructive, addicting death dance. The revelers talk and laugh and spill to the point where the alcohol plateaus with control and awareness. From then on it is downhill, saying things you do not mean, acting in bizarre ways, coupling with people you do not intend to. The psychological pain, the emotional remorse and grief, and the sense of uncleanness fills to overflowing in the wake. Then one returns at another time to re-enact the same inane gavotte. Seeing one's outer self behaving in a way unnatural to his inner self, yet imprisoned in a car named Desire heading nowhere, is one of life's greatest agonies. The pervasive philosophy of "I'll try anything once" *is* a deception—a mockingly cruel one.

Progression of the Addiction

Also, the more deviant the addiction, the faster and more securely it grips. The pimp will tell you that once he gets the young runaway to turn her first trick, she's hooked. The counselor will tell you that turning the homosexual to Christ and the "straight" life is next to impossible. The playboy will tell you that weaning oneself from the thrill of the hunt, the blast of the score, and the spice of variety is like switching from Snickers to broccoli. Sex is captivating, a convoluted maze from which there is no easy escape.

Part of the deception is our assuming that we do what we want, and we like what we do. This naiveté disregards the hook in addiction. Consider, for instance, the sad plight of Denny Mc-Lain, Detroit Tigers pitching star from 1963 to 1970, whose 31-6 record in 1968 makes him the last pitcher in major leagues to post a 30-win season. He was recently sentenced to 23 years in prison plus three concurrent 8-year terms for racketeering, extortion and conspiracy, plus 15 years for possession of cocaine with intent to sell. Said a tearful McLain, "I don't know how you get to where I am today from where I was 17 years ago."

The answer is painfully simple: one step at a time, starting with "I'll try anything once."

Jesus said, "Everyone who commits sin is the slave of sin."[16] There's the hook! People do things every day they wish they weren't doing. To try something once is a deception because every type of sin opens a door which cannot be shut, begins an appetite that grows into a hunger which cannot be satiated, begins a search for something which cannot be found, and initiates a yearning which cannot be fulfilled.

Many people who come to Christ after a wild past find dating and building meaningful courting relationships practically impossible. Their conditioning is too strong. It is foolish and naive, therefore, to think indulging one's appetite with Mr. Wonderful or Ms. Spectacular is justifiable because it is containable and controllable. It will prove to be neither, due to the addictive nature of sex. On to the next person . . . and the next . . . Like Gulliver, this person will find one thin thread of entrapment laid upon another until the accumulative effect is powerlessness and bondage.

Our desire to love and be loved gets us into this mess. We cannot seem to pay the high cost of celibacy, yet the down side of our erotic wanderings kills us inside. And because our sexuality is a biological part of normalcy, unlike drugs or addictive practices like shoplifting, it is difficult to single out and analyze. The mind, the will, and the emotions often function independently of each other, but sex functions differently. Part of that difference is that it brings all three of these aspects of personality into synchronization. A light switch in each room of a house turns on only the lights in that room. But all the rooms could be wired together so that one switch turned on every light in every room. Similarly, the act of sex plugs in the psyche, activating every filament and fiber of one's personality. In the heat of passion, the mind is numbed, blurring reason; the emotions are accelerated, and the will is whirled along at a boggling pace. All this holds out not only the prospect of extreme physical delight, but also exhilaration on every level.

All this meshing of mind, will, emotions and hormones can effectively camouflage the addictive nature of sex and confound our attempts to isolate our problems and understand ourselves.

Phases of Sexual Addiction

The narcotic element of sex is highlighted in Dr. Carnes's work, *The Sexual Addiction*,[17] in which he runs down the four phases that sexual addiction characteristically passes through:

1. Preoccupation; thinking a lot about sex.
2. Realization; serving the habit daily through masturbation, prostitutes, or sex with whomever.
3. Compulsion; the losing-control stage, the must-indulge phase.
4. Despair, guilt — lots of it — relieved only by re-entering the cycle at the starting point.

This study focuses on the extremity of the problem; nevertheless, we can draw some illuminating applications:

1. The addictive nature of sex is observable and definable.
2. Sexual addiction is perniciously progressive. One does not begin at some point of sexual involvement and remain

there — the whole involvement swirls into escalation.

3. Guilt and despair are real — not the imaginary invention of some stuffy, theocratic monk in a long black robe; guilt is a psychological — not just a spiritual — reality.

4. As with any other addiction, escape is elusive.

Self-sabotage

Everyone involved in sex is hooked, at least to some degree, simply because it is difficult to escape our hormones, our culture, and our conditioning. Combine this with the experiences shared in these pages, and a grim picture begins to emerge. We see nefarious psychological and emotional ramifications, destructive patterning and addiction, and paralyzing guilt taking shape. It hurts others and nullifies the ability to love. The gleeful tingle of sexual rah-rah is exposed as a sham masking a suffocating darkness. Ingrid Bengis finds herself at this point, having had her sense of self vanquished by her multiple affairs:

> Most of us are stuck, not knowing what the next step is, aware that we have stumbled upon a complexity we would never have dreamed existed. Having increased our expectations, we have also increased our disappointment; having taken the risks, we are feeling the consequences. . . . But spreading ourselves around, we discover that there is some thinness in our intimacies that leaves hollow spaces inside of us. Trying to be undemanding and independent, we discover that we are engaging in a new form of self-sabotage.[18]

This self-sabotage is what we have been looking at. The result is a hard-heartedness that is difficult to define but unmistakable when it is found. We become hard-hearted because our sensitive nature protects itself by walling out the physical sensations, depriving the inner self of being touched. Sexual intimacy becomes no more than the crass coupling of animals in heat, the impassioned thrashings of a double-backed monster. It may be exotic and ecstatic, but the core of the soul within becomes more and more untouched. We shut down emotionally and lose touch with ourselves, as Sheila did. Illicit sex may beckon like the cool, wet ocean with the promise of thirst-quenching refreshment, but in the ultimate analysis, like the salty ocean, it chokes and kills.

Concluding Thought

It may appear that the tone of this opening chapter is bleak.

That is the intent.

The lie that nonmarital sex is harmless and without consequences is so pervasive and widely accepted that we all need a hard slap to shake us loose from its somnolence. Our hope lies in the fact that exploring the gruesome darkness of the world of sexual lawlessness will arouse a repulsion that will move us toward the light.

▲▲▲

Here's What You Can Do

1. Look for, list, and then analyze the forces around you that influence your thinking and decisions.

2. What myth (if any) had you subscribed to in the past, and what is your assessment of it now?

3. Write out the things you believe that form a basis for your actions, desires and needs. All actions flow from thought; all thought comes from a philosophical base. For instance, what is more important to you, having a functioning relationship with a person, or with God? (NOTE: Your actions tell the answer, not your words.)

4. Identify and list separately: your needs, and your wants. Keep in mind Philippians 4:19: "My God shall supply all your needs according to His riches in glory in Christ Jesus."

5. Ask yourself this question about each need you have just listed. Write your answer for each one.

Is this need physical or emotional?

Attempting to meet an emotional need with a physical solution is the beginning of the problems of the heart.

2

Sex as Worship

Sex is more than the sharing of physical pleasure; it is more than bearing children, more than unifying two people, and more than bonding. It is different for humans from what it is for animals in that we do not go into heat, having sex only periodically with no thought of it otherwise. Our sexual drives or impulses are different from instinct. An animal cannot help acting the way it is programmed, by instinct, to act. Humans, conversely, have sex by choice, and can exercise control, using the mind and the will like rudders to direct the body.

This difference between the animals and us is so pronounced that we should not be surprised that God wants to say something to us through sex, to convey a critical truth. That truth is:

**There is a spiritual factor involved
in the sexual relationship.**

In addition to the psychological and emotional repercussions of sex, this dynamic parameter cascades throughout the chambers of our life.

God's Choice

God's relationship with His people is by choice; it is monogamous and contractual; it is a loving interchange; and it is forever. In a word, it has all the characteristics of a marriage.

Throughout the Old Testament, for instance, God refers to Himself as Israel's Husband, and to Israel as His wife. He says, "[I] swore to you and entered into a covenant with you so that you became Mine."[1] The Abrahamic Covenant was made when God initially chose a people, Abraham and his descendants, to be His alone.[2] This forever pact is reiterated in what is known as the Davidic Covenant in 2 Samuel 7.

The separating of a people unto God took a slightly different angle in the New Covenant, stated simply in Luke 22:17-20. God chose out a people from among others and, like a husband, committed Himself to them. When they, His wife, sin, it is depicted in sexually oriented language: "But you trusted in your beauty and played the harlot . . . and you poured out your harlotries on every passer-by who might be willing."[3] And: " 'You are a whore with many lovers, yet you turn to Me,' declares the Lord. 'Lift up your eyes . . . Where have you not been violated? . . . You have polluted a land with your harlotry and with your wickedness.' "[4]

The Spiritual Element

Spiritual unfaithfulness is expressed in sexual terminology for more than mere shock value or startling emphasis. One of the many purposes of sex is to make a statement about our relationship with God. Sexual purity reflects devotion to God—sexual promiscuity reflects spiritual wandering. This spiritual statement is made whether the participants in sexual activity are tuned in to the frequency or not. The judgmental results will come full force even if those who are involved are unaware of the spiritual implications. It may be the emptiness deep inside you or a consuming fire falling on Sodom and Gomorrah, but spiritual inconsistency spells dire consequences in the real world, *your* real world.

The spiritual is central to life regardless of who does or does not recognize it. Because it is central, it affects everything, and everything affects it. The extreme and flagrant immorality of the Sodomites was not just bad, as in the opposite of good, nor was it just breaking someone's arbitrary rules of morality. That behavior rocked the whole universe because sex is a statement of one's spiritual relationship with God.

Realizing that fact, we understand better David's cry of anguish to God in repenting of his adultery with Bathsheba, "Against Thee, Thee only I have sinned."[5]

We see that Joseph also was tuned in to this spiritual overtone of sexual misconduct. When tempted by his employer's wife to seduce her, he responded indignantly, "How then could I do this great evil, and sin against God?"[6]

Both David and Joseph understood the big picture. They understood the significant role they played because they were human, made in the image of God.[7] They understood the unique function of sex in the intricate point/counterpoint of the spiritual warfare being waged in and around us daily.

Conveying a Message

Of course, adultery is an offense also against the other person, that person's spouse, and even other members of the family. But comparing that offense with the offense against God is like comparing the heat of a candle with the heat of the sun. By extension, it impugns His name and His image among the powers and authorities in heavenly places.

Our inflated egos are repulsed at the idea of life being a big chessboard where the forces of light and darkness shift us around like pawns in some super–intellectual contest of wits. Nevertheless, one's life is played out in an arena far beyond the limits of time, space, and matter. We get a peek at this bigger game when we look at what Paul tells us about some of the new things that have come now that the church has been instituted: "The [multifaceted] wisdom of God might now be made known through the church to the rulers and the authorities in the heavenly places. This was in accordance with the eternal purpose which He carried out in Christ Jesus our Lord."[8] It is only a peek, but the impact is clear: There are rulers and authorities out there, and God has a point to prove to them. Man is His vehicle, chosen to convey the message of His purpose, which was established from eternity past and extends into eternity future.

Satan's Response

Satan understands the spiritual harmonic between sex and worship, and he uses it with an overt twist. He capitalizes on the "dark side" of this reality, warping sex and projecting into it his own style of worship as seen in the pagan religions of both the Old and New Testament. These religions employed temple prostitutes for sensory experience, which at that time was considered the highest form of religious expression. Today, group sex is the update in Satanic worship and occult facsimiles of ancient pagan religions. Not long ago, Paul Harvey reported that a number of junior high students at a gathering in Lompoc, California, were arrested for just such group sex in conjunction with Satan worship. In this fleshy, flip-side way, Satan mocks the spiritual reality.

Spiritual Unity

In the New Testament, Paul paints some graphic and incisive theological pictures which further clarify the aspect of sex as worship. In 1 Corinthians 6:16-17, using intricate reasoning, he contrasts oneness with God to oneness in a sexual union outside of marriage: "Do you not know that the one who joins himself to a harlot is one body with her? For He says, 'The two will become one flesh.' But the one who joins himself to the Lord is one spirit with Him."

This illicit sexual union being so sharply contrasted to the spiritual union graphically depicts the truth God wants us to see: One of the primary functions of sex is to illustrate the intended unity and identity with the God who created us because that oneness with Him is the essence of worship.

It is because the sexual is a spiritual issue that Paul's contrast makes sense. It is not possible to commit fornication with a woman and still be one with God. Sex is a spiritual issue!

The Body's Design

"The body," 1 Corinthians 6:13 points out, "is not for immorality, but for the Lord; and the Lord is for the body." The body cannot be for both, and it was not designed for the former. If one attempts to fit both the Lord and immorality into the body, he is trying to package a hurricane. Life will blow apart at the seams.

Recently Jim Bakker commented, as his ministry and empire lay in rubble all around him, "It's amazing how fifteen minutes can ruin your life."

Not just any fifteen minutes can do that, but fifteen minutes of immorality can because of its spiritual identity.

The body is literally the temple of the Holy Spirit, the spiritual worship place for God to dwell in. During Old Testament times, the Jewish Temple in Jerusalem was the holy place where God dwelt. The physical body of believers as the temple comprises a progressive update in God's program of worship. There were certain things you did in the Old Testament Temple and certain things you didn't do, and there are certain things you do with this temple of the body and certain things you don't. In that Temple one did not sit down, slay pigs on the altar, or copulate with prostitutes lest the Temple be profaned. Likewise, this temple, the body, is not to be profaned through immorality. Notice that what Paul says in verse 16 (of 1 Corinthians 6) about becoming one with a harlot is expanded into general immorality in verse 18.

The body is for worship; it is the place of worship—it is also the sacrifice for that worship. In the Old Testament economy, the worshipers sacrificed animals as their reasonable service, and the animal's shed blood foreshadowed the blood of Jesus Christ that would cleanse us wholly and forever.[9] Paul draws on this image in Romans 12:1: "Present your bodies a living and holy sacrifice, acceptable to God, which is your spiritual service of worship."

Sacrifice of the Body

Sacrificing my body to Him means relinquishing my rights to it. It means choosing with my body, not merely my words, to follow Jesus Christ as Lord. This is where the ax-head hits the tree: Does the walk match the talk? Paul says, "They profess to know God, but by their deeds they deny Him."[10] Your deeds, what you are doing with your body, are what is real in the spiritual realm. Talk means nothing.

Accepting eternal life from Him means surrendering my body to Him so He can take up residence in it. I do this by refusing to be conformed to the world's ways, as Paul goes on to say in Romans 12:2. Rather, my mind is to be changed into conformity to His value system. How do I bring about this change of mind? Paul expounds:

> Let us . . . lay aside the deeds of darkness and put on the armor of light. Let us behave properly as in the day, not in carousing and drunkenness, not in sexual promiscuity and sensuality, not in strife and jealousy. But put on the Lord Jesus Christ, and make no provision for the flesh in regards to its lusts (Romans 13:12-14).

Therefore, my spiritual service of worship is sacrificing my body to the exclusive dwelling of and use by God, by avoiding drunkenness, carousing, sexual indulgence, and anything else that would stir up the lust within me. Not exactly an easy assignment, nevertheless, one without equivocation. And, we might add, in light of chapter 1, an assignment designed to protect me from a lot of grief.

From God's perspective, the body is the worship site and the primary article of worship. And within sex, God has designed a built–in picture of man's identity with, relationship with, worship of, and conduit for God in his life. And Satan, desiring to deflect all worship from God, continually conspires to pollute the worship site, ravage the article of worship, and obliterate the picture of the God/man interrelatedness. How? By focusing our attention on self–fulfillment and on *sex for pleasure* — "Flesh for Fantasy," as Billy Idol croons.

Harlots and Virgins

Concerning the term *harlot* in 1 Corinthians 6, our cultural understanding of the word is usually confined to a woman who charges money for sex. Paul's reference here may well be intended in that direction since Corinth was a Roman port city well known for its pagan worship and temple prostitution. Certainly Paul wanted the Christians to understand clearly that visiting the temple prostitutes was not part of the program.

From the spiritual perspective which we have been examining, though, this is too narrow an understanding. More likely, using Corinth's religious prostitution as a comparative backdrop, Paul is saying that any fornication is tantamount to copulating with a prostitute and profaning God's temple, the body, the worship site. This interpretation is reinforced by the Scripture's definition of harlotry: A whore is a non–virgin.

This is a stunning acknowledgement in the context of today's culture.

Paul, the consummate Jew, may well have been speaking from this viewpoint, for he probably could quote Deuteronomy 22 from memory, in both Hebrew and Greek.

Deuteronomy 22:13–21 covers a situation in which a man is claiming that his new bride is not a virgin. The law says:

> If this charge is true, that the girl was not found a virgin, then they [the elders] shall bring out the girl to the doorway of her father's house, and the men of her city shall stone her to death because she has committed an act of folly in Israel, by playing the harlot in her father's house; thus you shall purge the evil from among you (verses 20,21).

She may have had only one previous lover, and she may have made love with him only once. Nevertheless, the fact seems inescapable that she was considered a whore because she was a non-virgin.

Monogamy Outside Marriage

One of the seemingly inexplicable puzzles many grapple with is why, or how, sex should play a different spiritual part in a monogamous love affair from what it does in marriage, which is also monogamous. Many believe the essential elements of both are identical, therefore the benefits and effects should be identical. The difference however, is that God designed marriage; man designed a live–in look–alike.

Sound like theoretical double talk? Consider this: "It is possible to analyze an apple and ascertain its chemical constituents; but all the chemists in the world cannot make an apple, nor anything that can substitute for it."[11] Neither can the world make any relationship do what marriage does, not even a monogamous love affair.

To our way of thinking, though, there is a vast separation between a monogamous lover and a street walker. Or, as the young coed in the previous chapter put it, between one who does it for love with her boyfriend and one who sleeps around. The biblical viewpoint, however, lumps all sexual activity outside of marriage into one heap. There may be variations of degree within all these social categories, but from a biblical perspective any type of deviation is unjustifiable because sex does make a spiritual statement. Inside marriage it is a melodious beauty of spiritual serenity; outside of marriage, even in a monogamous relationship, sex cries out a cacophony of spiritual chaos. And when that cacophony builds to a screaming pitch, look out! When indulging in immorality, sexual impurity, uncontrollable passion, illicit desires, or greed—all of which amount to idolatry since they are self–serving as opposed to God–serving—then, "on account of these things . . . the wrath of God will come."[12]

A Mystery

The parallel between sex and worship is stated in even stronger language in Ephesians 5. Paul speaks of the sexual union of husband and wife, then dramatically states that he is talking about our union with God. The shift is so sudden and shocking that it throws one into a quandary: "For this cause a man shall leave his father and mother, and shall cleave to his wife; and the two shall become one flesh. This mystery is great; but I am speaking with reference to Christ and the church" (Ephesians 5:31,32).

And it is to just this mystery that we now are addressing ourselves: spiritual oneness mirrored in the sexual encounter.

Comprehending the mystically spiritual aspect of sex, as we have seen, is what makes this passage meaningful and understandable.

The parallelism Scripture presents between the act of worship and the act of sex is consistent: the unity of God and man in the spiritual realm and the unity of a man and a woman in the physical realm.

Sex Within Marriage

In grasping this truth, we understand not only why God is so vehemently *against* sex outside the committed realm of marriage, but also why He is equally *for* it within marriage: It reflects the true intended union of God and man. Indeed, a marriage without sex is an anathema because it is a contradiction. By parallel it says that man and God are bound together in a relationship of commitment but with no interactional communion. This is nuts.

Just as Satan conspires to get singles sexually active in order to throw their spiritual life into a dark tailspin, so he conspires to build walls between marriage partners, blocking the sex and thereby blocking the flow of spiritual life. In Ephesians 5, Paul says he is speaking of the oneness of Christ and the church (i.e., people!) in the sexual union of man and wife. Therefore, if a man and his wife are not sexually united, spiritual ramifications will be felt.

Spiritual Death

We have seen that sex is a picture of worship that carries spiritual impact, but when it is reduced to a prosaic sport between consenting players for ego gratification and sensual pleasure, something more than some archaic religious edict has been violated. Not having sex is not just maintaining moral purity for the sake of self-righteousness, and having sex is not just chipping notches on the bed post to show how great a lover you are. Rather, sexual intercourse opens the way through an invisible, mystical veil into the spiritual realm. Within the covenental shroud of marriage, a spirit of bonding entwines the participants and tightens the joy and depth and, yes, the feelings of belonging, and of knowing and being known, satisfying one of the greatest urges of our innermost being.

However, when the sexual experience occurs outside this covenantal context of marriage, quite a different spirit emanates from beyond that mystical veil. Many of the physical joys are constant, but this spirit is a gripping force that permeates one's person like smoke pushing through a screen. It is a slow process, like a child growing: You never can see it; only by looking back six months or a year and comparing can you recognize its growth. This force, this spirit, continually increases, choking out any breath of togetherness, and evolves into a sense of emptiness, personal isolation and loneliness. Psychologist Froma Walsh of the University of Chicago says that it is this emptiness, loneliness and isolation that predominately characterize the casualties of the sexual revolution from the late '60s and '70s. The devastation within the ranks of the Baby Boomers is the result of their unshackled search for meaning and happiness.[13]

The Bible has a term for this force and its impact within the human spirit: It is called "death."

> When lust has conceived it gives birth to sin; and when sin is accomplished it brings forth death (James 1:15).

> She who gives herself to wonton pleasure is dead even while she lives (1 Timothy 5:6).

And what does the father of the prodigal son say upon his son's repentance and return to home?

> This son of mine was dead, and has come to life again; he was lost, and has been found (Luke 15:24).

To put it theologically, Paul says:

> Do you not know that when you present yourselves to someone as slaves for obedience, you are slaves of the one whom you obey, either of sin resulting in death, or of obedience resulting in righteousness? (Romans 6:16).

When death pervades the human spirit it is not surprising that its tentacles reach out and grasp other areas of life as well. That the loneliness and isolation mentioned by Ms. Walsh would be derived from a lot of interpersonal dealing on the most intimate level is highly ironic, but it corroborates the condition highlighted in chapter 1: emotional deprivation.

Sexual Disfunction

Another astonishing development is that of sexual disfunctioning. Some studies show that more than 10 percent of the men in our culture are impotent. In her book *Ordeal*,[14] infamous porn star Linda Lovelace said that not only did she never have one orgasm during the seven years she was involved in prostitution and pornography, but also that her husband/manager/pimp could be aroused sufficiently only on rare occasions and only under the most bizarre circumstances.

Those are extreme examples, but they do indicate that more is not better.

In another case, a wife credits her wild past before becoming a Christian for her disinterest in sex now and her inability to be orgasmic 90 percent of the time. "There are just too many walls inside," she says.

Self-Destruction

Ingrid Bengis, despairing of the pain and gloom resulting from her many intimate entanglements and despondent over her disintegrating social life, finally threw in the towel on romance and opted for celibacy. At the age of 27, when she wrote *Combat in the Erogenous Zone*, she had been celibate for two years. Life in the fast lane had brought her to a dead end.

Self–destruction can come even faster through mind–altering drugs and alcohol. These chemicals put the human faculties to sleep and open the gates of the soul to dark spiritual forces, forces which easily influence a person when his conscience is out for the count. Satan then can gain a firm grip on a person's inner life. Nancy testifies to this from her own experience:

> I drank a lot but I couldn't get off being drunk, and besides I was so locked up emotionally not being personally involved and all, that I couldn't really enjoy it, so if I'd fake the orgasm, it'd be over sooner. Maybe there'd be some tenderness afterward, but usually I was so out of it I didn't know or care if there was. Maybe I was afraid to care.
>
> Sometimes I'd think I was in love. But then I'd never hear from him again, or it would last a couple weeks or a month, then that would make me close up even more. They were just a piece of meat,

I'd tell myself. I'd laugh it off, but inside I knew that I was the piece of meat—and I was dying.

I loved life, but I hated myself; I loved men, but never any particular one, because I couldn't trust them; I loved sex, but I never really enjoyed it—that is, I was never really fulfilled. I was hungry but never filled. I never understood any of it, and I couldn't stop. The weekend would come and I was back on the roller coaster.

Nancy's hedonistic lifestyle is not different in kind or results from others' less flagrant promiscuity—it's just been compacted. She may have had six lovers in three months, and another may have six lovers in six years, but the results are the same. Stretching out the experiences over more time does not nullify the reality of their effect. Spiritual death, along with the emotional and psychological factors, is irrevocably constant. Nothing will forestall it, dissuade it, or negate it.

Spiritual Parallels

Sex is an image bearer, delivering a message. It reaches to our depths, seasons our life, and enables our relationships to scrape the heights of both racing joy and wrenching agony. It is a double–edged sword that cuts both ways, often brandishing about in a blur of confusion between right and wrong. How can sex be two things at once? How can it be both negative and positive? How can it build in a good way here and devastate over there? Perhaps if we can acknowledge how something else in life may offer this same dual function, how it may deliver at the same time both positive short–range results and negative long–range results, then we can see more clearly and understand more comprehensively its two sides.

Fire

Take fire, for instance. Fire is good. It heats our homes, cooks our food, strengthens steel for building, and softens iron to shape horseshoes.

Fire is also bad. It burns down our homes; it burns up crops and forests; it kills animals and people; and doctors say the pain from a severe burn is the most intense that can possibly be endured.

So, which is it? Is fire good? or bad? Yes. The context determines everything.

Likewise, sex is exciting, euphoric and cementing. It has

these elements no matter what the context. In the dynamics of a life–long committed relationship, these factors are enhanced and they grow. In a non–committed relationship, or in an affair that eventually ends, these factors tear up the turf of the heart. The mental and physical euphoria, the sense of closeness with the other person, and the heightened sense of self-actualization all camouflage the duplicity inherent in the nature of sex. The elements of sex themselves are good and constant; where they are expressed determines the positive or negative effects.

One Sunday at church we ran into Mary, a friend we had been talking with over a period of time. The pastor's message had been on the rich young ruler, and he had pointed out that anything in our lives could be like money was to that young man: a barrier between God and ourselves. The message reduced Mary to tears. After the service we all stopped at the cafe to talk, and through coffee and more tears Mary related how she was certain that her job was coming between her and doing the will of God. Granted, her job was not the greatest, but it was not illegal, nor was it in any sense immoral. What floored me was Mary's blank–faced indifference toward the obvious: She had been living with her boyfriend for five years! The Holy Spirit was knocking on her heart through the message at church but her mind sent it on an inconsequential tangent. I shared with her what God says about sex apart from marriage (cf. chapter 6) and her open–faced incredulity turned to stone–faced rejection.

"I don't think that's the problem," she said.

She never attended church with us again. She did not drop her job, and nothing changed with her boyfriend—until a year later when it all came crashing in.

He said, "Over," broke up with her for good, and moved out. Then she knew deep down what the ripping and tearing were all about. She moved back to the state her parents live in to take up life again, six years thrown away. Her heart may never recover from that experience.

Sex in a relationship is not just one factor among many, arbitrarily singled out to carry the blame every time something goes wrong. It contains a spiritual something that mystically permeates all aspects of a relationship. Mary touched the edge of what many have drowned in: ardor turned to bitterness, love turned to resentment, and the folding in of trust and hope and joy like dying flowers.

Summary

Because sex is a doorway to the soul and the heart, it is also a doorway to the spirit—and that makes our bodies a spiritual battleground. Therein lies the connection between sex and worship. Illicit sex distorts God's message to man about the relationship with and commitment to Him. The absence of celibacy, with its discipline, diverts our focus from our relationship with God and centers it on self and sexual fulfillment. Illicit sex pollutes the worship site, the body, with what is essentially a Satanic deception. And when the spiritual forces of darkness win their first battle here, each successive battle—and each successive step in dominating the person—becomes easier. Each successive sexual encounter pulls you further from your spiritual roots, like an undertow pulling you out to sea.

Celibacy means biting the bullet today. It is the narrow way, the road less traveled, that puts others before self and God above all. It purifies the soul, cleanses the worship site, and allows the mind to reach for higher ground. It clarifies inter–personal relationships instead of confounding them. Because the channels of communication with and worship of God are free of clutter, we can hear from Him concerning important directions and decisions of our life, and we can be moved along toward our intended destiny by the Spirit.

ΔΔΔ

Here's What You Can Do

1. List insights that have crystalized for you as a result of seeing the correlation between spiritual oneness and sexual oneness.

2. Look for other parallels in your own experience—like fire—that help you to grasp the elusive essence of this understanding.

3. Share these insights with a friend. Talking out new concepts helps to bring them into focus.

3

Profaning the Symbols

Beyond Sight and Sound

> Anger, fear and aggression. The dark side are they. Once you start down the dark side, forever will they dominate your destiny.
>
> Yoda, "The Empire Strikes Back"

Long, long ago in a galaxy far, far away, somebody invented football. He drew up a field of arbitrary length and width, with a pair of poles at each end. He chose a peculiar shaped ball, not used in any other sport at that time—never has been, never will be. He then called upon a certain number of rather large fellows to stand just so, each one to perform this task or that, divided the game into four time periods, blew the whistle, and they've been bashing each other to bits ever since.

Blue and gold symbolize one team, red and black another. A bear symbolizes this team over here, and a dolphin that team over there. Above the playing field flies the American flag, the symbol of our great nation, and those who raise and lower it are sure never to let it touch the ground. If it gets too dirty to fly proudly, it is burned, but it is never washed. And, oh yes, those who win the big one get a trophy or a ring or some symbol of accomplishment. When the game is over, each of the heroes drives off in his Mercedes, a symbol of success, to his home in a neighborhood which is also a symbol of success.

Our lives are filled with symbols, not just the games and the teams and the schools. Every company has a logo, a symbol that stands for that company alone. Every product has a symbol, and some symbols, like the Mercedes, function on multiple levels. The hood ornament, for example, distinctly announces the brand of car; it further represents a degree of quality; it even can symbolize the success of the owner.

God is the inventor of this really big game called "life," and He has come up with some symbols of His own—symbols with a difference.

God's symbols have a life of their own. They have power, and they have beginning–to–end significance. When these symbols teach and instruct, they carry punch. When the Corinthians failed to observe the Lord's Supper rightly, for instance, they were becoming sick and dying.[1] When the blood of the Passover lamb was applied to the doorposts,[2] it represented the shed blood of Jesus Christ[3] and as such protected the people who had the faith to apply it. That blood, that night, applied by those people, saved their children from death.

Sex is such a symbol,[4] and it, too, has its own intrinsic power. It represents the oneness of man and God, their communication and identity with each other, and the commitment of each to the other. Because of the significance of its symbolism, God makes a number of pronouncements concerning sex, its use and its misuse. But before we pursue that in chapter 6, we are going to look at three of the symbols God has used to communicate, and what happened when they were treated disdainfully. If we can appreciate how seriously God considered these symbols, then it will be reasonable to appreciate the fact that sex, as a symbol, is also serious.

An Ounce of Skin

Did you know that God was going to kill Moses for disobedience before he had appeared on Pharaoh's doorstep the first time? It was after God had appeared to Moses in the burning bush. In that brief interval, between the times when God announced to Moses that he was to lead the people out of Egypt and when Moses returned to Egypt to get the program under way, God actually was going to kill His prophet before he even had a chance to call down the first plague! Obviously, God was upset about something.

Exodus 4:24-26 briefly tells of how Moses almost became "Prophet for a Day"—literally. Why was God angry enough to cancel the exodus? Because Moses had not circumcised his son, as commanded in Genesis 17.

That's it? God was going to kill him for that? That's right.

Circumcision is cutting off the "extra" skin on the end of the penis, and the Hebrews were the only people who had that practice in ancient times. To not do it, therefore, was tantamount to identifying with the heathen and not God's people. Indeed, it was probably through his circumcision that Joseph made his kinship with his brothers irrefutably known.[5] Also, circumcision was healthier and cleaner because if urine got under the fold of the skin, it could cause infection.

As important as these reasons may be, however, none of them is why Moses was almost killed by God. The symbolism of circumcision is light years beyond these. The flesh on the end of the penis symbolizes the reign of the flesh, the sin nature, over us, and circumcision speaks of cutting away the control of sin in our lives:

> In Him you were also circumcised with a circumcision made without hands, in the removal of the body of the flesh by the circumcision of Christ; having been buried with Him in baptism, in which you were also raised up with Him through faith in the working of God, who raised Him from the dead. And when you were dead in your transgressions and the uncircumcision of your flesh, He made you alive together with Him, having forgiven us all our transgressions (Colossians 2:11-13).

In the progression of revelation, that command which was delivered to the Jews to be obeyed as an act which had medical and cultural significance was explained two thousand years later:

> For he is not a Jew who is one outwardly; neither is circumcision that which is outward in the flesh. But he is a Jew who is one inwardly; and circumcision is that which is of the heart, by the Spirit, not by the letter (Romans 2:28,29).

That this explanation came a couple of millenniums after the fact did not, in God's eyes, lessen the seriousness of Moses' offense. Moses may not have been able to expound the profound theological tenets of Romans 2, nevertheless, the Grim Reaper had his scythe raised and Moses was moments from the cutting blade when Zipporah, his wife, jumped into the breach, flint in hand, to save the day. She circumcised the boy, and Moses lived to become a legend.

The seriousness of Moses' mission, the plight of the hundreds of thousands of Israelites, and the preparation and character of the man himself were not as weighty before God as was Moses' obedience to that one issue. An ounce of skin, seemingly so insignificant; a religious rite, seemingly so inconsequential. There is obviously more here than meets the eye. And that something more is the symbolic power.

Golden Cups

In 605 B.C., the Babylonians, under Nebuchadnezzar, dealt the death blow to Judah, the Southern Kingdom of the nation of Israel. They wiped out the army, leveled Jerusalem, and took many captives back to Babylon, among them Daniel, who rose to prominence within the Babylonian Empire. He became a trusted confidant of Nebuchadnezzar, and eventually, also of the Persians who took the territory from Nebuchadnezzar's heirs. After Nebuchadnezzar's death, a number of rulers came and went, with much intrigue, increased degradation, assassination, and religious pollution. The last of the Babylonian rulers was Belshazzar, and chapter 5 of the book of Daniel breaks in on his last night, in the midst of a drunken orgy.

He had more than a thousand of his nobles there, along with plenty of women, and was probably making a great show of confidence in the midst of a threatening situation. The Persian armies were right outside the gates of the city, and had been for some time. But the walls of Babylon were noted for their impregnability. They were high and thick, and within the city was a storehouse able to sustain the inhabitants an incredible twenty years! Belshazzar had no plans for immediate retirement.

Unfortunately, Belshazzar had not learned much from his forefather, Nebuchadnezzar, who had quite miraculously repented of his arrogance and turned his heart toward the true God of heaven. Belshazzar's life and kingdom had been on the slides morally for some time, but this night he made a fatal error that put him over the edge: "He gave orders to bring the gold and silver vessels which Nebuchadnezzar his father had taken out of the Temple which was in Jerusalem, in order that the king and his nobles, his wives, and his concubines might drink from them."[6] The revelers profaned the sacred utensils from God's Temple, using them in a common manner, joining them with bovine debauchery, and audaciously toasting the gods of gold, silver, bronze, wood and stone. It was Belshazzar's crowning act of folly. In the midst of the ruckus, the hooters stopped dead still:

> Suddenly the fingers of a man's hand emerged and began writing
> . . . on the wall . . . Then the king's face grew pale, and his
> thoughts alarmed him; and his hip joints went slack, and his knees
> began knocking together (Daniel 5:5,6).

Belshazzar was scared! Nobody knew what the message said, so eventually Daniel was called to interpret the cryptic words on the wall. Cutting to the bottom line, we find that Daniel said, in essence, "You knew how God had dealt with your father,[7] Nebuchadnezzar, yet you have exalted yourself against the LORD of heaven and have brought the vessels of His house to drink to other gods, who are no gods at all. The days of your kingdom have been numbered and they are up; you have been weighed and found deficient; your kingdom has been given to someone else!"

Belshazzar didn't live to see the sunrise. The Medes and the Persians had diverted the Euphrates river and entered the city through the underground river bed. They took the city *that night*.

Belshazzar lost his life and his kingdom over a gold cup and a silver tray? In a summary sort of way, yes. The artifacts from the Temple symbolized God's house and worship (which biblically is the most important of our relational aspects with God), so Belshazzar's disregard for the intended sacred use of those things typified his disdain for God's ways in general and His symbols in particular. This misuse of the symbols was the final act that brought it all crashing in on him.

Substantiating the severity of Belshazzar's error is the fact that there were a number of rulers between Nebuchadnezzar and Belshazzar who are not mentioned, and none of Belshazzar's life except this one night receives any comment whatsoever. In fact, this famous scene at Belshazzar's orgy bears no contextual relationship with what went before in the text or what follows. It simply breaks in on a beautiful quote from Nebuchadnezzar after he is recovered from the insanity God inflicted on him for his unbridled arrogance . . .

> Now I Nebuchadnezzar praise, exalt, and honor the King of
> heaven, for all His works are true and His ways just, and He is
> able to humble those who walk in pride (Daniel 4:37).

. . . and is then followed by Daniel being thrown into the lion's den, an incident which occurred after the Medes and Persians took over. Belshazzar's party is singled out to take up a full chapter in this important book, indicating that this incident with the Temple artifacts bears significance worthy of reflection. Yes, it illustrates the truth of Nebuchadnezzar's words concerning the honor due God and the humbling of the proud—but more, it is a statement on misusing God's symbols. The consequences of doing so, as we are seeing, can be disastrous indeed.

The Temple in Jerusalem

The Jewish Temple in Jerusalem was a symbol of the true Temple in heaven.[8] Whereas God indwelt the Old Testament Temple, after the resurrection of Jesus Christ and Pentecost, the physical bodies of born-again believers replaced stone and mortar as the residence of God.[9]

During Jesus' time, the Old Testament temple in Jerusalem still stood as the focal point of national worship and the primary symbol of God's dwelling among men. Jesus never raised an eyebrow to defend Himself against false accusation or adversaries who continually ridiculed His teaching, impugned His lifestyle, mocked His authority, condemned His motives, and chastised His associates. Yet there were some things that definitely brought Him to His feet. Misusing the Temple was one of them.

When the money changers and salesmen did business in the Temple, they were essentially doing what Belshazzar did: They were taking something set aside by God for a specific and holy purpose and using it for a common, self-serving end. Jesus did not stop to teach on the subject. He acted.

Whip in hand, Jesus strode purposefully into the Temple, putting passion and blood to righteous indignation, and drove the merchants out. The Temple was a place of worship and prayer, the house of God, the representation of God on earth. The commercial villains had to go because that building of stone was more than mere stone. It was the communication of a message from God. In the expression of Jesus' white-hot anger as He drove out the sheep and oxen, overturning tables and deliberately dumping out the money of the traders onto the ground, we *see* how God perceives the improper or casual abuse of symbolic realities. His symbols matter. They exist for a purpose, to make a statement. To desecrate their significance and prostitute their destined use is to mar the message God wants to communicate through them.

Sex as a Symbol

Sex is a symbol. It is a symbol of the unity of God and man—their interrelatedness. Marriage is a symbol. It bespeaks the breadth and depth of God's commitment to us and (ideally) our commitment to Him. Encompassing sex, marriage echoes the interrelatedness and oneness of man and God. It also shadows the uniqueness of the one chosen: God has chosen man only among all His creation to image Himself, to commit Himself to contractually, to suffer and die for, and to dwell with forever. Man, for his part, chooses God as his Head, his Master, his Husband, putting the kingdom of God first, having no other God, and no other "thing" that would supplant God in the relationship.

The symbolic feature of sex is not its totality. But the point of these illustrations is that this symbolism does not diminish the wholeness of sex but rather amplifies its power—a power, as indicated in earlier chapters, to destroy two individuals or to build, bind, and bond two people. The destructive personal repercussions are real when this spiritual dynamic is ignored. Like Moses or Belshazzar, we may be bewildered when something we thought was no big deal suddenly takes on overpowering proportions and consumes us. The results may be dramatic, or they may evolve over time; they may be simple or complex. But to abuse God's symbols is to lose.

Again I refer to Ingrid Bengis. Her glimpse into the hidden chambers of the soul when sex is misused and its power unleashed in a negative setting elucidated for me the extent of the loss experienced:

> There were a number of things I hadn't counted on, things which none of my friends who wanted to be "free" had counted on. The first of these was that my attachments to men usually deepened the longer I knew them and the more I shared with them, whereas their attachments [to me] seemed to lessen.
>
> The second was that when love didn't turn out as planned, there was some peculiar pain that I refused to acknowledge, a pain of separation that had not been part of the design. . . Even though being emancipated meant being willing to take chances with your life, it also meant you might take chances that sent you reeling when you lost. I had never even thought about the "odds of winning" and the "price of losing."
>
> The other thing I didn't count on was the power of sex. I didn't realize that sex made a difference. I thought sex was an expression

of love, a part of love. What I didn't think was that it transformed everything, that for me—and for most women— making love with a man several times created unpredictable bonds, which weren't broken by saying, "This was a trial marriage for which the contract has expired."

I didn't realize that physical intimacy had unknown properties, that it created deepening needs [and] highly unprogressive bursts of possessiveness and jealousy . . . I didn't realize that love could reverse itself, could be withdrawn, or that consequences of such withdrawal could be so powerful as to crush vast expanses of one's own potential for feeling. I didn't realize that there actually was such a thing as falling apart over the loss of love.[10]

As we see in Ms. Bengis' account, to ignore the symbolic power of sex is to put life into a tailspin. It may seem inconsequential to thrust aside God's commands, as Moses did, not realizing the reverberating importance those commands might bear beyond their own simple design. Yet to do so is to be suddenly face to face with death.

It is easy to look only at the beauty of something and its usefulness to oneself, as Belshazzar did, yet he paid with his life for disdaining the sanctifying design behind the obvious. It can appear trivial to put practical concerns ahead of theological fine points, as the merchants did. Yet they found themselves thrown out on their faces.

And aren't we guilty of these same offenses? We disregard God's commands about sex, ignoring the serious repercussions of the issue. We focus on the beauty of sex and what it will do for us, neglecting the holy design behind the physical pleasure. We forever posture about our great need for sex (even sex education classes in schools do not present celibacy as an option!), esteeming ourselves modern and practical, all the while overlooking the spiritual ramifications because they are too remote, too rarified.

The fact that sex is symbolic of meaningful eternal values places it on the same shelf as the other symbols we have looked at. To take it down at whim, to play with it as a child would a loaded gun, is to find ourselves, like Ms. Bengis, shot full of holes— and wondering why.

△△△

Here's What You Can Do

1. Identify three symbols that have been meaningful to you during your lifetime, and write what differences they have made.

2. Pray that God will impress your heart with the true symbolism of the sexual relationship and write what difference you expect that understanding to make in your life.

3. Can you share this concept with someone?

4

Meanwhile, Back at the Garden

Is Satan a real, live entity, who can influence and direct the lives of people? Does he have a personality, with a purpose, goals, attributes and characteristics? And were Adam and Eve two real people who had no youth, no parents and no problems until . . . well, you know the story. But is it a real story? These aspects of the Christian faith can sometimes sound pretty foolish, especially when discussing them with non-Christians. Friends might give you this pitiful "Oh, really?" look, when what they actually are thinking is, "Get me out of here!"

Fact or Fiction

This chapter is not a defense of creationism. Nevertheless, before we can examine the relevance of the garden scene to our topic, it is critical to acknowledge that if there were no such scene, and if Adam and Eve were merely fictitious, merely two ideals representing humanity in someone's overblown mythology, then we need to deal with two inescapable conclusions. **First,** the basis of salvation, as explained by Paul in Romans 5 and in 1 Corinthians 15, is reduced to inconsequential noise. And **second,** Jesus Christ was a liar.

When Jesus Christ was challenged on the issue of divorce, He based His answer on the words of Adam, as quoted in Genesis

2:24, and stated, "He who created them from the beginning made them male and female."[1] There is no indication that Jesus assumed anything other than the biblical account of creation, which should give that account considerable weight.

Paul's argument for salvation and justification hangs on the historicity of Adam. The parallels Paul draws are meaningless if Adam is not an actual, historical figure who brought irrevocable consequences for all through his encounter with the tree. Paul's arguments run something like this:

Adam . . . one transgression . . . . many died

Christ . . . one act on the cross . . many receive the gift of grace

and

Adam . . . .sin . . . . condemnation . . . death

Christ . . . .righteousness . . . justification . . . . . life

The validity of the Bible, the virtue of those who wrote it, and the veracity of history's central figure, Jesus Christ, all crumble if Adam and Eve were not real people who had a conversation with Satan in a garden somewhere back in time. It would mean some of the central teachings and critical assumptions of both Jesus and Paul were based on a lie. If we don't approach the garden scene as dealing with real-life people in an actual historical situation, we are as foolish as a traveler plotting his course based on last night's dream.

In addition, although the account of Adam and Eve in the Garden of Eden has nothing to do with sex, the actions of Satan, the reactions of Eve, and the elements of the situation are too instructive to pass up, because they parallel our subject.

The Person and Work of Satan

Like all of God's creatures, Satan was created in beauty and perfection in a sinless universe.[2] From within him, however, sprang an arrogance that got him kicked out of the inner circle of God's government in heaven, though he still has access to God's throne.[3] Sometime in the future he will be barred from heaven and restricted to earth.[4] After that he will be sealed in the bottomless pit.[5] Satan is not unlike the villainous emperor of the Star Wars saga in his current-day role as God's adversary. He is pure evil with amazing powers. Why God allowed Satan to live, and why He allows him his powers and his somewhat restricted freedom, will be covered shortly.

As we will see in the next chapter, the major element of sin is deception, and Satan is the master deceiver. He plays no game fairly, he is never up front, and he never concerns himself with delivering on his promises. He wants to have the biggest team possible, but he, himself, is not at all into fame—indeed, many of his top players do not even believe he exists. And he hates you with a passion beyond your comprehension! His purpose, his goal, is your ultimate destruction, though in the meantime he will ply you with any trinket that will distract you from your awareness of your need for God.

He is skillful in deceiving others;[6] he is a tempter;[7] he is constantly on the prowl and relentless in the pursuit of his goal;[8] he snatches away the gospel from those who hear it;[9] he uses sexual temptation as a primary weapon,[10] and he constantly strives to gain an advantage over believers[11] and to blind the minds of unbelievers.[12] Through his subtlety he is capable of corrupting the minds of believers,[13] for he is constantly attacking them,[14] tempting them to unbelief;[15] he also can work in and through and can manipulate unbelievers.[16] He put Peter through a meat grinder,[17] hindered Paul's missionary travels,[18] put betrayal into the heart of Judas,[19] and filled the heart of Ananias to lie.[20] We live in his domain, and life is not a piece of cake—it is a battle. He is our enemy.[21] The whole world lies in his power.[22]

Not True—Not False

This is the one who, from the outset, wove a web of discontent in Eve's thinking. If you'd like to follow along in the Scripture with me, open your Bible to Genesis 3. First, Satan approached the woman, circumventing the headship of the husband, a tactic he is still employing with great success. In the case of Eve, she was duped into a foolish pursuit of doubt by his deception. As she later exclaimed, "The serpent deceived me." He led her to believe things that were wrong. Though what he told her was not wholly untrue, her conclusions were totally false.

He began by throwing tarnish on God's image as a good provider: "Has God said you shall not eat from any tree of the garden?" Implication: "God is a killjoy who is limiting your freedom. He obviously does not have your best interest at heart!" Eve corrected the serpent, but Satan had already sown the seed-thought of a jealous, narrow God who was not trustworthy, an idea he would build on in his next statement.

When Eve stated the penalty for eating (and touching, an addition she apparently threw in for added emphasis), Satan came at her full force, confronting God's condemnation as false: "Surely you shall not die!"

Did she die when she ate? What did she think when she ate and gave to Adam? Chances are Eve had never seen anything die, but had she been quizzed on the subject, she probably would have assumed it referred to physical death. When she didn't drop dead, she undoubtedly concluded that Satan was telling the truth.

But reality caught both her and Adam, coming and going. No, they did not die suddenly leaving good-looking corpses; they died slowly. They got old. The pains, diseases, and disabilities of age and the inevitable approach of death was (and is) a much more awful fate than just dropping dead. They had not counted on that.

Also, they died spiritually. Paul says, referring to his own experience, which is universal in nature, "Sin, taking opportunity through the commandment, deceived me, and through it killed me."[23] Sin, in the form of Satan's deceptive tactics, took opportunity through the commandment, "Thou shalt not eat of the tree," deceiving Eve, and thereby killed her.

So, did they die? Yes, but not in the way Eve was led to believe by Satan that they would. That is the key! What ultimately transpired she never could have guessed at.

Satan continued, "God knows that in the day you eat from the tree your eyes will be opened, and you will be like God, knowing good and evil."

True? Again, yes and no. God Himself later says, "Man has become like one of Us [a clear reference to the trinity], knowing good and evil."[24] So they did become like God, and Satan was telling the truth? No.

By way of analogy, I might say to you, "I will give you a rock like gold." You assume that I mean it will be gold the way gold is gold. But I merely paint a rock a gold color and give it to you. Is it "like" gold? Yes and no, and it is worthless anyway!

Eve *assumed* from Satan that she would be like God. She jumped on that! Satan infused into her heart the same lust toward

God-equality that he had, which got him kicked out of heaven. When she ate, she perceived good and evil all right, like God said she would, and like God does — but it was a worthless gain for her. She was not anything like God! Again, there was an element of truth in what Satan had said, but he led Eve to believe a lie.

The final push of persuasion came when she "saw that the tree was good for food, and that it was a delight to the eyes, and that the tree was desirable to make one wise." And with that, she put innocence behind her.

Satan and the Single

Correlating this with our subject, Satan weaves a web of discontent in the heart of the single person, causing him to focus on what God has prohibited rather than on the bounty God has provided. Satan causes us to be agitated over the limits of our personal freedom, rather than being focused on the needs of others and the freedoms we do have. This negative focus sows doubt about the goodness and wisdom of God. Satan does this by persuading us with truths and half-truths that motivate us to act: Sex is good. Sex is fun. Sex will enhance the relationship and bring you closer together. Sex is an expression of love that feels wonderful.

Once doubt is wedged into the heart, Satan begins with the lies: Sex will not hurt you. You can control it. It will enhance you, not detract from you, because your eyes will be open and you will have a greater awareness of life.

He fogs over the obvious problems and dangers with the unsupportable belief which we all have embraced at some time: "It won't happen to me." He convinces you that *you* won't get pregnant, *you* won't get a disease, *you* won't be hurt. He is a deceiver.

If and when you decide to be sexually active, the half-truths bear themselves out, but the results are all wrong. Sure, it is good. Yes, it is fun. Yes, it brings you closer together — but with devasting results, as we saw in chapter 1. No, God is not trying to keep you from having any fun. He is trying, as we have been laboring to convey, to spare you a great deal of grief. Once the lid of Pandora's Box is opened in your life, it cannot be shut.

Temptation

Even in the garden, at the beginning of relating to man,

Satan knew man better than man knew himself. When Satan addressed Eve, he used a form of reasoning to secure her defection. He appealed to her latent pride and desire to be more, to have more. Between the lines was a subtle appeal to "freedom." Shouldn't she have the right to eat of any tree she wanted? After all, the tree was very appealing. It certainly was not ugly and tasteless. How could such a tree be bad? Why is God prohibiting *this* tree— this *good* tree?

The catch was that she listened! She followed Satan's line of reasoning and permitted self-aggrandizement to displace the Word of God. This is not to say that reason itself, nor the mind per se, is bad. But when mind and reason are used to back the Word of God into a corner of "unreasonableness," the outcome will be alienation from God. God did not say it was a bad tree, an ugly tree, or a tasteless tree. Satan is getting Eve to reject God's prohibition on false premises. This is one of the strongest parallels in our analogy. We think that, because sex looks so good and is so intensely pleasurable, God must not really know what He's talking about by prohibiting it.

Furthermore, this allure of sexual pleasure, combined with the belief, *I ought to be able to do what I want, when I want,* separates us from that essential ingredient Jesus so esteemed in children: trust. Aldous Huxley, the famed atheist, reflects this mode of thought in an illuminating passage from his work, *Ends and Means:*

> I had motives for not wanting the world to have meaning; consequently assumed that it had none, and was able without any difficulty to find satisfying reasons for this assumption. The philosopher who finds no meaning in the world is not concerned exclusively with a problem in pure metaphysics; he is also concerned to prove that there is no valid reason why he personally should not do as he wants to do, or why his friends should not seize political power and govern in the way that they find most advantageous to themselves . . . For myself, the philosophy of meaninglessness was essentially an instrument of liberation, sexual and political.[25]

Satan's Goal

Satan recognizes that he is not going to get you into hell just because you commit fornication, but as Huxley reveals, the sexual appetite, and the desire to fulfill it in a lawless way, is enough to cause you to look for "reasons" to drop trust in God's ways, as Eve did. Pursuing that course resulted in Huxley rejecting God.[26] *That* is Satan's aim with all of us.

Satan's goal is to get you headed in the wrong direction, to cut you off from God as he did Eve. Premarital sex can do just that. To him, it's simply a means to an end. He doesn't care about sex any more than he does about trees. He's after *you*, and one of the easiest doors to knock down to get inside of you is labeled SEX.

You cannot run from your sexuality. Satan capitalizes on that in one way by incessantly bombarding you with it through the media. As the tree beckoned Eve, so the world system beckons you with the joys, promises, and glories of sexual indulgence. And it can seem a bit corny and foolish, even repressive, to remonstrate against such innocent pleasure. God is made to appear prudish and His position on sex inanely narrow, especially to the unsuspecting who are heady with the sweet juice of forbidden fruit.

But like Eve's images of the tree and what it would deliver, it all comes crashing down, resulting in broken hearts, fractured lives, incurable and deadly diseases, murder (i.e., abortion), broken homes, et. al. None of this concerns Satan. His goal is to get you to the other side of innocence and to keep you going.

Another lure of the tree of knowledge of good and evil is simply that it was forbidden. As the siren sings to the unsuspecting, naive, young man:

Stolen water is sweet;
And bread eaten in secret is pleasant (Proverbs 9:17).

The desire to have what we should not have is temptation enough to stir up lustful desire. Such is the appeal of immorality in all forms: premarital sex, extramarital affairs, group sex, homosexuality, incest, sex with children, and even sex with animals. Perversion runs a course. Fornication is only the first bite, a starting point. This is the inverse of the "seed principle" of John 12:24—every action, like a seed sown, bears much fruit. Satan is counting on that. His desire to destroy our innocence and start us running from God is fulfilled. Adam and Eve hid from God because of their shame. So do we. If Satan can keep us running and hiding, he can get us where he ultimately wants us. The companion verse to the one above concludes:

He does not know that the dead are there,
That her guests are in the depths of Sheol [Hell] (Proverbs 9:18).

Sex is not just another appetite, another element of life. It is a testing ground, a tree in the middle of the garden of life. A fulcrum upon which so much of life turns. A pressure point that can break you.

Testing, Testing: One, Two, Three . . .

The BIG question is, of course, why have a tree at all? If there were no tree, Satan would be robbed of his angle to tempt Eve. He would be standing around, his hands in his pockets, and nothing to bother her with. No tree, no problem. God created everything, and He created that tree. Therefore, He did not have to have that tree in the garden. Why does God want to present the means for causing problems? That tree was a dumb idea!

Yes, dumb — if God's aim for your life and mine is tranquility. When we realize that tranquility is not His aim for us, we have begun to comprehend the game behind the game. There is something else going on here. Life is more than naming animals (a job) or walking in the garden (recreation).

The spiritual is central, and that involves testing.

The refining pot is for silver and the furnace for gold,
But the LORD tests hearts (Proverbs 17:3).

When we see clearly that God is going to put us through the gamut, so much about life makes sense. Of course, like anyone else, I would rather dwell well within the comfort zone, and I wish God were not in the testing business. But He is, and knowing that prepares me to encounter life more sure-footedly. Again, it is His game; I cannot escape. There are winners and losers, and the stakes are exceedingly high. He says:

I, the LORD, search the heart,
I test the mind,
Even to give to each [person] according to his ways,
According to the results of his deeds (Jeremiah 17:10).

God is very much into rewards. The concept of earning rewards springs from God Himself. There is no way to determine the convictions of one's heart without testing the heart. And God rewards according to His tests. Man did not create performance orientation, though he has definitely gotten side-tracked into his own game-playing for awards which have no eternal value. But the performance ethic emanates from God's image within us.

Sometimes the test is strange and disrelated to anything else — on the surface anyway. Like the tree in the midst of the garden, or Abraham being told by God to kill the son he had been given. Hebrews loathed human sacrifice, for it was contrary to everything they and God stood for.

Nevertheless . . .

Now it came about after these things, that God tested Abraham (Genesis 22:1).

After He tested Abraham's obedience and spared the boy, God said:

Because you have done this thing, and have not withheld your son, your only son, indeed I will greatly bless you (Genesis 22:16-17).

Abraham believed and he obeyed. Faith and obedience earn rewards with God. Pharisaical do-gooding and complying with an endless list of man-made rules are not what we are talking about, however.

Sometimes the test is from God but through the hand of Satan. This was the case with Job, and with Jesus.[27] In all situations, testing is a part of God's plan for every person: "The LORD tests the righteous and the wicked."[28]

There are basically two kinds of tests. One is the kind that frightens beyond despair. It is as if God turned His back, turned out the lights, and walked out. It is the discipline of darkness. Job cried out in deep agony, "Why dost Thou hide Thy face, and consider me Thine enemy?"[29] The anguish of such an experience is almost beyond description and for our purposes, certainly beyond the scope of this subject.

The other kind of test, the one that concerns us, is the temptation to soften God's design for us and blend it with our own ambitions. Satan's offer to Jesus Christ, to make him king of the world, was like his approach to Eve: offering what only God can give. Had Jesus capitulated, He would have received no more than Eve did, for Satan is a deceiver and has no burden to deliver on any deal. We will never know what "Plan A" was for Adam and Eve, but we can see from the unfolding of the New Testament what God's plan was for Jesus, because it came to pass. From these two examples, we can conclude that God's way, His initial plan, is better than having to work it out some other way. As will be clear from the next chapter, God certainly forgives, but the consequences of our actions stay with us. Adam and Eve were forgiven, and they will be in heaven to greet you when you get there. But every day of Adam's long life, he had to work and sweat for the produce of the ground, fight the weather, and encounter pestilence like every farmer since. And every baby Eve bore came through indescribable pain.

God's Ways

God's way requires trust in who He is, faith in what He says, and patience to wait for what He has for us. Satan's way is a shortcut that leads to a dead end as we reach for goals and strive for completeness. Those shortcut methods attempt to achieve love through sex, peace through drugs, fulfillment through accomplishment, joy through fun and satisfaction through taking. Learn from others: These methods do not work.

God's way is quite contrary:

> We . . . exult in our tribulations, knowing that tribulation brings about perseverance; and perseverance, proven character; and proven character, hope; and hope does not disappoint, because the love of God has been poured out within our hearts (Romans 5:3-5).

Temptation is a test. It is a tree in the midst of a garden. Your sexuality is a tree in the midst of the garden of your life. The "why" of that test may make no more sense to you than the why of Eve's tree. Why all the hoopla over a piece of fruit? Why all the vexation over sex?

Can you not hear the wranglings of your own mind at these questions? Can you not recognize the philosophies of our culture ringing in your ears as you contemplate the simple joys of sexual coupling? Eating fruit is so natural . . . and sex is not far behind in acting out natural appetites. Chapters 1, 2, 3, 5, 9 and 10 highlight some of the troubles that can occur with premarital sex, so we are not talking about blind faith in God's prohibitions. But the test is one of faith. Of identity. Of allegiance. A test of faith not just in God, but in His ways. A test of manifest destiny that will reach to the depths of your being and to the end of your life.

Knowing

> [Wisdom speaking:]
> Power is mine! . . .
> He who sins against me injures himself;
> All those who hate me love death (Proverbs 8:14,36).

There are times when life is a glassy, tranquil sea, . . .

then suddenly it happens! From a blind corner lust strikes like a ninja, raining down heavy blows! Immediately you are knocked off balance. A vicious struggle ensues. The mind works frantically to compute weaknesses and strengths, and to come up with a winning strategy against the pull of lust.

Compounding the problem, the insidiously deceptive nature of temptation steps in, and you are not sure which is the win—to cling to integrity, or to let lust have its run. Unfortunately, clarity usually comes only after pleasure has turned to ashes. One way or another the experience is dealt with, and eventually life slows down to an easy roll, again leadening the spiritual senses.

Then, wham! Lust gushes like a torrent again! With maturity comes commitment, but the wrestling is still necessary. Like an evil grappling hook, lust clutches your desires and pulls you inexorably toward an abyss of pride and shame.

How does one resist? Quote Scripture? Stand firm? Pray?

Yes.

But above all,

Know the cost.

Thrill is short-lived. Contentment in Christ is long and peaceful. To succumb to lust brings inevitable regret.

To resist strengthens the inner man.

His own iniquities will capture the wicked,
And he will be held with the cords of his sin.
He will die for lack of instruction,
And in the greatness of his folly he will go astray.

(Proverbs 5:22-23)

At those times, I would rather die than fight! Relinquishing control is so much more delicious than the agony of hanging tough. Where is the power, the overcomer's sufficiency? Where is the Lord of victory?

Maddeningly, platitudes fail and promises turn to smoke. And the test of faith begins.

Somewhere in the maelstrom—if we persist in our reading and listening and learning (otherwise, we are no better for our experiences than a fly battering against the glass)—we touch the reality of knowing.

And our knowing rises from rocky ledge to rocky ledge, like

a mountain climber on a cliff. Every truth learned is a pinion driven into the granite of life, and our survival depends on those pinions. In the burgeoning explosiveness of our own passions, though, we sometimes forget what we have learned, consequently slipping and sliding and tearing ourselves up. We swear we will not forget again, we will not neglect, we will not ignore. And we begin to climb once more. It is a tough learning process, but there are no shortcuts.

> Suddenly he follows her,
> As an ox goes to the slaughter,
> Or as one in fetters to the discipline of a fool.
> Until an arrow pierces through his liver;
> As a bird hastens to the snare
> So he does not know that it will cost him his life.
>
> (Proverbs 7:22-23)

He does not know. He does not know!

As we learn the truth, and come to rely on the truth, and as we struggle with temptation and blurred vision, and as we comprehend the self and the Lord, the natural and the unnatural, the Lord blesses our life with breakthroughs which transcend experience. Our knowledge is the arsenal with which we fight the battle.

> The mind of the prudent acquires knowledge,
> And the ear of the wise seeks knowledge (Proverbs 18:15).

Knowing is the beginning of victory. God went to the time and trouble to write a book. He wants us to know. Knowledge is the beginning to understanding Satan, understanding temptation, understanding yourself, and understanding testing.

> I pray that the eyes of your heart may be enlightened, so that you might know:
> 1. what is the hope of His calling;
> 2. what are the riches of the glory of His inheritance in the saints; and
> 3. what is the surpassing greatness of His power toward us who believe (Ephesians 1:18,19).

Knowing.

Knowing is the defense against our shrewd adversary who incessantly lays traps for us, deceiving us with lures which can never produce the satisfaction they so loudly promise. By our knowing, no advantage can be taken of us by Satan, for, as Paul says, "We are not ignorant of his schemes."[30]

We can know that we are going to be tempted, as Eve was, to have it "all" now, and to want what we cannot or should not have. We can know the seed principle, that one action is the source of future actions and reactions. We can know that Satan's aim is merely to get us to take the first step toward the other side of innocence, then one more step, then one more . . .   We can know, with David, that the Lord is going to test us in the crucible of life:

I know, O my God, that Thou triest the heart,
And delightest in uprightness (1 Chronicles 29:17).

Knowing is a safe–guard. It is a weapon. It provides me with power, insight, wisdom and endurance to persevere. I can know the Lord. I can know His ways. I can know that He tests the hearts of men, and that one of the basic tests in the garden which is my life is the temptation to sexual indulgence outside the prescribed dimensions He has instituted. And I can know the cost—the high cost—of free love.

Apply your heart to discipline,
And your ears to words of knowledge . . .
Buy the truth, and do not sell it,
Get wisdom and instruction and understanding.
(Proverbs 23:12,23)

ΔΔΔ

Here's What You Can Do

1. Look for and list areas in your life where you can differentiate between testing and tempting.

2. Identify and list specific people, places and things that tempt you. Resolve to avoid them.

3. Consider and list those people, places and things in your life that may be testings from God. Give thanks for each of them—whether you want to or not.

5

Consequences

Playing the Hand You Deal

> The last public reference to sin we can recall offhand
> was President Coolidge's remark that his minister had
> preached on sin and was against it. In these new times
> sin is known by nicer names, such as delinquency, im-
> propriety, indecorum, indiscretion, irregularity, laxity
> and moral turpitude.
>
> *New York Times Magazine*

We have discussed the dark side of romance and the
weighty effects our errant sexuality can have on the mind, emotions and heart. We have explored the role of sex as an image, a
statement on the worshipful corollary in our relationship with
God, and why as a spiritual factor it manifests both positive and
negative power. And as a symbol, God has imbued it with wall–
to–wall significance, as He does all His symbols. They are serious,
and unleash an explosive force when misused. And Satan's crafty
tactics have been exposed in the account of the first sin.

The Principle

The obvious thread of consequences has run throughout our
discussion. Our actions cause residual effects in others' lives as
well as in our own. In chapters 9 and 10 we will deal with some
disastrous consequences of giving in to our passions (i.e., venereal
disease, abortion, and pregnancy). But here we will discuss the nature of sin and its consequences, the principle—the why—of
consequences from the divine viewpoint, and how that principle

has been played out in others' lives.

First, two observations:

1. Biblical illustrations are used almost exclusively because often the accompanying text illuminates the mind of God. The whys and wherefores of a contemporary story would be merely conjecture, because each of our lives is so complex, and simple answers are difficult to nail down. The biblical account, however, provides answers, and we can see "the news behind the news" with greater accuracy and insight.

2. "The fear of the LORD is the beginning of wisdom,"[1] according to what Solomon taught his son. The purpose of the following illustrations is that we might learn, and thereby fear, in order that we might live in peace and joy.

Nehemiah, a governor of Judah after the Babylonian 70-year captivity, says he did not do many of the things former governors had done "because of the fear of God."[2]

Job quotes God Himself, saying, "To a man He said, 'Behold, the fear of the Lord, that is wisdom; and to depart from evil is understanding.' "[3] We learn, in order to know, that we might fear. The old saying, "Fools rush in where angels fear to tread," means that an angel knows better than to go barrelling into a situation — he knows enough to have a healthy fear of it. The person who is ignorant, or who is stupid, goes charging in anyway, either unmindful or uncaring of the consequences.

David sums it up succinctly: "Who is the man who fears the LORD? He will instruct him in the way he should choose."[4] If we learn but do not apply the knowledge, we make foolish and costly mistakes. Wisdom is knowledge applied. The reason fear is the beginning of wisdom is that it can keep us from a great deal of pain and from those costly mistakes.

"Therefore," says Paul, "be careful how you walk, not as unwise [people], but as wise, making the most of your time, because the days are evil. So then, do not be foolish, but understand what the will of the Lord is."[5]

Deception of Sin

In evaluating the consequences of our actions, there is one realization which, when fully grasped, will give a 60 percent head start in achieving spiritual growth. It is the daily, conscious awareness of a truth so pervasive that just knowing it will cut through the fog and clarify most of the confusion that impedes progress. It is simply this:

The most elemental and predominant ingredient of sin is DECEPTION.

Sin appears to be what it isn't, and it is not what it appears to be. It promises what it cannot deliver; it commands you when it has no authority; it creates feelings and desires which are an illusion and convinces you that those feelings *must* be believed, and those desires *must* be fulfilled, which are lies. It gives you thoughts and convictions which you believe are your own, and they are not. These delusions occur to Christians and non–Christians alike. Actually, one of the cruelest deceptions of all is the conviction that one is a Christian when there is not a shred of evidence to support it. The Christian has the capacity to recognize the deception and back away; the non-Christian does not have that ability.

One aspect of the deception is in the slow–acting nature of sin's consequences. Today it is rah, rah. Tomorrow it is grief, loneliness, emptiness — and herpes. Because the results are so late in arriving, we are inclined to think there are no consequences. Of course, that is part of the deception — no consequences. One can enter a throbbing disco or attend a gyrating party and be overwhelmed by the dense wave of sensuality undulating through the crowd, defying the universal principle of cause and effect. In the throes of passion, time is suspended. There is no consciousness of the insufferable damage waiting around the corner, however distant that corner might be.

When at a university during the drug and sex revolution of the raucous '60s, a couple of students took LSD one morning and spent the afternoon staring at the sun, rejoicing in the kaleidoscopic unfolding and blending of colors. By nightfall they were blind. And if they are still alive, they are still blind. That's an operational definition of sin in a nutshell:

Foolish action causes irreversible consequences.

The five illustrations in this chapter will convey these factors of deception and consequences. From them an amazing, awesome reality will emerge: The consequences of each situation will seem totally blown out of proportion to the cause, the sin itself. There will appear to be no fairness on God's part. The cause will not seem commensurate with the effect, as in the usual Newtonian laws of action and equal reaction. Rather, sin creates an event as in quantum physics: A particle as minuscule as an atom produces a cataclysm like Hiroshima. It appears this way to us because we are not clear about sin, we do not grasp how God views sin and why, and we are not convinced of the centrality of the spiritual in life.

The Power of Sin

Therefore, it is necessary to understand this term *sin* in order to comprehend its consequences. Sin is not a humanistic nor a psychological term, but a theological one. It describes a power which influences every aspect of our lives; it affects our every thought and action. God said to Cain, "Sin is crouching at the door; and its desire is for you, but you must master it."[6] We can only hope to master it if we understand it.

Sin—What is it? What does it do? How does it do what it does? And what consequences does it create? How does God feel about sin and why? How does He see it, and what does He do about it? We hope that what follows will help crystallize your thinking.

God's law is the writing down of His perfection. It is the expression of His righteousness for the purpose of directing our thought and action. There is no arbitrariness in God's law because it is a statement of who He is, not just what He demands. When civil government decrees a 55mph speed limit, that may be in our best interest but that "law" does not emanate from the nature of the governors. It is an arbitrary assessment of what is right at the moment. Due to experience and judgment the speed limit may be moved up or down at another time, and then that new speed limit would become law.

God's Law

Understanding this difference is critical because then we can see two additional realities that complete the picture:

1. We do not *break* God's law—it is not a "thing" to be broken; it is the outward expression of His holiness. You may ignore it, transgress it, or swear at it, but you cannot circumvent it or break it. It's like when a man wanted to "break" the law of gravity. He jumped out the window of an 87-story building, and as he passed each floor he yelled to the people, "I'm okay so far!"

From Hugh Hefner to your next-door neighbor, many

people are in various stages of sin and it may look as though they are suffering no ill effects. They may even seem to be leading incredibly charmed lives, but they are just in free-fall. They haven't hit the ground yet.

2. Sin is the contradiction of God. The common notion that sin is essentially selfishness is so limiting as to miss the mark completely. Selfishness is not a true assessment of either sin's nature or its gravity. God's law is designed to regulate one's life to be consistent with God's perfection. Transgression is violation of that which God's glory is and what it demands. Sin is aimed against God. As unlikely as this may sound, we will see this perspective in the passages of Scripture to be cited. This concept is difficult to accept because most of us sin with other apparent motives than setting out to hurt or displease God. Yet Paul makes clear that in sin we are enemies of Christ.[7]

When we understand that God's law is not arbitrary, it does not break, and that sin is going against who God is, then we can begin to grasp the seriousness of sin and understand the severity of its consequences.

In chapter 4, we looked at the garden scene, evaluated the nature of temptation, and saw how Satan works. Here we will again look in on that conversation between Eve and Satan, this time to see how sin works, and to see the results, or the consequences.

Adam and Eve — Taking It From the Top

SATAN: Indeed, has God said, "You shall not eat from any tree of the garden"?

EVE: From the fruit of the trees of the garden we may eat; but from the fruit of the tree which is in the middle of the garden, God has said, "You shall not eat from it or touch it, lest you die."

SATAN: You surely shall not die! For God knows that in the day you eat from it your eyes will be opened, and you will be like God, knowing good and evil.[8]

Satan's words to Eve actually were directed against the integrity and honesty of God. As for Eve, the promise of a tree to make one wise drove a wedge of defection into her heart immediately. When she took the fruit, it wasn't just going against what God had said. It was repudiating His authority, doubting His goodness, disputing His wisdom, rejecting His justice, contradicting His veracity, and spurning His faithfulness.

This is the character of every sin in every instance: We are foraging for our own deification. Simply put, we want to call our own shots and be our own God. Because Adam and Eve went against the expressed dictates of God about the tree, consequences have been put in motion that are still crashing through the lives of every one of us:

1. Man's Attitude Toward God

Adam and Eve, like all of us, were made for fellowship with God. After the sin, they hid themselves.[9] Don't we all? Shame and fear predominate our approach to God. How much easier and calmer to decide there is no God to approach, as some have done. If there is no God, there is no shame or fear. But there is no fulfillment, either; there is only a vacuum. In *Sex Addiction,* Dr. Patrick Carnes notes in passing, "The void that sex attempts to fill remains the same."[10] Shame, fear and hiding are manifestations of sin in our lives.

2. God's Attitude Toward Man

Sin is one-sided. Its consequences are not. We talk about God hating sin and loving the sinner, but often this becomes a blurred caricature that perverts reality. The fact is, Adam and Eve's sin elicited from God reproof, condemnation, curse, and expulsion.

Any sin brings forth wrath and displeasure from God like a fulminating tidal wave, and it must be so, because sin is a direct contradiction of what God is. For God to be complacent about sin is an impossibility because He cannot deny Himself. Hence, all sin ends with the sinner ultimately in the Lake of Fire because all sin has its roots in spurning God Himself. This is why a Savior was necessary. He deflected the wrath of God away from us and onto Himself. He had to be perfect, otherwise He could not qualify to pay for someone else's sin. He would have had to pay for His own, just as we would have had to do.

If we choose not to receive pardon through His shed blood for our sin, we repudiate God's authority by rejecting the only avenue of escape from death. We are saying we don't need a substitute or, if we do, we're not interested. We are saying, "You have no right to be the Master of my life!" The core of sin, as this reveals, is a reach for God-equality. But in the eternal state there will be only one God. The new heavens and the new earth will not become battlegrounds for individuals to assert their claims to personal deity.

3. Consequences for the Human Race

The history of man furnishes an abundance of evidence that man inherited evil from his original parents. Man is unique in this aspect among all living things on the earth.[11] We witness with tract in hand and say to someone, "Sin is falling short of the glory of God." That's true, but it is a little like taking a teaspoon of water from the ocean to someone who has never been there and saying, "This is the Pacific Ocean." All the component parts are there, but the impact of the immenseness is lost.

Similarly, the dimensions of sin are staggering—beyond our comprehension. When David committed adultery with Bathsheba, he later cried out, "Against Thee, Thee only, I have sinned."[12] Our inclination is to say, "Wait a minute! Didn't David sin against Uriah, Bathsheba's husband, by taking his only wife, seducing her, killing him, and then being responsible for the death of her first baby?" We are incensed at David's nonchalance about the pain and injustice he inflicted on other people because we are not aware of the magnitude of the pain he caused God. Comparatively, their pain was insignificant—that is the point! When Jesus said, "If anyone comes to Me and does not hate his own father and mother and wife and children and brothers and sisters, yes, and even his own life, he cannot be My disciple,"[13] He was speaking comparatively. Hating our parents is not His goal for our lives; a disproportionate love for Him is. How our sin has affected others is bad; how it offends God is incalculable.

4. Consequences for Creation

The fall of man necessitated the cursing of creation.[14] Otherwise, creation would have been "higher" than man. The cursing of the ground (so that man has to work for a living!) was part of the consequences, but the ground is not all that was cursed. Sin, an event in the realm of the human spirit, had emanating effects throughout all of creation. It roars through time like a typhoon crashing through a border town, destroying everything in its path. Nature itself has suffered, so severe are sin's results.

5. Death

Death was the epitome of sin's effect, and God warned us of it in His initial prohibition.[15] It became part of the curse.[16] Today a paradox exists: We are surrounded by death and the dying, unlike Adam and Eve, yet we are no more aware of it than they were.

If you *really* believed Christ was coming back next Friday, or if you *really* believed that a week from Tuesday you would die in an auto accident, wouldn't you fill your remaining days with preparation? Instead, we plan our future as if life will never end. Its presence pervades all we do with an aspect of absurdity. So what if we learn this, accomplish that, or earn so much money? We're just going to fall into the ground and disappear anyway. Death is the dictator of hopelessness, and by far the cruelest consequence of sin.

6. Depravity

Sin never consists of a mere voluntary act. Every volition has a source. A sinful act is the expression of a sinful heart.[17] Until we recognize this problem, there is little recognition of the need of a Savior: "The LORD saw that the wickedness of man was great on the earth, and that every intent of the thoughts of his heart was only evil continually."[18] "For the intent of man's heart is evil from his youth."[19] Until you can say Amen to that, dealing with your sexuality is the least of your problems. Hell is going to be peopled with well-meaning do-gooders who claim they never knew what the problem was.

Sin always includes the perversity of heart, mind, disposition, and will. The theologians call it "depravity." David says, "I was brought forth in iniquity and in sin my mother conceived me."[20] That does not mean he was born out of an illicit relationship on his mother's part. It means that sin, that which will evolve into sinful acts, was woven into the fabric of his personness while he was developing in the womb. The witness of Scripture, therefore, is that sin is deepseated, pervasive, and continual.[21] Genesis 6:5 and 8:21, just quoted, spell out the components as the Creator evaluates them:

conception . . . . "the intent of the thoughts of his heart"

totality . . . . "every imagination"

constancy . . . . "continually"

exclusiveness . . . . "only evil"

early manifestation . . "from his youth"

Concerning this source of sin, Jeremiah says, "The heart is deceitful above all things and desperately wicked: who can know it?"[22] From whatever angle you consider, you see that man is hopeless: "There is none righteous, no, not one; there is none who understands; there is none who seeks after God . . . there is none who does good, no, not one . . . There is no fear of God before their eyes."[23]

The Common Fault

As we consider the consequences of sin in the lives of a few biblical characters we will look at, and in our own lives, and the ultimate penalty of death, the above verses will illuminate God's viewpoint.

Many people, of course, do not think about God or about His righteousness one way or another, nor do they usually consider themselves deceitful or desperately wicked. They may not be depending on His Lordship, or even sensitive to His presence, but after all, they're not an Adolf Hitler!

Therein lies the common fault. We compare ourselves to Jack the Ripper, and fail to recognize that the issue is sin directed at God: "The mind a person is born with is naturally inclined toward non-spiritual things and hostile toward God. It does not subject itself to the ways of God because it is not able to do so."[24] Through God's evaluation of the situations, we shall see this hostility toward God clearly in the upcoming passages.

God's Program

It may be helpful to add, by way of illumination, that this "depravity" is not necessarily the absence of either cultural virtues nor civil rightness. Every person has a conscience, and the law is written upon each one's heart to influence him to do right.[25] Man can compose beautiful music, produce great art and strive to understand his world through science—and it all contributes to our quality of life. But those things do nothing for the meaning of life.

God's criteria for judging actions lies beyond outward civility and productivity. They are:

- His love as the animating motive of life;
- His ways as the directing principle of life; and
- His glory as the controlling purpose of life.

The natural absence of these things causes our need for someone who will impregnate us with these characteristics, which Jesus does when He comes to live in us. Paul says, "If any [person] is in Christ, he is a new creature; the old things passed away; behold, new things have come."[26] We do not have the ability to work up these values or anything close to them on our own, hence, Jesus' words, "I am the vine, you are the branches; he who abides in Me, and I in him, he bears much fruit; for apart from Me you can do nothing."[27] On our own, every thought and action is a slice from the same loaf that Adam and Eve cooked up.

The question may be asked: Is God an egomaniac that He has to have everybody bowing to Him, depending on Him, standing around His throne saying, "Holy, holy, holy is the Lord God Almighty"? We may not understand all we know, but this I do understand: That very question springs from the insolence and insubordination we have just been dealing with. God is more worthy to run my life than I am, and I see within myself and all around me the evidence that any other way would be a short-cut to disaster. Submitting to the program as He outlines it is the only reasonable solution. And not only is it reasonable, it also brings peace, joy, purpose and fulfillment in the midst of the mess of our lives. Dr. Carnes acknowledged that sex does not fill the void; knowing God does.

The very fact that so radical a measure as a new birth is required is evidence of the hopelessness of our sinful condition.[28] It is simply impossible to extricate oneself physically, psychologically, morally, or spiritually from the vise–grip of sin. In fact, the fantastic message we find proclaimed by Jesus Christ and unfolded throughout the New Testament is not that our nature is *changed*—for our corruption is so complete that even He cannot renew it—but that the power of God is capable of birthing in us a *new* nature, virtually His nature. He alters our identity from the old self to this new self, and thereby releases us from that grip we ourselves are powerless to break.

I am laboring this point about sin because in every instance of consequences we will see, the dimensions are mind–blowing!

Saul—A Kingdom in the Balance (1 Samuel 15)

Saul was the first king over the nation Israel. He was a fearsome warrior and a popular leader, though he did not always rule wisely. In the beginning he was humble and unselfconscious,[29] but eventually he became conceited about his "kingliness," and arrogance replaced humility. One act of folly ended the possibility of establishing his royal line forever; the second mistake ended his rule abruptly.

What single devastating fault could cause God to turn His back on Saul and choose another to replace him? Did he attempt to lead the people against God to serve foreign deities? Did he burn his children alive, as was customary among many of the pagan religions? No. Saul just did not wait for Samuel, God's prophet, to show up to offer the sacrifice before a battle. He offered the sacrifice himself, and he felt justified in doing so.

He had waited the amount of time Samuel had told him to wait, seven days, and Samuel had not arrived. Isn't seven days long enough to wait for someone? Then to compound the problem, the people who were to go to battle with Saul began to scatter as the enemy— assembled its forces nearby. Logistically it looked bad and was getting worse, and the whole thing began to unravel before the battle could ever get underway.

Saul made an executive decision based on the factors as he saw them. He executed the sacrifice himself, asking the favor of the Lord in order to unite the people and prepare for war. Put another way, situational ethics dictated a pragmatic solution, disregarding biblical principle. God's prophet had said to wait until he came, for only a priest could offer sacrifices.

Samuel's judgment: You have not kept the commandment of the LORD your God.[30]

Circumstances, no matter how perilous, do not justify disobedience.

Saul's second mistake was even more acceptable from a human viewpoint. He had been told by God through Samuel to "go and strike Amalek and utterly destroy all that he has, and do not spare him; but put to death both man and woman, child and infant, ox and sheep, camel and donkey.[31] Instead, Saul took Amalek prisoner and spared the best of the sheep, oxen, and lambs. Why? "To sacrifice to the LORD"[32]

Noble motive! But as the text makes emphatically clear, there is no reason for disobedience. These were only transparent excuses thrown up to camouflage a willful pride that craves, like Eve's did, to be its own boss. Samuel unmercifully ripped off the mask of Saul's partial obedience in one of the most dramatic scenes in all of Scripture, revealing fullblown rebellion equal to idolatry![33]

Saul had initially deceived himself into thinking that he actually had obeyed the Lord by doing part of what God commanded. When confronted by Samuel's blazing anger, though, he deflected the heat from himself by blaming the people he was leading. When incessantly pressed by Samuel's indignant wrath, he confessed, but it was too late. The kingdom had been taken from him.

Now, by way of parallel, let us be realistic and blunt. There are an amazing number of "Christians" in our time who have deceived themselves into thinking that monogamy with their boyfriend or girlfriend is equal to celibacy before God's eyes. They attend church, Bible studies and camps, sing in the choir, and say with Saul, "Blessed are you of the LORD! I have carried out the command of the LORD."[34] They are no less deceived than was Saul. John McArthur, recently asked what he thought of all the Christians living together, replied, "Simple. They aren't Christians."

Narrow? Absolutely.

Wrong? Absolutely not.

Our lip service and glib compromise of God's ways with the world's style are no different from Saul's burnt offerings and sacrifices with partial obedience: "Has the LORD as much delight in burnt offerings and sacrifices as in obeying the voice of the LORD? Behold, to obey is better than sacrifice . . . and insubordination is as iniquity and idolatry."[35] Even though Saul was not rejecting God outright, his sin was no different from the sin of worshipping foreign gods.

Regarding assimilating the world's ways, James says, "You adulteresses, do you not know that friendship with the world is hostility toward God? Therefore whoever wishes to be a friend of the world makes himself an enemy of God."[36] (Notice how James uses the image of sexual unfaithfulness to indicate spiritual pollution — the mingling of the world's ways and God's ways.)

Paul puts it just as strongly: "For many walk, of whom I often told you, and now tell you even weeping, that they are enemies of the cross of Christ, whose end is destruction, whose god is their appetite, and whose glory is in their shame."[37]

Today many people have an enlarged appetite for sex, and satisfying that hunger is easily more important to them than conforming to the will of God. What Samuel nails in Saul is a common duplicity that loves God but rejects His narrow ways. Samuel clearly points out for all of us that to disregard God's ways is insubordination and rebellion, and rejection of God Himself. This hearkens back to the earlier discussion that to disregard God's law is an attack on God Himself. Though many choose to differentiate between loving God and conforming to His ways, Samuel's incisive words here make that impossible.

Would Saul have chosen *not* to wait for Samuel, or to spare Amalek's life, if he had *known* it would cost him his kingdom? Would you? Maybe. But once he chose his course of action, the consequences played themselves out beyond his control. They always do.

Moses—Hitting the Rock (Numbers 20)

Moses walked from the presence of the Lord right into sin, the consequence of which cost him the goal of his life and mission: to enter the promised land for which he had led the Hebrews out of Egypt. One act of disobedience in a moment of rage canceled the purpose of his efforts on God's behalf. Again, looking at it from our vantage point, the consequences can seem cruelly disproportionate.

The people were grumbling, as usual, complaining that they were in a wretched place with no food, and no water, and it was all Moses' fault. Moses and Aaron sought the Lord, who said, "Speak to the rock before their eyes, that it may yield its water."[38]

But Moses had a better idea.

> Moses and Aaron gathered the people before the rock. And he said to them, "Listen now, you rebels; shall we bring forth water for you out of this rock?" Then Moses lifted up his hand and struck the rock twice with his rod.[39]

Humanly speaking, Moses can certainly appear justified in his anger against his unbelieving, faithless charges who doubted God at every turn and condemned him at every difficulty.

"But the LORD said to Moses and Aaron, 'Because you have not believed Me, to treat Me as holy in the sight of the sons of Israel, therefore you shall not bring this assembly into the land which I have given them.' "[40] Moses disobeyed God, and the disobedience was judged as *unbelief*, which was indistinguishable from the people's unbelief. Indeed, belief and obedience are two sides of the same coin. If you have not one, you have not the other.

From that perspective, Moses' anger and Samuel's anger are absolutely dissimilar — the one was from human frustration that put a self-righteous twist to the order from God; the other was a reflection of God's anger at Saul's disobedience. Also clear is that the people's sin did not justify Moses' sin. Neither can the fact that "everybody's doing it" justify anything. We can see from these illustrations that we are soundly held responsible for our actions and our obedience regardless of anything else. God was personally offended at Moses' hitting that rock. Moses, in his mind, may have been impassioned at the people's stupid faithlessness, but God saw Moses' action as also a lack of faith. And "without faith it is impossible to please Him."[41]

Definitely worth noting in this situation is that Moses goes straight from face-to-face fellowship with God right into sin. He did not progressively slide from fellowship. *That* is how deceptive sin can be! It can come on like righteous indignation, a smoke screen to cover supercilious condescension.

Also, in spite of the judgment against him for this slip, Moses does not waste a minute apart from his walk with God and his momentous calling. He immediately gets back into fellowship with God. No time for guilt trips or self-pity because of God's heavy hand.

Furthermore, it is sobering to realize that while the relationship between God and Moses is maintained, there is no alleviation of the consequences. God is not vindictive and He does not hold grudges, yet forgiveness does not make the consequences disappear like a mirage on the horizon.

Similarly, you can walk straight from Bible study into bed with your girlfriend if you are not careful. We must *know* the truth, *hold* tenaciously to it, and ruthlessly *ignore* any justifications screaming in our minds.

Once again we can ask ourselves, would Moses have given vent to his anger and allowed his own disobedience if he had known his ticket to Canaan would be canceled? Don't you think he grieved with that deep, hard ache inside him as he lay quietly in the dark at night reflecting on the price of that moment of foolishness? Could he have penned this passage in tears, hoping against hope that some of us would realize that sin wears a million masks, and that whatever benefit we might derive from it is quickly crushed by its overwhelming cost? Free will is alive and well *only at the point of action* — then the consequences will play themselves out, as though directed by an unseen conductor.

The consequences of sin are irreversible, but like Moses, we must go forward, walking in the light. Paul says, "One thing I do: forgetting what lies behind and reaching forward to what lies ahead, I press on toward the goal for the prize of the upward call of God in Christ Jesus."[42]

Samson — If Wishes Were Horses (Judges 13-16)

In the depths of a dark, dank Philistine dungeon sits a broken man. This dungeon is particulary dark for this person because there are only hollow pits where his eyes used to be. He has not washed in . . . how long has it been? He's fed only enough to keep his muscles fueled for the arduous labor that fills each day: turning a great stone to crush grain. The Philistines used to use two oxen to tread the circle hour after hour under the blistering sun. Now they use Samson.

At night they throw him back into the dungeon with a bowl of slop for dinner. No one talks with him. They only taunt him, spitting at him, mocking his incapacity. There is no warmth of human comfort, no tenderness, only vast loneliness, deep, deep pain, and an unquenchable grief. Each night tears fall from the empty sockets. And Samson replays the litany of agony burning inside him: "What should be, isn't; what could have been never will be." Satan has won again.

What happened to the lusty, powerful Samson whom the world feared? Who but Samson could catch 300 foxes, torch their tails, and set them running through the standing wheat fields of the Philistines? Who but Samson could kill a lion with his bare hands, or, when bound with two new ropes and handed over to the enemy, could break the cords like melted wax, pick up the jawbone of a dead donkey and kill a thousand soldiers? Who but Samson could uproot the doors of the city gate, posts, bars and all, and carry them thirty-eight miles uphill? How could someone like this come to such a crude and ignominious end?

Samson was called of God to be a judge during the time judges governed Israel. Samson judged Israel for twenty years, and that was about 150 years before Saul was chosen as the first King. But Samson's call was unique because he was a Nazarite, and as such was not to cut his hair, drink alcohol, or go near a dead person or animal. Unfortunately, Samson did not take his responsibility seriously, and continually used the gifts of his calling for personal vengeance. His position made him, like Saul, drunk with the delusion of invincibility. While brandishing godliness, he broke all his Nazarite vows, and he never married, preferring the fast lane with enemy whores. Samson's life has become a beacon warning of the results of unrestrained sensuality for the believer. His pompous arrogance and cavalier disregard for eternal values got him betrayed and stripped of his eyes, his strength, his calling, what little integrity he still had, and ultimately his life.

Between personal exploits harassing the Philistines, Samson seemed to spend a lot of time with women. One fair female with whom he was particularly taken was Delilah. She had been paid highly by Philistine rulers to discover the key to Samson's great strength. He had no reason to trust her, but his sense of reason and judgment were blinded by lust. She continually pressed for his "secret" until, exasperated, he told her. That he revealed the source (more accurately, the symbol, for his source was God) of his inhuman power was only the proverbial tip of the iceberg. The reality of compounded sin in Samson was the same as it is for all of us: payday someday!

Samson, the James Bond of the Old Testament, always got the girl, and escaped from every trap without a scratch, all the while breaking all the rules. Like many of us, Samson thought he could live a forever-charmed life, but reality is so painfully different. We all get into trouble when we identify with James Bond and consider ourselves beyond the reach of consequences.

The story of Samson may not have a particularly happy ending, but what it lacks in happiness it makes up for in drama. The Philistines were having a great feast in one of their huge temples, with thousands in attendance and another 3 thousand spectators on the roof looking on. They called for Samson to be brought in so they could be "entertained" by humiliating him.

When led into the assembly, Samson said to the boy holding him by the hand, "Let me feel the pillars on which the house rests, that I may lean against them." Then he called out to God, "Please remember me, and please strengthen me just this one time, O God."[43] Paul said, 1200 years later, "The gifts and calling of God are irrevocable."[44] It was true for Samson. God, who had called

Samson to judge Israel and kill Philistines, heard Samson's prayer, and gave him the grace to accomplish something as he died: "And he bent with all his might so that the house fell on the lords and all the people who were in it. So the dead whom he killed at his death were more than those whom he killed in his life."[45]

There is an old saying:

If wishes were horses, beggars would ride.

You and I can learn from Samson: You can't sin and win. Having God in your corner is not going to mitigate the consequences at all. We cannot just wish things were different, wish things would change . . . and after the destruction is wrought in our lives and in others, wish it hadn't happened. Wishes will not get you around the block!

David and Bathsheba—Lust in High Places
(2 Samuel 11–18)

David was the second king of Israel, after Saul, about 900 years before Jesus Christ. He was undoubtedly the most colorful, charismatic and deeply spiritual leader Israel ever had. Time and space do not allow us to cover all the exploits of David as a warrior and faithful man of God, but he was the first person to consolidate all the tribes under one rule and the first to conquer all the nations around Israel who had harassed them for centuries. David was the only king ever referred to as "a man after God's own heart"; he and his son Solomon were the only kings to write inspired Scripture. But when David blew it, he really blew it.

Most of us are familiar with the story: David should have been at battle and was home instead. He saw the beautiful Bathsheba and sent to have her brought to his palace, where he seduced her. Since we have covered this ground three times already, we can expect two things:

1. If he had it to do over again, he undoubtedly would have made different choices.
2. The results of this sin would be stupendous, like a worm giving birth to an alligator.

Let's make a list of the consequences and backtrack from there. Remember that David not only already had a number of wives, but he also could take just about any single female of his day to be either a concubine (a legal mistress) or a wife.

1. David kills Bathsheba's husband and brings her into his house permanently. He does this in order to hide the fact that he had made her pregnant.

2. The baby with which she is pregnant dies shortly after his birth.

3. David is exposed by Nathan, God's prophet, for his stupidity and evil and is humiliated before many of the people in his inner circle—he had "given occasion to the enemies of the Lord to blaspheme."

4. David had killed an innocent man, and therefore the sword would never leave his house. One of David's sons would kill another of his sons, and the killer would in turn be killed by David's own army.

5. David had taken another man's wife and had lain with her in secret. David's killer–son would not only drive David out of his house and city in an attempt to usurp his throne, but the son would lie with David's wives and concubines on the palace roof, in broad daylight, the very same roof from which David first saw Bathsheba!

This is a lot of bad news for a one–night stand. But as we learned in the results of Adam and Eve, this sin, like all sin, is directed at God even though the participants may not have been cognizant of that fact: "The sword shall never depart from your house, because *you have despised Me* and have taken the wife of Uriah the Hittite to be your wife."[46]

When confronted by Nathan with his sin, approximately nine months after David first committed adultery with Bathsheba, David repented. He didn't hide, he didn't excuse, and he didn't dodge. Like Moses before him, David sprang back and kept on going; nevertheless, the consequences spun out over time.

First the baby died. Later, one of David's sons raped his sister. Another brother plotted revenge, and after waiting for two years, he killed the rapist-brother. The killer went away, and David mourned the loss of one son through death and another through exile. Years passed. The runaway reconciled with his father, but then plotted the overthrow of David's government. He drove David out of the city and raped all of David's women on the rooftop to totally emasculate and humiliate his father—to say nothing of the women! David eventually got the upper hand militarily and the son was killed in battle with David's army. David went back into mourning.

Because Nathan told David up front the general outline of the consequences of his sin, we know that the death of the baby, the rape, the murder, the overthrow, et al., are directly linked to that one night with Bathsheba. David lived out the shuddering truth, that even though the pleasure of sin is real, it is temporary, but the pain goes on and on.

Psalm 51 records David's repentance:

Be gracious to me, O God, according to Thy lovingkindness;
According to the greatness of Thy compassion blot out my transgressions.
Wash me thoroughly from my iniquity,
And cleanse me from my sin.
For I know my transgressions,
And my sin is ever before me.
Against Thee, Thee only, I have sinned,
And done what is evil in Thy sight,
So that Thou art justified when Thou dost speak,
And blameless when Thou dost judge (Psalm 51:1-4).

This is one of the most beautiful and magnificent passages of Scripture in the Bible because it beats with a life that springs from our own experience.

The twentieth century is a difficult time to live in as a Christian. Ours is a peculiarly sensuous age that reaches deep inside us and plucks the cords of our cravings, so we must know where we stand and why. The bombardment of our lascivious culture is relentless. The world's viewpoint increasingly infiltrates today's church and deceives the bewildered Christian.

The clamor of lasciviousness in our time exacerbates the Christian's desire for holiness, and it illuminates his stand, making him a light in the darkness as never before. Our protagonists lost their cutting edge when they blended in. Saul was forever being swayed by the people because popularity was more important to him than anything else; Moses became angry like the people; Samson was as lustful as his heathen neighbors; and David used his office for selfish pleasure, mistaking the blessing and protection of God for personal invincibility.

Know this—there are consequences to sin, and they will be worse than you can possibly imagine. Being aware of that, believing that, may do more than any other thing at the point of temptation to keep you from believing the deception of sin's lying promises.

Let us not "live and learn." Let's learn, then live.

Do not be deceived, God is not mocked; for whatever a [person] sows, this he will also reap. For the man who sows to his own flesh shall from the flesh reap corruption, but the one who sows to the Spirit shall from the Spirit reap eternal life. And let us not lose heart in doing good, for in due time we shall reap if we do not grow weary (Galatians 6:7-9).

△△△

Here's What You Can Do

1. Think through some recent decisions and actions in your life and identify the consequences, both positive and negative. Write down your conclusions.

2. What changes would you make if you were faced with the same circumstances now? What plans can you make for future decisions and actions?

3. Discern, in the case of wrong choices and detrimental consequences, if your regret is because you "got caught" (i. e., pregnant, STD, broken heart, etc.), or because you really feel a "godly sorrow" for your sin against God. Only godly sorrow begets change of lifestyle. Ever seen someone who is truly remorseful, but then ends up in the same mess again and again? Misplaced regret is the reason for that.

6

What God Says

> It isn't what I don't understand in the Bible that disturbs me. It's what I do understand.
>
> Mark Twain

When Eve chose to defect from God's team, it was not just transgressing a law that was involved in her reasoning. She knew God. She and Adam had walked and talked with God in that garden. She had the light of experience and understanding to guide her in choosing God's way and rejecting Satan's poisonous polemic. Unfortunately she chose not to.

Similarly, we have more than just a list of prohibitions illuminating the path of our choices. There are:

- Life-experiences of others that can demonstrate the psychological and emotional validity of sexual abstinence.
- The spiritual overtones and undercurrents of sex that go far beyond the sensory experience.
- The powerfully symbolic significance of sex, expressed within and without its design, paralleling other symbols that have acted out God's purposes in the drama of human history.
- The shrewd tactics of our adversary and the understanding of temptation and testing that make our wrestling with our sexuality obvious.
- The crushing consequences of lust and sin, as we are able to view them in the lives of others.

God's Absolutes

All these have come before this chapter, "What God Says," in order that we might have a well-prepared turf to receive God's absolutes.

God never requires blind faith. That is why we have first covered the rationale for believing and obeying what God says. Faith is always the issue—blind faith, never.

Also, I have waited until this juncture to cover the clear statements of the Bible in order to avoid the stigma of presenting holiness in negative terms. Merely blasting out with a list of "Thou shalt nots" can certainly make God, and Christianity, sound like a bad-news no-fun program. Hopefully, this five-chapter lead-in will shed light on the fact that God's prohibitions about sex emanate from love and concern for our best interest.

For instance, in *Time* magazine's recent exposé on drugs, the writer refers to cocaine as "promising momentary escape and delivering long–term misery and waste," and he reveals that "the easy tolerance of the '60s, when turning on was a statement of personal freedom, has turned to dread."[1]

These doomsday reports are no longer viewed as uninformed condemnations from square politicians and uptight parents. They are seen as warnings of real, not imagined, dangers. When we view God's laws in the same light, we will rejoice in knowing the truth, and we will not kick against the limitations of abstinence.

The value of looking at what God says lies in clearing out the cobwebs of our vague impressions and facing the absolutes of God's mind. Such an exercise might seem redundant, but I am continually amazed at people's incredulous response to the simple statements of the Bible that reveal God's position on sex. They never knew it was so clearly laid out, so all-encompassing. But the simple truth in black and white stares you in the face and never blinks. It is convicting.

Do not be deceived; neither fornicators, nor idolaters, nor adulterers, nor effeminate, nor homosexuals . . . shall inherit the kingdom of God. And such were some of you; but you were washed, but you were sanctified, but you were justified in the name of the Lord Jesus Christ, and in the Spirit of our God . . . The body is not for immorality, but for the Lord; and the Lord is for the body . . . Flee immorality. Every other sin that a [person] commits is outside the body, but the immoral [person] sins against his own body (1 Corinthians 6:9-11,13,18).

Do not let immorality or any impurity or greed even be named among you, as is proper among saints . . . For this you know with certainty, that no immoral or impure person . . . has an inheritance in the kingdom of Christ and God. Let no one deceive you with empty words, for because of these things the wrath of God comes upon the sons of disobedience. Therefore, do not be partakers with them; for you were formerly darkness, but now you are light in the Lord; walk as children of light (Ephesians 5:3–8).

Consider the members of your earthly body as dead to immorality, impurity, passion, [and] evil desire . . . which amount to idolatry. For it is on account of these things that the wrath of God will come (Colossians 3:5,6).

Let us behave properly as in the day, not in carousing and drunkenness, not in sexual promiscuity and sensuality, not in strife and jealousy. But put on the Lord Jesus Christ, and make no provision for the flesh in regard to its lusts (Romans 13:13,14).

We know that the Law is good if one uses it lawfully, realizing the fact that the law is . . . [made] for those who are lawless and rebellious, for the ungodly and sinners, for the unholy and profane, for those who kill their fathers or mothers, for murderers and immoral [people] and homosexuals and kidnappers and liars and perjurers, and whatever else is contrary to sound teaching (1 Timothy 1:8-10).

I am afraid that when I come again my God may humiliate me before you, and I may mourn over many of those who have sinned in the past and not repented of the impurity, immorality and sensuality which they have practiced (2 Corinthians 12:21).

This is the will of God, your sanctification; that is, that you abstain from sexual immorality; that each of you know how to possess his own vessel [body] in sanctification and honor, not in lustful passion, like the Gentiles who do not know God; and that no man transgress and defraud his brother in the matter because the Lord is the avenger in all these things, just as we also told you before and solemnly warned you. For God has not called us for the purpose of impurity, but in sanctification. Consequently, he who rejects this is not rejecting man but the God who gives His Holy Spirit to you (1 Thessalonians 4:3-8).

Effects of Christian Morality

In his book, *Mere Christianity*, C. S. Lewis points out that there are three elements to Christian morality. The celebrated "Does it hurt anybody else?" viewpoint is valid in evaluating one's actions, but it is only the first of the three criteria. "Does an action enhance or detract from one's inner person, his piece of mind (i.e., conscience), the delicate balance of 'rightness' within him?" is the second. The third is, "How does this action influence or impact the direction of one's life?"

All three factors must be considered in any course of action, along with one additional factor: the perspective of eternity. Lewis quickly points out that choices might take on considerably different sway if seventy years were the extent of life. This was certainly Huxley's angle in the earlier quote from his work, *Ends & Means.* He was a writer, thinker and renowned atheist, and he believed that the extent of life determined everything. Choices and actions were totally free of the restraints of absolutes because physical death ended it all. Lewis, acknowledging that life does not end with death, recognized that every action and choice sent repercussions into a very distant future.

Choices, therefore, affect not just other persons, but also have an impact of staggering proportions upon the inner self and one's own destiny. Not simply in the sense of "Where am I going to end up, heaven or hell?" but in the larger sense of "Who am I for eternity?" In light of our earlier look at rewards, we would guess that the eternal state is not going to be a mass of white beings floating on ethereal harp music as it echoes throughout the galaxies forever and ever. Whatever else I am doing here in this life, I am shaping my future for eternity as well.

When I embrace these absolutes regarding the divine limits for expressing my sexuality, others will be safeguarded. I will be protected from harm, and my future destiny will be enhanced.

Ecological Niches

By way of example, consider the fish. He has definite limits: the boundaries of the water. Within those limitations, however, he has wonderful freedom and joy. Outside of the water, beyond the limits that God established for him, is agony and death. Similarly, birds are free in the air, vulnerable on land, and dead in the water. Interestingly, man, who is outside the systems of nature, has no ecological niches. Since he is the only created "creature" with morals, ethics and God-consciousness, unlike animals which function by instinct, it is fair to say that his niche of freedom is found within the psychological, emotional, and spiritual limits

God has set for him. Outside those limits he will meet agony and death, just as surely as any other of God's creatures. Inside his limits man experiences his ecological, natural purpose, which is to glorify God. Paul puts it stirringly:

> There is but one God, the Father, from whom are all things, and we exist for Him; and one Lord, Jesus Christ, by whom are all things, and we exist through Him (1 Corinthians 8:6).

When we understand that freedom and purpose are experienced within these narrow "laws," we begin to see the rationale behind the tempting/testing syndrome. Satan incessantly conspires to keep us from flowing into a deeper life with God, from growing into the fullness God has for each of us, and from grasping the destiny He desires for us all. We begin to realize that conforming to God's limits on our sexuality is not a high-water mark of achievement, but merely the necessary first step toward being transformed and used purposefully by God.

Because it is a first step, a doorway, a testing ground, Satan throws everything he has at us in this area. The lure of sexual lawlessness is so strong that we can forever wrestle with it, starting, stopping, gasping, wretching, agonizing—and never get it behind us so we can move on. A decision must be made to conform to the Scriptures just quoted. As long as we are grappling over surface issues, divided in our commitment to truth or doubleminded in our direction, we will go nowhere in our spiritual growth.

> The one who doubts is like the surf of the sea driven and tossed by the wind. For let not that [person] expect that he will receive anything from the Lord, being a double-minded [person], and unstable in all his ways (James 1:6-8).

God and His Ways

> Not everyone who says to me, "Lord, Lord," will enter the kingdom of heaven; but he who does the will of My Father who is in heaven (Matthew 7:21).

At a local high school, the banner stretching down the hall announced the coming game: "We're #1!" That's fine—except they have not won a game in three years.

God is not after perfect people. If He were, He'd have a long, long wait. Our lives often ring with the same hollowness as that high school banner. While we ourselves are capable of tremendous self-delusion, God and others quickly see through the hypocrisy.

Some have vague impressions of God's prohibitions against pre-marital sex; others are crystal clear about what the mind of God is on it. But a surprising number from both these groups share a common delusion: They believe they can transgress God's ways with eternal impunity. They may have to endure the consequences of their actions on this earth, but after death, they are "eternally secure." They believe it is possible to love God, reject His ways, and have eternal peace with Him. Don't count on it.

Unlike many traveling evangelists and deacons' boards, God is not after decisions. He is after changed lives. Hearing the message is not the meal; it is the menu. Reading a book on scuba diving is not scuba diving. Never in Christ's teaching, nor anywhere else in the New Testament, is there a recognition of dead-end believism. Conversely, there *is* clear condemnation of such. Paul refers to those who are "always learning and never able to come to the knowledge of the truth" (2 Timothy 3:7). God will not be mocked. It is not our doctrine but the Word of God that will live and breathe and last forever. Jesus said:

> The gate is wide, and the way is broad that leads to destruction, and many are those who enter by it. For the gate is small, and the way is narrow that leads to life, and few are those who find it (Matthew 7:13,14).

If, by the actions and values that characterize my lifestyle, I look no different from those who travel the broad way, then which way am I on? Is this not James' point, when he says those who are hearers only of the Word, and not doers, delude themselves?[2] They think they are on one path when they are actually on another.

Changed Lifestyle

We just looked into the mind of God to see what He thinks and says about premarital sex. Let's look again, this time to see what He says about conforming to His ways. From this, we can see that identifying with God, saying we are on God's team, saying we love God, must necessarily encompass a transformed lifestyle:

> And by this we know that we have come to know Him, if we keep His commandments. The one who says, "I have come to know Him," and does not keep His commandments, is a liar, and the truth is not in him; but whoever keeps His word, in him the love of God has truly been perfected. By this we know that we are in Him (1 John 2:3-5).

> He who believes in the Son has eternal life; but he who does not

obey the Son shall not see life, but the wrath of God abides on him (John 3:36).

Everyone who comes to Me, and hears My words, and acts upon them, I will show you whom he is like: he is like a man building a house, who dug deep and laid a foundation upon the rock; and when a flood rose, the torrent burst against that house and could not shake it, because it had been well built. But the one who has heard, and has not acted accordingly, is like a man who built a house upon the ground without any foundation; and the torrent burst against it and immediately it collapsed, and the ruin of that house was great (Luke 6:47-49).

If you love Me, you will keep My commandments . . . He who has My commandments and keeps them, he it is who loves Me; and he who loves Me shall be loved by My Father, and I will love him, and disclose Myself to him . . . If anyone loves Me, he will keep My word; . . . He who does not love Me does not keep my words (John 14:15,21,23,24).

You are My friends, if you do what I command you (John 15:14).

Again, sinless perfection is not the issue. Indeed, the closer we get to Jesus Christ and the farther we walk down that narrow road, the more sensitive we are to sin, selfishness, narrowness of faith and attitude. As Paul says,"[We] groan within ourselves, waiting eagerly for our adoption as sons, the redemption of our body."[3] We yearn to be set free from the confines of this body and experience the real freedom of sinlessness. We have no control over when that time will be, but meanwhile, we do have control over some things, and lawless sexual indulgence is one of them. Many people stumble and fall right at this point. They assume that, because we cannot be totally sinless, giving our natural urges free reign leaves us no worse off spiritually than if we restrained them. Wrong!

An example of this would be humorous if it weren't so sad. In the magazine *Film Comment,* an article covered the Golden G-String Awards in Las Vegas, the "Academy Awards" for strippers. Of one aspiring dancer it said, "Among those auditioning is a show-girl stripper named Janette Boyd, a six-foot, 37-year-old, born-again Christian, recently divorced."[4] Somewhere God draws a line that separates the narrow way from the broad way of the world. It does not take much self-analysis to see if your life is distinguishable from your heathen neighbors in fundamental areas.

Perhaps the classic passage evaluating lifestyle is Hebrews 3. It refers to the Israelites who left Egypt under Moses and saw

God work for forty years. They took the name of Jehovah and identified with Him, leaving Egypt and following Moses. They were
not rank heathen like those Canaanites! Yet, they did not embrace
God's ways; therefore, they were just as rejected by God as the
Canaanites who gave their children as burnt offerings to deities
of stone:

> I was angry with this generation, and said, "They always go astray
> in their heart; and they did not know my ways"; as I swore in my
> wrath, "They shall not enter my rest" (Hebrews 3:10,11).

The writer of Hebrews goes on to warn the readers against
being "hardened by the deceitfulness of sin" (verse 13):

> And to whom did He swear they should not enter His rest, but to
> those who were disobedient? And so we see they were not able to
> enter because of unbelief (Hebrews 3:18,19).

Faith and Obedience

Notice the flip from obedience to faith in that passage. It is
the same in John 3:36. When we believe, we are obedient. When
we are unbelieving, we are disobedient. Obedience is faith.

To disobey is to believe, as shown in action, that God really
does not want what is best for me, much less know what is best
for me. To obey is to act upon the belief that God knows better
than I do what is best for me. To obey is to act as if God is trustworthy. To obey is to believe that the Scripture is true and is reflective
of the mind, heart, and will of God. To obey is to believe that God
loves me. It is the operational outworking of believing. And, to be
sure, such believing is the only type of believing the Bible knows
anything about.

These two concepts, belief and obedience, are not merely
compatible, like the proverbial hand-in-glove; rather, they occur
only together, like roses and thorns. They are as inseparable as
God and His ways.

Though a Christian, no matter how mature, can be deceived
for a time and slide into gross immorality, it is so against his inner
nature that he will not stay there. He will be like a cork under
water and he will suffer terribly for having done so—the consequences are unavoidable. But so-called Christians who live an
immoral lifestyle are a wholly different matter. Hence the writer
of Hebrews continues, "Let us therefore be diligent to enter that
rest, lest anyone fall through following the same example of dis-

obedience" (4:11).

The story is told of Alexander the Great reviewing his troops after a fierce battle. He came across one of his captains disciplining a soldier for cowardice. Alexander approached.

"What is your name, soldier?" he asked.

"Alexander," replied the soldier.

"What?" exclaimed Alexander the Great.

"Sir, my name is Alexander!" said the soldier.

Trembling with rage, Alexander the Great yelled, "Soldier, either you change your ways, or you change your name!"

As we saw from the Gospels and the writings of Paul and John, the issue of lifestyle is neither incidental nor obscure. As soldiers in His army, we simply must choose: We either stop acting cowardly, or we change our name.

The kingdom of God does not consist in words, but in power (1 Corinthians 4:20).

Whose Am I?

I have mentioned more than once that the game of life is His game, and we cannot escape. I trust this does not sound fatalistic or morbid. But it is true, and the truth of it illuminates many other avenues of understanding. I have determined in my life to take reality by the throat and shake it to see what comes loose, and what has come loose is a lot of philosophical double talk and empty presuppositions, which may be painted pretty but crumble like a paper doll under the slightest pressure. Individual freedom is one such issue that shook loose right away.

Personal choice is not what I am referring to. From those choices, however, flow the person's lifestyle, the building of his future life, and the shaping of the inner person. I may believe that I am the ultimate determiner of my destiny, that I am directing my life and its course of events, but am I? When I look into the Scripture, I find quite a different scenario.

Before a person accepts Jesus' death on his behalf as payment for the penalty of his sin, he has a master to whom he is a slave: sin.[5] After being saved (i.e., washed clean of all past, present and future sins, and declared righteous, spotless, and perfect before a holy and just God), one could continue submitting to that old master,[6] or become a slave of righteousness.[7] Suddenly, the idea of being the captain of one's own ship is revealed to be a bad joke. There never was, and there never will be, such an option.

To say I have one of two masters is another way of saying there is a narrow gate and a wide gate. God's ways and Satan's ways. Yet an overwhelming number of people sincerely believe that there is a third way, a middle road, which is not fanatically holy but which is certainly not flagrantly lascivious. Because there are no orgies, drunkenness, or whores in their lives, these people may consider it to be a dignified individualism. This is a deception. It is "the Emperor's new clothes" about which everybody may nod approval, but in reality, are simply nonexistent.

By dignified individualism, which essentially is humanistic existentialism, I mean doing what seems right to a person within the present circumstances. But remember, the unsaved person has no choice. He is a slave of sin. He is chained to the broad way. For him, immorality is as natural as breathing.

In high school, I had a good friend named Chris. When I returned to school for my senior year, after I became a Christian during the summer, Chris's excessive profanity became increasingly unnerving to me. So I challenged him.

"Chris, could you not swear if you chose to stop?"

"Of course," he said.

"Would you be willing to bet?"

"Sure. I'm in control of my life."

"Okay," I said. "You pay me a quarter every time you swear."

"Fine," said Chris.

Before the day was over, Chris owed me more than ten dollars. He absolutely was out of control, and it was humbling for him. I didn't bother collecting the money, but the experience seemed to make an impression on him just the same.

Regardless of Frank Sinatra's famous song, there is no path in life marked "My Way." Determining my own design for my life is a deceptive illusion, a false front covering the broad path to hell. Satan and his ways or God and His ways are my only two options. It always comes back to that.

There are many reasons to choose God's ways, but my focus at this point is one specific aspect. That is, when contemplating whether or not to conform to God's narrow and rigid standards, I need to recognize this truth: I was a slave in the slave market of sin. I was bought at a very high price—the blood of Jesus Christ.[8]

True Freedom

And that brings me to a fundamental, cataclysmic and inescapable conclusion: *I am not mine!* I do not belong to me. I don't have either authority over nor title to me. I was not mine before, for I was a slave to sin; and I did not become mine. Someone else paid the price for me; I didn't. I was transferred from one master to another.

All of us were designed for freedom, just like that fish in the sea. We were also designed for God, to glorify God. Therefore, when I am functioning according to design, I am experiencing maximum freedom. Slavery to Jesus Christ is freedom!

> It was for freedom that Christ set us free; therefore keep standing firm and do not be subject again to a yoke of slavery (Galatians 5:1).

> And having been freed from sin, you became slaves of righteousness . . . But now having been freed from sin and enslaved to God, you derive your benefit, resulting in sanctification and the outcome, eternal life (Romans 6:18,22).

To the person who has not been enlightened to this perspective, there may seem to be no greater restriction than slavery to anybody at any time. But to those who see, believe, and embrace this truth, it is the most liberating realization imaginable. Why? Because if I grasp this fact, then I realize how stupid it is to attempt to go any other way than God's way, the narrow way. And I am free from the burden of having to choose celibacy if I am single, or monogamy if I am married. Those choices are out of my hands. Having chosen Jesus Christ predetermined those choices.

> Do you not know that your body is a temple of the Holy Spirit who is in you, whom you have from God, and that you are not your own? For you have been bought with a price: therefore glorify God in your body (1 Corinthians 6:19,20).

The Christian life is designed to move in only one direction: forward. If we rankle and squirm at the idea of handing the reigns of our life over to Jesus Christ to control, the frustration and anxiety will mount within like a blocked boiler building toward self-destruction. Peace, joy and the experience of freedom come from living within the confines God has established.

The Yoke of Lordship

A yoke is a wooden frame fastening two oxen together for drawing a plow. It is a picture of submission, of belonging to whomever put the yoke on. Jesus said, "Take My yoke upon you, and learn from Me, for I am gentle and humble in heart; and you shall find rest for your souls. For My yoke is easy and My load is light" (Matthew 11:29,30). In that last sentence, put the emphasis on *MY* and you will get the point.

The choice is not between Jesus Christ's lordship and no lordship—it is between His lordship and another of an infinitely more burdensome kind! The comparison is with the yoke of the legalism of the Pharisees, and all cults and religions. They all burden their followers with a seemingly infinite array of do's and don'ts designed to appease a distant god. Also in view is the yoke of sin, the growing, crushing burden of life's failures and disasters as they pile up on you with no help, no relief.

When Jesus refers to "rest for your souls," He is speaking of the constant, ultimate, everpresent aim of our innermost being: peace. Not relaxation from the burdens of living this life, nor release from the battle with the enemy, but peace with God and peace with oneself.

I take on His lordship; I conform to the narrowness of His ways; I adopt His commandments, and He takes the load of all my guilt, shame, humiliation, fear, anxiety, pain, heartache, anger and hatred.[9] Augustine beautifully compares this yoke of Christ to a bird's plumage, an easy weight, which enables the bird to soar into the sky!

This exchange—the yoke of sin for the yoke of Christ—is the only exchange going in the universe. There is no other. If I think I have been relieved of my burden of sin, but I refuse the yoke of His Lordship, I am living a delusion. The Word of God knows nothing of such an arrangement. It simply does not exist.

> Whoever believes that Jesus is the Christ is born of God; and whoever loves the Father loves the child born of Him. By this we know that we love the children of God, when we love God and observe His commandments. For this is the love of God, that we keep His commandments; and His commandments are not burdensome (1 John 5:1-3).

And that is what God says.

ΔΔΔ

Here's What You Can Do

1. Pick one of the verses listed on page 85 and one on pages 88-89 of this chapter to memorize. Write each of these out on a 3" x 5" card and carry them with you. Refer to them often in order to "hide God's Word in your heart."

2. In what ways will you allow these verses to be put to work in your life?

3. List all the verses mentioned in both sections by chapter and verse in the back of your Bible. Be sure to work with a "modern" translation. Recommended are: Ryrie Study Bible, New American Standard Bible, and New International Version Study Bible.

7

Pornography

A Message of Madness

> It is an indescribably horrid situation when you are afraid to die, but can't stand the thought of living through the pain of another day. I could find no purpose for my existence. Now I had even come to the point where I abhorred sex. It no longer held any pleasure or enjoyment or satisfaction for me.
>
> Brenda MacKillop, *Playboy* Bunny

One of the ways that mankind is different from all other created beings on the planet is that his mind has the ability to imagine. That power to imagine then gives rise to his individual reality. If you see yourself a loser, you will be a loser. If you see yourself a victim of circumstances, that will be your interpretation of your life. If you imagine yourself an achiever within a limitless spectrum, you will undoubtedly accomplish quite a lot.

Imaging emanates from the content of the mind. Because of what our mind has received, for instance, we imagine what women are like, what they desire, how they relate and how a man relates to them. From that imaging we direct our actions toward the opposite sex.

In the same way, pornography, which depicts perverse sex, degradation through sex, transient meaningless sex, violent sex, etc., becomes a shaper of reality as it flows into and through the viewer's mind. It is unbelievably powerful and lasting in its impact on the mind, but it is a reflection of incomplete and abnormal human development.

However, if you find pornography stimulating and exciting, that is not surprising. When we understand man, Satan, and the dynamics of human interaction, we can realize why pornography has such appeal.

Women, for the most part, are turned on sexually by touch, atmosphere, and enduring words of love. On the other hand, men were designed to become aroused by just the sight of a female body. Pornography capitalizes on these features of our nature and mixes them with the God-designed capability to experience vicariously. To experience vicariously means to identify with, learn from, and essentially experience something without going through it. When you see a film or read a book that creates feelings in you of peace, fear, anger, anxiety, resentment, tenderness or sadness, you are experiencing vicariously. The reason so much of the Bible is history and the recitation of personal experiences is that people have the ability to benefit from what others go through. Animals do not have this capacity. It is part of the image of God within us and it allows us to learn from another's past, project into the future, and shape the present.

Pornography blends, on film and in print, sight arousal and vicarious experience to ignite the imagination — and the impact is enormous. It reaches down inside a person and snaps a captivating grip on the sin nature, that part of us that clings to darkness and is drawn toward the degrading of the natural.

One may ask, "What is so unnatural about people making love?"

Pornography is not people making love.

But, let's back up a bit. God created sex. He designed it to take a couple beyond words into communicating something deep and tremendously meaningful. It speaks where nothing else can. It heals and binds and blends two people into one in a miraculous way — that is, if its ideal purpose is not interfered with.

But pornography lifts the fleshly component of love out of its designed context and turns it every which way but loose. The film "Doing Debbie Dirty" is not about a girl who falls down in the mud, and it has nothing to do with love and marriage, or even making love. It is dashing, daring Debbie and thirty-seven guys in one protracted orgasmic spermathon.[1]

Pornography is cold, mechanical sex; it rarely involves only two people; it usually encompasses violence, and it is totally male centered. It is sensation without feeling and sex without relationship. Then it goes downward from there, incorporating the arcane and the bizarre, beyond the imagination of most people: torture, bondage, children, animals, blood and death.

The Magnitude of Pornography

As an industry, pornography is flourishing. It is the third highest profit enterprise of the mafia, after gambling and narcotics, with roughly 90 percent of all pornography being produced and distributed by organized crime.[2] Though ten to fifteen years ago pornography was a minor element of interest and production, it is now spreading rapaciously. The number of current pornography outlets in America exceeds that of McDonald's franchises.[3] The market for X-rated video tapes alone in the Los Angeles area was $200 million in 1982, and bounding upward.[4] *Forbes* magazine estimated in 1978 that pornography gleaned $16,438,000 a day, but amazingly that is a trifle compared with the $8 billion annual figure in 1987. Today *Penthouse* magazine alone sells four thousand copies an hour, every hour of every day. One tragic statistic, according to Henry Boatwright, Chairman of the U. S. Advisory Board for Social Concerns, is that 70 percent of all pornographic magazines end up in the hands of minors.[5]

This growing industry is making an impact on our society, and one of its most jarring repercussions is what happens to our children as a result. According to Senator Christopher Dodd (D. Connecticut), "By even the most conservative estimates, a child is sexually abused somewhere in this country every two minutes." Of the 1.5 million children who run away from home each year, 40 to 75 percent do so because of incest.[6] What is the connection between incest and pornography? Police vice squads report that 77 percent of the child molesters of boys and 87 percent of the child molesters of girls admitted they were imitating the behavior they had viewed in pornographic publications.

But we are not here concerned primarily with the social implications of pornography, as horrendous as they may be. Rather, our concern is more personal: **your** relationship with pornography. What effects will it have, can it have? What is its nature and how does that nature affect you if you expose yourself to its influence? Many people on many levels believe pornography is harmless. It is not. It is dangerous. It is a mind-altering drug of deceptive appeal.

The Purveyors of Pornography

Since the early '70s pornography has reached deeper and deeper into the shocking. According to P. E. Dietz and B. Evans, in their study published in the *American Journal of Psychiatry,* the November 1982 issue, the changes in the pornography industry both create and respond to the demand for the increasingly bizarre, in a reciprocal, downward spiral. Twenty years ago, 90 percent of the "adults only" literature featured nude women posed alone. Today that mild fare accounts for a mere 10 percent of the market. What is depicted in today's pornography, they say, is an accurate representation of what is going on in the viewer's mind, and what is transpiring in the viewer's mind is created and extended by what he sees or reads. And, apparently, the more gruesome, the better. Retailers complain that pictures showing blood and death concurrent with the sexual antics sell out so fast they cannot keep them in stock. This symbiotic relationship between the pornographer and the consumer accounts for much of the impact of pornography on our culture.

The Effects of Pornography

One of the leaders in the field of studying and documenting the effects of pornography is Dr. Victor Cline, Professor of Psychology at the University of Utah. He has categorized four phases one goes through in the assimilation of pornography and its cascading consequences:

1. *Addiction.*

Within the scope of pornographic literature and films, there is something for everybody's degree of twist, from the artistic to the outrageous. Wherever one plugs into it, pornography is like a drug: It takes more and more to fill the ever-growing need it creates as one becomes increasingly distorted in his perception of reality. Indeed, the confines of his mind become his reality, and eventually he attempts to contort his circumstances into the shape of the images in his head. Many studies show that repeated exposure to pornography, whether simple and soft or hard and perverse, leads to alterations in attitudes, appetites, and even behavior. Said one man, "The cumulative effect of pornography caused me to devalue my wife as a sexual being. The great lie of *Playboy,* films, and even commercials, is that the physical ideal is obtainable and oh, so close . . . "[7] The young, beautiful, flaw-less female is smiling at me, and she is just around the corner! But this wrinkle of perception is just the beginning of the problem.

The drug-like property of pornography is the hidden snare within the seemingly harmless. What is so horrific about a picture of a naked woman? Isn't that the way God made her? Could not that be considered art? So go the defenses of nudity before the camera.

But that is not really the point. The real point, the absolute-ly pernicious point of pornography, is that, initially, the picture of the naked woman sets off sirens, but after repeated looking it does not merit even a second glance. A man becomes hooked; he keeps going back for more. Soon it takes a couple on the couch, then a group on the floor involved in every conceivable position and aber-ration, to stimulate him. As his imagination becomes continuously stretched, it eventually fails to return to normal, and ever-increas-ingly explosive jolts of the outré are required to fill the outsized parameters of his inner reality. He is hooked. "Men will give up grapes and lettuce and orange juice and Portuguese wine and tuna fish, but men will not give up pornography."[8]

2. *Escalation.*

Addiction leads to the need for rougher, meaner, more bi-zarre, more way-out, more explicit sexual imagery to get "turned on." Even in marriages where a woman may attempt to placate her husband by participating in his bizarre fantasies, she even-tually realizes there is no end to it. Other men or women may be brought into the bedroom to continue to maximize the orgasmic thrill as the imagination continues to stretch.

Addiction and escalation negate the myth that exposure to pornography breeds boredom, soon people will stop buying it, and eventually the whole business will starve itself out of existence.

Both academic studies and the financial gains of the bur-geoning empire prove the biblical judgment on the nature of man: He who sins is the slave of sin. Indeed, the slavery/addiction/es-calation syndrome of pornography is sufficient to demonstrate that its character is intrinsically evil.

3. *Desensitization.*

As one's addiction escalates, to him other people take on a one-dimensional focus — sexual. And the sex depicted in pornog-raphy becomes not only something outside the bounds of human normalcy, but also something other than animalistic. No animal engages in sex the way it is depicted in pornography, quite simply because animals are not moral creatures capable of scraping the fringes of depravity. Dr. Cline also states that through desensitization the shocking and repulsive soon become commonplace, then legitimized, then acceptable, then attractive.

That is truly frightening, because you can be pulled along until you're into something you didn't even like but now you need! This is what is referred to in both psychological and theological circles as the "searing of the conscience." And it is just as true for the participant in pornography as for the consumer of pornography. One actress recounts her evolution from nude posing to hard core films and how it forever altered her perceptions, or inner reality, and therefore ultimately her life:

> Things won't ever be the same for me. My sex life will never be normal. I can't equate sex with affection. I have the images that never stop running in my head of women as passive victims of violence and abuse. The scenes disgust me but I can't stop them. I want to be able to be in a loving situation without having these scenarios going through my head, but I can't. I hate myself for having them, but I can't get off sexually if I don't have them . . . I've been in years of therapy but nothing's changed. I just feel damaged. I relate sexually to women now. The psychic damage has never really healed.[9]

Furthermore, the conscience can be seared in a surprisingly brief span of time. In a case study, men were tested both before and after viewing rough pornography to determine their feelings concerning rape. Before the viewing, they were repulsed and sympathetic to the female. After the films their attitudes became flippant toward it, seeing the women as either deserving it or actually liking it. This is because 20 percent of sexual episodes in pornography are rape, an additional 6 percent are incestuous rape, and 97 percent of both clearly focus on the victim's fear being transformed by the rape into orgasmic exaltation.[10]

The Malamuth and Spinner report points out that "the information conveyed in much of the sexually violent materials is that women are basically masochistic and in need and want of male domination," and that a lot of ordinary men commit rape, suffer no remorse, and gain sexual and ego satisfaction from it.[11]

Corroborating these findings, Christofer Wetzel, Assistant Professor of Psychology at Rhodes College, says that the effects of pornography include increased aggressiveness, less sympathy for rape victims and increased belief that women want to be raped, and pornography makes many men feel freer to act out the same thing.[12]

4. Acting Out.

Acting out is the mind's way of bringing outward reality into conformity with its own inner world. Only when the inner world of the mind and the outer world of a person's life are aligned can there be sanity. The human organism knows this instinctively and contrives to bring it to pass.

Over the period of time that the mind is taking in the pornography, the mind is being shaped by it. The more that happens, the more the mind is out of step with outside reality. As the gulf between the inner reality and the outer reality widens, one of two things must happen: (1) The intake of pornography must cease allowing the mind to slowly come back to normal; or (2) the person will act out what is in his head.

This is the point of Proverbs 23:7: "As [a person] thinks within himself, so he is." The power of thought is again pointed out in the New Testament:

> Whatever is true, whatever is honorable, whatever is right, whatever is pure, whatever is lovely, whatever is of good repute, if there is any excellence and if anything worthy of praise, let your mind dwell on these things (Philippians 4:8).

The mind cannot distinguish in its imagery between what is real and what is artificially imposed from without. It functions much like a computer receiving and recording input without evaluation.[13] Judgment is the prerogative of the spirit and choice is the prerogative of the will, but the mind takes in whatever it is given. The will is the policeman designed to stand at the door of the mind and block the entrance of material that will distort and destroy. And the spirit is designed to enlighten the will and thereby assist its function. If the will chooses to allow pornography in, the influence will affect the mind and eventually the outward life of the individual. It cannot be otherwise.

Those who do not ingest pornography are outraged and incredulous at rape, violence toward women, perversion, and the seduction of children. To the pornography addict, however, all this is unshockingly normal because he views it in light of his inner, contorted values. With his conscience immobilized, his appetite cultivated, and his perception altered, the consumer of pornography eventually believes the myth that "everybody's doing it."

The reason the impact of pornography is so powerful that it spills over into action is explained in part by Dr. James L. McGough from the University of California, Irvine. He points out that experiences—vicarious or real (remember, the computer/brain does not distinguish between the two)—at the time of emotional (or sexual) arousal get locked into the brain by the chemical epinephrin and become virtually impossible to erase.[14] Hence, the memory of the pornography is bigger than life, banging noisily on the walls of the brain and drumming up an insatiable lust that demands expression but defies satisfaction. This was the effect described by the actress quoted earlier.

An ex-policeman now turned writer says his books often reflect cases he was involved with, but, he adds, some were too gruesome even for fiction. One example he gave was a case where a woman assisted her boyfriend in raping her own 12-year-old daughter. What could possibly influence two people, especially the mother, to participate in such a tragic perversion that could ruin her daughter's entire life? Pornography.

Because of the elements of escalation, desensitization, and acting out, pornography is becoming recognized as an attack on the family. Not only does it glorify recreational sex and devalue monogamy as stupid and unsophisticated, but it also causes men to become unappreciative of their wives, move into adultery and/or drag their wives into fantasies, fathers begin raping their daughters and sons, and the fabric of the marriage and the home begins to unravel. The spirit of pornography simply does not submit itself to containment.

The Evil of Pornography

Torture, blood and death have little to do with sex. Normally, that is. However, when we recognize the spiritual foundation of life, that man is a spiritual being, that there is a spiritual war waging, that Satan is intent on diverting our attention, creating destruction, and destroying the work of God, then the violent associations within pornography all fit. Jesus Christ is life and peace. Satan is the opposite—pain and death. The fact that so much of pornography incorporates pain and death reveals the stamp of Satan. It is his program. Therefore, from a spiritual perspective, the blood and gore make sense.

Also, Satan is not a creator as God is. His aim is to take what God has created and twist it, distort it, and mar it. By doing so, he deadens it, ripping the life out of those involved.

At this time, snuff films and child pornography are at the end of the line of the pornographic gamut. Snuff films portray the literal, actual torture and murder of the women and/or children in the midst of the man's sexual climax, all in living color while the cameras are rolling. For a growing number in our culture, this is entertainment. There are an estimated 260 child-porn publications in the U. S. alone, and in 1983, a conservative estimate indicated that 300,000 children, mostly eight to twelve years old, but also from fifteen down to less than six months, were raped and sodomized before the camera for commercial purposes.[15] There are even two national organizations that actively promote the justification of this: the René Guyon Society, whose motto is, "Sex by eight or it's too late," and the North American Man/Boy Love Association.

Deviation From the Norm

And make no mistake—it is a straight shot from the pristine pages of pretty *Playboy* pinups to the dregs of beastiality and kiddie-porn. The one who thinks there is an essential difference in kind and not just degree is either blind or uninformed, and knows nothing of the spiritual ramifications involved. Indeed, *Playboy, Penthouse* and *Hustler* subtly encourage child molestation. Surprised? With her research team, Dr. Judith Reisman, of the American University in Washington, D. C., conducted a page-by-page review of virtually every issue of all three publications since 1953 and found more than 6,000 images of children that implied sexual activity in photographs, cartoons, advertisements and other pictorial material.[16]

Hugh Hefner, himself, advocates sex with animals, as revealed in an interview with the *Los Angeles Times:*

> What I'm saying is this, what difference does [sex with animals] make if it turns somebody on? Isn't that a positive thing? The only thing I see in beastiality that is hurtful to people is the fact that people used to go to prison for it . . . I think that's a very sick attitude on sex.

Of course, what is usually meant by "if it turns somebody

on" is that the man will be turned on by watching women have sex with animals. Linda Lovelace, in her autobiographical work, *Ordeal*, relates how she was coerced by her husband and Hefner to have sex with a dog in Hefner's back yard. It was not her idea, and she was not the one turned on by it.

Deviation from the norm in sex is learned, not inherited. There has never been any study or claim that desiring and pursuing sex with corpses, animals or children springs from our genes. It is what Professor Cline calls an "accidental condition." In other words, one does not start out to learn how to become a rapist or child molester. In the report to the Attorney General on child pornography, the California Attorney General's Advisory Committee on Obscenity and Pornography noted, "In interviews with a great many police officers the Committee was frequently told, 'I never arrested a child molester who did not have pornography in his possession.'" Also, a Los Angeles Police Department investigation studied more than forty child molestation cases during a five-month period and pornography was found to be present in every case. It is therefore no surprise to realize that child sexual abuse has increased as adult pornography has spread.

By way of illustration:

A 31-year-old father in Milwaukee was recently arrested and charged with sexually assaulting his 11-year-old daughter and taking pornographic photographs of her. The incidents occurred while the girl was visiting her father under the terms of her parents' divorce. According to Captain Thomas Perlewitz, police obtained a search warrant and confiscated several pornographic videotapes and hundreds of porno magazines and books.[17]

In Bonney Lake, Washington, Bert Mendenhall was charged with two counts of first-degree statutory rape involving the three- and five-year-old children of a woman he had known from childhood. Searching Mendenhall's home, police found foreign and domestic child pornography.[18]

Timothy Rains of Newark, California, was recently arrested for the rape and torture of two girls, a 16-year-old and an 18-year-old. Detective Lance Morrison said, "Both victims were tortured to the point of believing they would be killed any second." In Rains's residence, police found sadomasochistic videos and magazines.[19]

Sex Criminals

What is the profile and background of the perpetrator of sex crimes? Consider Eugene Pyles, 29, military veteran, no criminal record, and an enviable family background. In December of 1984, he forced a 16-year-old female into his car at knife-point, took her to an isolated area, raped her, stabbed her repeatedly and cut her throat. Thinking her dead, he went home. The girl, naked and covered with blood, crawled to the road, where she was picked up and taken to the nearest house. Her description of Pyles got him arrested. In Pyles's apartment, police found a scrapbook of nude magazine photos, a journal describing brutal sex acts and torture written by Pyles, portions of sexually and brutally explicit novels stapled together, and a number of videos of the same caliber. Pyles had reached the acting out stage.[20]

When Edna Buchanan, a staff writer for the *Miami Herald,* was writing a series of articles on the "pillowcase rapist," who had been active in her area for some time, she contacted scientists at the FBI Academy in Quantico, Virginia, for facts on rapists. Said the Academy, "He collects pornography magazines of all types, dreams of rape, then slips over the threshold of fantasy into the reality of sexual assault."[21]

The impact of pornography cannot be over-emphasized. In Minnesota prisons, which probably do not differ from many other state prisons, sex offenders now outnumber any other single category of inmate. Two sex offenders from one prison testified last fall before the U. S. Senate Subcommittee on Juvenile Justice at the federal courthouse in Pittsburgh.

"I see pornography itself as a catalyst to the fantasies of a sex offender," said one.

The other then added, "There is no doubt it was a contributing factor to my problems. It gives you ideas. It gets your mind stimulated, your head going, your body going, and your fantasies going . . . pornography okays the act. The only way I could find gratification was to victimize someone younger, weaker and less knowledgeable."[22]

Denials

For some, the idea of acting out the seduction, rape, and violence of pornography cannot be "proved." According to Berry Lynn, counsel for the American Civil Liberties Union,[23] "No study now or ever will demonstrate that sex offenders and abusers are caused to be the kind of people they are because they look at pornography."[24]

And, "We would not be a safer society for women and children if pornography disappeared. There is no basis for making that conclusion."[25]

If a man had the nature of a horse or a rabbit, that would be true. But his nature being what it is, man responds to pornography as Dr. Cline enumerated, and the above examples illustrate the validity of that conclusion, a conclusion corroborated by law enforcement personnel.

For instance, in Pasco County, Florida, police experimented with a one-year crackdown on pornography. Says Sheriff Jim Gillum:

> I have concluded that there is a correlation between our anti-porn campaign and the drop in rape. This is also the view shared in the Attorney General's Commission on Pornography. For purists, of course, there is no "scientific" evidence to support this conclusion, but for that part there is no scientific evidence to support the correlation between the decline in automobile homicides and the raising of the drinking age in Florida, or the correlation between the increase in home burglaries and the raising street cost of cocaine and other drugs. Yet almost everybody accepts those conclusions.[26]

Pasco County had a 35-percent drop in rape against a rising 18 percent in the rest of Florida. That is a 53-percent disparity. Conversely, Alaska and Nevada have the highest rape rates of all other states — and they also have the highest readership of pornographic magazines (i.e., *Chic, Club, Hustler, Genesis, Forum, Gallery* and *Playboy*). This correlation appeared in a carefully researched study by Muerry Strauss and Larry Baron, sociologists at the University of New Hampshire.

Dr. Reo M. Christenson, Professor of Political Science at Miami University, Oxford, Ohio, says:

> Science cannot tell us whether love is better than hatred, democracy better than dictatorship, peace better than war, or about anything else in the realm of values — that is, in the things that matter most. But if science cannot give us assured answers, let us use our common sense. Pornography leaves the impression with the viewer that sex has no relation to privacy, that it is unrelated to love, commitment or marriage, that bizarre forms of sex are the most gratifying, that sex with animals has a specially desirable flavor, and that irresponsible sex has no adverse consequences — no venereal disease, illegitimate births, abortions, premature marriages, single parent families or moral erosion. I see no way that a

torrent of materials with this subliminal message, which ultimately fans out to reach people of all ages, can fail to have pernicious effects. As has often been said, if destructive material can do no harm, then constructive material can do no good, and everything conscientious people have believed since the dawn of the family is wrong.[27]

Altered Realities

It has been stated that pornography alters one's perceptions, influences his inner reality, and eventually spills over into his life. However, imitating in life what one sees and reads is not limited to pornography. Such carry-over is indeed the natural outcome and response to any material one is exposed to. Seeing this influence in other areas may help us grasp the seriousness of the truth we are dealing with.

Violence and suicide are classic examples. In a *Los Angeles Times* interview of film directors by Jack Mathews, moderator Stuart Fischoff pointed out how at least three women and one man had imitated the murder depicted in the television film, "The Burning Bed," in which a wife had incinerated her sleeping husband. They each murdered their spouses in the same way.

Kotcheff, director of "First Blood," said he learned early of the lethal impact of his work. When he was 24, he directed a play in London that opened with a scene depicting a man leaping to his death from a subway station. He was warned not to duplicate the subway platform realistically, but he did anyway. The following day, five people killed themselves in identical leaps.

A more academic approach to this factor of identity emulation was done by Rowell Huesmann, Ph.D., and Leonard Eron, Ph.D., both professors of psychology at the University of Illinois at Chicago. They did a 22-year study of the members of a third grade class in a school in New York County. They discovered that those who watched more television violence as children were convicted as adults of significantly more violent crimes than others from the same classroom.

"Children who watch more violence on television learn to behave more aggressively," says Dr. Huesmann, "and they are likely to carry this behavior over into adult life."

Just the headlines of newspaper articles bear out the validity of Huesmann's statement: "Boy burns house, imitating Superman II," "Child gets burglary idea from television," "Man copies movie in murder case," "Teen hangs himself after television movie on suicide" ("Silence of the Heart"), "Teen suicides follow television movie" ("Surviving"). Mental health workers Bernard Ceskik and Karen Stevenson said their social/psychological profile of an 11-year-old boy indicated nothing abnormal about him. The only explanation for the fact that he hung himself with a belt in the bathroom was that he had just finished watching "Friday the 13th, Part III" in which a character named Jason had done the same.

These are not disadvantaged crazy people. The immense impact of visualization can drive anyone to one of these actions. Dr. Christenson says:

> It is interesting that while dozens of studies have demonstrated that violent entertainment stimulates violent behavior on the part of those who witness it, entertainment which features irresponsible sexual behavior is alleged to have no effect on its consumers. You can't have it both ways.[28]

Pornography is at the fringe of humanistic ideology, which says that man is a self-determining animal with no outside absolute moral restraints and that pleasure is the ultimate goal of life, regardless of the cost to others. Mainline culture, being equally secularistic, inevitably moves in the wake of the lunatic fringe. This play-off of fringe elements with center-stage commerce is revealed in advertising, where the bizarre puts spice and snap into commercialism. "Obsession" perfume shows a woman and three men in the throes of sexual heat. A high-fashion magazine shows a well-dressed man violently slapping a woman. *Time* magazine's review of the PG film "Howard the Duck" states, "Movie-goers who are in search of a porno zoo parade may enjoy the bedroom tryst in which the duck's human sweetie discovers a contraceptive in [the duck's wallet] and snuggles up and asks, 'You think I might find love in the animal kingdom?' "

Group sex to sell perfume, violence against women to sell clothes, and sex with animals as chic drama in a child's movie are all mild forms of erotica that dull the edge of repulsiveness toward pornography. Just like an inoculation is a little of the real disease that stimulates the body to build up immunities against getting a full-blown case, dribbles of pornography in mainstream media inoculate the senses against the grotesque harshness of its full impact. This way the conscience of an entire culture is blunted, and society as a whole drifts closer and closer to the edge. Quoting again Dr. Christenson in his address to the National Consultation of Pornography, Obscenity, and Indecency:

> Whatever conditions people to regard destructive sexual behavior as harmless, or worse, as desirable, will inevitably weaken those barriers which society erects against irresponsible sexual conduct. If this is not true, then black is white and up is down.[29]

Because of the widespread nefarious effects of pornography on a society, even Sweden, long heralded as the sex capital of the world, is reversing its attitude of unrestraint. Two decades after liberalizing their laws, the country is cracking down on pornography, with a constitutional amendment in the works to have it banned. The Swedish Sex Education Association, organized in 1933 as an advocate for greater sexual freedom, is now asking for controls on the grounds that pornography is "dangerous and degrading."

Hans Nestius of the Association said, "We had hoped that liberalization would lead to the open and honest portrayal of all aspects of sexuality. Instead, the sex capitalists moved in and what we got was pornography, which was cold, mechanical, violent and degrading."[30]

Apparently Mr. Nestius and his associates were not conversant with the nature of man.

The thrust of all this sensationalism of the flesh may not move you to rape, but move you it will. Pornography is a pictorial representation of a crumbling culture cascading down a tall, moral precipice. Sex with one, then two or three simultaneously, sex with the dead, with children, with animals . . . one or more of these options may not turn you on today, but don't go away—if you keep pumping into your mind what does turn you on, eventually that will be too tame and you, too, will be moving on down the line. The diabolical insanity of this is that you can know this truth and still get hooked if you expose yourself. There is a dangerous spirit in pornography that imbues it with the power of hell.

The Lies of Pornography: A Summary

Brenda MacKillop is an ex-*Playboy* Bunny who currently travels to testify of the sham behind the gleaming *Playboy* façade. She knows what it is to go from bad to worse, even though she walked the aisle in her Baptist church at a young age. Sex felt so good and refreshing when it began at 16 in the back seat of Ron's car, but before it was over she was giving herself to casting directors for bit parts in television spots and doing orgies at Hefner's mansion. She says she had lost count of the number of married men she slept with and, due to the crushing misery of her life, the number of genuine suicide attempts. How do you get from the front of a church to the thrashing anguish at the depths of despair? One step at a time. Sound familiar? The slick image of everybody having a good time, women loving it, no pain, no remorse, no regrets . . . **is a lie.**

Many types of entertainment are "lies" but it is not quite the same. A Disney cartoon is a "lie" because animals cannot talk and birds do not sing in English or in harmony, but that is harmless fabrication. Such is the nature of all story telling. But the lie of pornography is dangerous because it shapes the viewer's beliefs and alters his reality.

Lie #1: Pornography depicts love.

The first lie is that pornography depicts love—lots of it. But the women are not smiling for the love of it. They are being told to, paid to. The reality is that it is essentially misogynistic, filled with the hatred of women. It creates a climate where a man comes to believe that his being rough and violent is what a woman really wants and what fulfills her, and because of his sin nature, it is basically what he wants. Ms. Dwarkin puts it crudely, but gets the point across:

> Pornographers, modern and ancient, visual and literary, vulgar and aristocratic, put forth one consistent proposition: Erotic pleasure for men is derived from and predicated on the savage destruction of women. The fact is that the process of killing—and both rape and violence of any kind are steps in that process—is the prime sexual act for men in reality and/or in imagination. The knowledge of an imperial right to kill, whether exercised to the fullest extent or just part way, is necessary to fuel [their] sexual appetite and behavior.[31]

The attitude of the filmmaker that the woman is a prop to be used as desired comes through to the viewer. For the pornographer, his material is an extension of his reality:

> One does not violate something by using it for what it is. Neither rape nor prostitution is an abuse of the female because in both she is fulfilling her natural function; that is why rape is absurd and incomprehensible as an abusive phenomena in the male system and so is prostitution, which is voluntary, even when the prostitute is hit, threatened, drugged, or locked in.[32]

In time the viewer absorbs and adopts these attitudes and beliefs. He eventually believes that anything done to a woman is merely releasing natural impulses and fulfilling a natural carnality. To the realist, of course, this reasoning is beyond the bounds of reason. Replies Ms. Dwarkin:

> Every charge, by women, that force is used to violate, rape, batter or prostitute them is dismissed by the reasoning that female nature is essentially fulfilled by these acts of aggression, which, thereby, transform aggression into merely using a thing for what it is, and blames the thing if it is not womanly enough to enjoy what is done to it.[33]

Not unlike a psychedelic drug, pornography infuses into the psyche its own internal world of images where women are different, sex is different, and the whole world revolves around these differences. But, the one hooked on pornography still lives and acts in this world, and like a drunken driver, endangers others as he careens wildly down the street.

Ray Bauer was one such man who lived within his internal world of pornography while acting out in the real world. He undoubtedly was quite shocked when his wife of twenty-nine years pulled out a gun and shot him dead. When she answered the door for police in a skimpy costume her husband had her wearing, her back, buttocks, and chest were etched with whip marks. "He wouldn't stop beating me," she said. Discovered among Bauer's personal effects was an extensive collection of violent pornographic videos, magazines, books, and a variety of sadomasochistic devices. Apparently the wife had endured this treatment progressively for twenty years. Ray Bauer had become addicted and his addiction had escalated, with the result that he was desensitized to the brutalization of his own wife, which he then acted out.[34]

Lie #2: The female's sexual nature is like the male's.

In addition to the lie of women loving violence directed at them, a second, equally serious lie is the nature of the female's sexuality. Sex for a woman is totally encompassing, but in pornography it is localized, immediate, and similar to a man's sexual nature. Sex was intended to deepen relationships, but in pornography there are no relationships. A woman needs to feel special, and she responds to communication, tenderness, thoughtfulness and esteem. All these elements are lacking in pornography. She is shown to be totally excited by raw intercourse, copulating with strangers and animals in unrestrained ecstasy, panting like a dog in heat after other women, begging for anal sex like it's the greatest experience since Christmas, and other such nonsense.

There may be a certain element of "star" status that goes with being in the movies, and some women may feel that it is better than getting a real job for less money, but those factors do not alter women's innate nature. They all are wired essentially the same, and what they are doing before that camera is not a turn-on for them. They don't love sex and men the more for it, and they aren't fulfilled by it.

Lie #3: Pornography meets a need.

The third lie is that pornography meets a need, but in reality it creates a need, a sense of unrest. Like a drug, it begins a craving for itself, and the more of it that is supplied, the greater the craving becomes. Whereas God-ordained desire can be satisfied, sinfully inspired lust cannot. The artificially created craving pulls one out of natural orbit and leads him into a cold abyss of darkness where there is no satisfaction.

As we said at the beginning of this chapter, when we understand man, Satan, and the nature of the interaction among the principles of life, then all these things become obvious. But nothing is obvious apart from total dependence on the Spirit of God. The biggest mistake we can make is to believe that the fundamental makeup of the sex offender, the suicidal person, or the violent aggressor is different from yours and mine. It isn't. We are all sliced from the same loaf. The "garbage in, garbage out" truism functions regardless of persons.

Several years ago the mayor of a major southern city, concerned about the flow of pornography through his community, appointed a task force of five known and respected professional persons to evaluate the films and make recommendations. Within one year, four of the five, all who were professing Christians, were involved in adulterous affairs and related scandals.[35] What they had considered out of bounds had become justified, then comparatively harmless, and they ultimately embraced it.

It could happen to you or me.

> *Sin is a monster of such awful mien,*
> *that to be hated needs but to be seen;*
> *but seen too oft, familiar with face,*
> *we first endure, then pity, then embrace.*
> — Old English Proverb

∆∆∆

Here's What You Can Do

1. Recognize the significant difference between those sins one is continually working on (i.e., lack of love, lack of gentlemanly conduct, etc.; cf. Galatians 5), and using pornography. One can control his feet and keep them from entering a store that stocks porn, from entering an establishment that rents porn videos. One can keep his hand from reaching for that which invariably pollutes the mind.

2. Repent of past use of pornography. Foreswear it. What will you replace it with in your life? Where will you find the emotional and spiritual support you will need?

3. Realize that withdrawal is inevitable in the discontinuance of pornography, as with any other addiction. And, as with any other addiction, the withdrawal will pass. The desire will probably resurge (Satan will occasionally grip you with a sense of "gotta have it"), but, applying obedience and self-control, it, too, will pass (i.e., "Resist the devil, and he will flee from you," James 4:7).

8

Sex and the Single

It's a funny thing about life. If you refuse to accept anything but the best, you very often get it.

Somerset Maugham

A group of university students desired to stump the old philosophy professor with an enigmatic quandary in which he couldn't help but fail. One of them held a small robin in his two palms as they approached the professor. The plan was this: They would ask the professor to guess if the bird was alive or dead. If he said, "Alive," the boy would crush the bird; if he said "Dead," the boy would open his hands and the little bird would fly free. They reached the professor and presented the question. The old philosopher stroked his gray beard and thought a moment, then replied, "Son, the answer lies in your hands."

As a single person you see marriages and relationships foundering all around you. Today, over 50 percent of all marriages in our society collapse and burn, devastating the lives of not only the husband and the wife, but also whatever children there might be. But for you, your future lies in your hands . . . virtually the power of life or death, depending on how you handle it.

Desire for Marriage

Studies show that most people want to be married and have the kind of close intimacy and deep friendship that can come only through time and commitment to one person. Of course, there are the Elizabeth Taylor types who marry everybody they're infatuated with, and the Warren Beatty types who marry nobody, regardless. But as the majority of dynamic, wealthy, creative, beautiful people choose marriage, even though they have limitless options for a variety of companionships, sexual or otherwise, I am greatly encouraged—marriage is not dead.

A smashing example of this is seen in the comments of film star Ava Gardner, one-time wife of Frank Sinatra, Artie Shaw (famous big-band musician), and Mickey Rooney. She said she would gladly have exchanged all the glitter and fame for a long, happy marriage. She grew up hoping to find "one good man I could love and marry and cook for and make a home for, who would stick around for the rest of my life. I have never found him."[1]

It is therefore fair to assume that you, too, plan on marriage someday, and these thoughts are designed to cover some basics in the meantime.

Virginity

Within the past couple of decades, virginity has fallen on hard times, being scorned like a disease. Both guys and girls can be ridiculed mercilessly by "friends" with, "You're still a virgin?! You've got to be kidding!"

Recently, in *New Woman*, a national magazine, this statement appeared in the "Advice" column:

> I am 26 years old and still a virgin. Once I was proud of this but not anymore. People make fun of my single bed, friends tell me that sex will cure some of life's frustrations, and people who assume I'm sexually active ask me intimate questions about my sex life. If I met someone I wanted to have sex with, I would be afraid to tell him for fear that he would laugh at me.[2]

So, not everybody's doing it, though peer pressure is certainly doing a number on this young woman. In an interview, Priscilla Presley said of daughter Lisa Marie, "I'm not going to say she hasn't tried alcohol and drugs. She's gone through everything every other teenager does."[3]

But there are a lot of things "every other teenager" hasn't gone through, including sexual indulgence, contrary to Ms. Presley. Assuming "everyone is doing it" is not only inaccurate, but also dangerous. It is a thinly-veiled rationale for the ideas that abstinence is an impossibility, fornicating with *somebody* is an inevitability, and virginity is something nobody is interested in.

The impression that virginity is outmoded, unpopular, and

pointless is certainly enhanced, though, by the fact that not only are most of one's friends falling for this fatalistic fallacy, but "the system" also encourages it. For years the availability of contraceptives and abortions has been progressively expanded by laws, even allowing these things to be provided without parental consent. The newest jag is School Based Clinics (SBCs) — health care clinics, situated on the grounds of junior highs and high schools, which provide a cornucopia of services including athletic physicals, general health assessments, laboratory and diagnostic screenings, immunizations . . . and on-site dispensing of contraceptives to students. The message is clear: You are going to have sex, so you might as well be protected.

Ms. Mosbacher of the Family Research Council says:

> Perhaps the greatest problem that SBCs pose is a moral one. SBCs give an implicit endorsement to premarital sex. Moreover, free and easy accessibility to contraceptives encourages adolescent sex behavior and undermines parental teaching in the home.[4]

Concurrent with this message is the fact, indicated earlier, that abstinence is not presented as a practical option in school. The health aspects of abstinence are not even covered. In Chicago, pro-family groups had to get a court order in 1980 before schools would include abstinence as part of the sex education curriculum.[5] At this writing, roughly 38 percent of females and 20 percent of males are virgins at age 19. With increasingly liberal views, liberal laws, and acceptance and availability of all types of contraception, the non-sexually active person can feel increasingly alienated and just plain "weird," as did the young lady speaking in *New Woman*.

In spite of the insidious press of culture, however, it is through virginity that disease and pregnancy are totally avoided; emotional, psychological, and spiritual scars are circumvented; and patterning and addiction never become an issue. Beyond these there is also an extra strength that comes only to those who have maintained sexual purity and molded their lives from trust rather than just ricocheting off bad experiences. Even though dealing with temptation, rejection, and harassment are constants, embracing celibacy is easiest for a person who never has had sex. To the virgin, God gives something He gives no one else.

The best way to describe this is by analogy. After leaving Egypt, Moses and his two million followers journeyed to the edge of Canaan, their goal territory. This was the promised land they

had left Egypt to enter. Unfortunately, they blew it by choosing
to be cowardly, and they voted not to go in. So God had them
wander around in the wilderness desert for forty years until all
the adults who lacked the faith to trust God for victory had died.
The second time they came to the edge of Canaan they went in.

But the *first* time God was to lead the people in, He planned
to do it quite miraculously and uniquely:

> I will remove sickness from your midst. There shall be no one mis-
> carrying or barren in your land; . . . I will send My terror ahead
> of you, and throw into confusion all the people among whom you
> come, and I will make all your enemies turn their backs to you.
> And I will send hornets ahead of you, that they may drive out the
> Hivites, the Canaanites, and the Hittites before you (Exodus
> 23:25-28).

Hornets! No fighting, no loss of life in battle, no loss of babies,
no wives without children. Incredible! Conditional? You bet! They
had to go in the first time, not worship foreign gods, and make no
covenants or agreements with the people of the land (Exodus
23:20,24,32). Three conditions. All unfulfilled.

If you are not a virgin, you can learn from the books of
Joshua, Judges, 1 and 2 Samuel, and others how God loves us,
never abandons us, accepts us as we are, where we are, and takes
us forward, blessing us as we look to Him and giving us victory in
the battles of life.

But if you are a virgin, here's another boost to get you
through the jungled entanglements of relationships. It is more
than just not getting ripped up inside by the inevitable trauma
that lingers from sexual intimacy; it is more than avoiding pregnancy. It is an extra lift, an extra strength, an extra blessing for
doing it right, God's way, the first time. It is as if someone else is
fighting the battle for you. Life is still a battle, but it is nowhere
near as difficult when hornets are doing the fighting as when you
are having to wield your sword.

Regardless of What He Says . . .

Another reason for virginity—particularly for women—is to
avoid the con job that men work on them. Men say one thing and
mean another. Oh, they say, "sex now" and mean it; but a woman
hears "sex now and a relationship on-going." Actually, the man is
saying, "sex now and no promises for tomorrow."

Most women don't get into sex because of some inner hunger for sex. For the woman, sex is predominantly a means to an end. That is not to say they do not enjoy it. But women are naturally pleasers, they are essentially responders. If sex is what he wants, then she'll go along, silently hoping that there is a payoff for her. Often she does not realize that guys are wired differently; they do not need much of a relationship, now or in the future, to want to enjoy sex for sex's sake. Not understanding this, the woman can end up feeling "taken." Girls may be charged by romance, but rarely by mere sex.

And what is it that women want that they will not find through sex? Lasting love, permanent esteem, enduring desire, and a sacrificial heart. Not gaining these is what mothers are talking about when they tell their daughters, "If you give in, he won't respect you." That is hopelessly simplistic, however, because a guy can have tremendous respect for a girl's prowess in bed. (On second thought, I don't think that's what Mom was talking about.)

What guys want now, girls want ultimately. What girls want now, guys want ultimately. And what is that again? Lasting love, permanent esteem, enduring desire, and a sacrificial heart. Here are two opposite perspectives on this reality.

The Value of Waiting

Women were supposed to be "equal" to men. That meant that being a virgin was nonsense, and having affairs wasn't. Girls in my class at college spent whole evenings talking about whether or not to "give" their virginity to the boys they were going out with. Guys, in the spirit of true equality, offered to take it. By the time a girl was a sophomore, she wasn't supposed to be a virgin anymore. True to the tone of the times, I wasn't.

But two years later, I had a long talk with a male friend, three years older than I, who was planning to get married. He, as I, had always said that the idea of virginity was anachronistic. Except now, as he talked, he admitted that his prospective wife was a virgin, one of the few he had met, and said that it really meant something to him. I was astonished. And retrenched to think things over.[6]

Is that a slammer, or what?! "Except now . . . it really meant something to him." Ladies, take note. Regardless of what he says, regardless of how passionately he remonstrates for the value and virtue of sexual intimacy now, he wants to marry a virgin. It may be covered over with a lot of *Playboy* philosophy, and he indeed may not end up marrying a virgin, but even if he doesn't, he will wish he had.

And, in the final analysis, the woman will wish she were if she's not, and may wish he were, also, because in every serious relationship, the past eventually comes out. You end up telling your story. At that time, with your husband or prospective husband, you would give anything to be able to say, "Darling, there is no story to tell. There's never been anyone else [because non-sexual "romances" don't count in anybody's estimation]. There is only you. You're the only one who will have all of me." What man or woman wouldn't want to hear that?

Elisabeth Elliot gives us another perspective on this viewpoint, and she puts it as hard and bold as I have ever seen it:

> I took it for granted that there must be a few men left who had the strength to swim against the tide. I assumed that those men would also be looking for women of principle. I did not want to be among the marked-down goods on the bargain table, cheap because they had been pawed over. Crowds collect there. It is only the few who will pay full price.[7]

Mrs. Elliot was a virgin when she married, and she expected the same from the man she would give herself to. And many men expect to marry a virgin whether they themselves are or not. On this point, beware; God hates hypocrisy! Jesus ripped into the Pharisees time after time after time, hammering home the intrinsic evil of this single point: expecting from others what they themselves couldn't deliver!

Mrs. Elliot's words reflect a truth of ingrained values: That which costs us nothing—in time, patience, effort or waiting—means little. The greater the price, the higher the value. If you have to pay the price of waiting for sexual favors of another, especially waiting till after the bells have rung and you are picking rice off your sleeve, then the value of those pleasures is proportionally increased. This may not be the only reason for waiting, nor the most significant, as we have seen, yet it is a powerful one.

Inner Strength

Through the waiting, God is shaping. Under pressure you are forced into reliance on the Spirit; you are forced to seek higher ground. Indeed you will probably never make this trip without His help. We all have a need for love, and if we refuse to gratify that need for love through sex, then that hunger will throw us at His feet. There alone is strength and comfort for the core of life.

This reliance on God's strength, this refusal to buckle under the pressure of "everybody's doing it," is preparation for marriage as well. That's a twist, isn't it? So often we hear of trial marriage, or living together to see if it works, or the stupid argument, "Would you buy a pair of shoes without first trying them on?"

As we have seen, although sex is a physical act, the issues which are involved are spiritual, psychological, emotional and relational. Whether the parts fit is hardly in question. The realities are: Life is a battle, and the spiritual is central, and that is why many marriages fall apart. Not because parts don't fit, but because partners are not prepared spiritually; they are not strengthened inside to withstand the pressures and testing of marriage.

No single person ever believes this, but being married *is* more difficult than being single. And if we cannot fight and win battles when we are single, we are not going to be able to fight and win them when we are married. When David faced Goliath, he was prepared.[8] He had already fought a lion and a bear when they were trying to kill his sheep, and he had acquired confidence, strength, and inner power. To King Saul, he said:

> The LORD who delivered me from the paw of the lion and from the paw of the bear, He will deliver me from the hand of this Philistine (1 Samuel 17:37).

To Goliath he said:

> You come to me with a sword, a spear, and a javelin, but I come to you in the name of the LORD of hosts, the God of the armies of Israel, whom you have taunted. This day the LORD will deliver you up into my hands, and I will strike you down and remove your head from you . . . that all the earth may know that there is a God in Israel! (1 Samuel 17:45,46)

What is a raging bear, as strong as he might be, compared to a nine-foot, fully-armored, trained soldier? Similarly, God has designed our battles to become progressively more difficult. If, in encountering the test of celibacy, we lie down and allow ourselves to float with the current of the times, we will be in no shape to encounter and successfully deal with the giants that come against us in marriage. There may have been a time, in eons past, when these words would appear melodramatic. Today, when Western society is virtually crumbling due to the disintegration of the home, they are merely a sobering indication of what must be if your marriage is going to be all you want it to be.

Handling Date Pressure

How do you deal with the come-ons of sexual pressure from dates? Decide where you stand and commit yourself to no compromise, regardless of the cost. Then decide what you will say before it needs to be said. Be honest, without condemnation. You are stating your position. Sounding like you are judging the whole world never quite comes off right. Here's an idea for the guys that you could use in some form. It is a letter from Jim Elliot to his future wife, and both his honesty and commitment come through:

> I'm hungry for you, Betts. We're alike in our desire for God. I'm glad for that. But we're different too. I've got the body of a man; you've got the body of a woman. And frankly, I want you, but you're not mine.[9]

Women, it helps if you give a response that has both reason and strength. The suggestions below may sound unlike you — and, after all, they are only suggestions — but remember, they are not for you, they are for him. They carry punch, even if it is too much punch for you. If you are with someone who is not much of a prospect and he is coming on strong, say something like:

> It's too bad that your impulses are more important to you than my integrity. I had thought you had more going for you than that. I guess I was wrong.

If you are really tight with a guy and you think this could be a lasting thing, but you want to clarify your position with honesty and finality, this statement will blow his socks off! Frankly, I think it would generate a great deal of awe for you:

> My body is valuable to me, to God, and to my future husband, whoever that may be. I have made this promise, therefore, to myself, before God, and for my husband, and I'll share it with you so you'll know where I'm coming from. When I get married, my man will never want for thrill or excitement. I will apply every ounce of imagination and energy to pleasing him. I will be the most uninhibited sexual vixen to ever walk an aisle, but until that time, I have no burden to prove anything. And it is not up for discussion. I hope you can accept this. If you can't, I'll understand.

Don't let anyone intimidate you by saying there is something wrong with your hormones, your brain, your social adjustment, or anything else just because you are not willing to jump into the sack. Recognize that those who are pressuring you are Satan's pawns, yet don't be condemning. Remember Jesus' words to Peter when Peter tried to dissuade Him from walking into a death trap in Jerusalem: "Get behind me, Satan!" He said that to Satan as He stared Peter in the face! Peter was no slouch apostle, but on that occasion his mind and mouth were under the influence of Satan. It can happen to any of us. Of course, if it continues incessantly, you'd better spend time with people who will respect your values. The whole world is conspiring to convince you that virginity is not only worthless, but also foolish. Put yourself where you can get some positive feedback.

The virgin really can feel left out if he focuses on what he does not have, or what he has not felt, or is not experiencing, while the world and life seem to go sliding by. But that is all an illusion. The dirty snowball of compromise and self-deception now rolling through our culture will eventually melt under the white-hot heat of Him who is the Truth. Only dirt will remain.

Desire

Handling the hormones is one of the challenges in the juggling act of growing up, whether one is approaching thirteen or thirty. In chapter 4, "Meanwhile, Back at the Garden," temptation was dealt with as an aspect of Satanic attack. Here we want to make a critical differentiation between sexual drive and lust. In fact, desire, a positive motivational force, and lust, a negatively perverted force, are both derived from the same word in the original language of the Bible. It's no wonder we get confused.

By way of indicating the innocent side of desire, consider this comment about Jesus Christ:

> For we do not have a high priest who cannot sympathize with our weaknesses, but one who has been tempted in all things as we are, yet without sin (Hebrews 4:15).

Jesus Christ was a man in every way a man is a man. And that includes sexual desire. But that natural, human desire was always under rein, never out of control. The difference between desire and lust is the difference between a wild stallion and a trained race horse. The one is lawless and submits to no one; the other is "broken," made useful, and channeled. Both have the power. The difference is control.

This is a critical understanding, especially for the guys who can really get turned on at the quick sight of something lusciously female. That's physiology, not lust. If one is to desire holiness, he must be clear on what he is shooting for. You cannot root out your chemistry with some kind of spiritual trowel. Purity is not the absence of virility. Jesus Christ was sinless, but it wasn't because He had no hormones — He had them — He was sinless because He also had control. Unlike many role models, He was the master of His body, not the slave of His impulses.

When you feel desire, rejoice! That is the way God made you. The problem comes when we believe either that we must act on those desires or that the desires themselves are evil and harmful. Neither belief will direct you to holiness. The one will drive you into alienation and sin; the other will tie you into neurotic knots.

Often the problem is our own foolishness, however, rather than strictly hormones or natural desire. Paul says:

> Put on the Lord Jesus Christ, and make no provision for the flesh
> in regard to its lusts (Romans 13:14).

Enter outside stimulation, which can be like throwing gasoline on a fire. We've already covered pornography, which is part of that which can trip desire and send it plunging headlong into lust. Like an athlete in training, you must be shrewd in evaluating what enhances your competitive edge and what detracts from it. We're not talking about legalistic do's and don'ts — you be the judge of your own life. What bends your focus and inflames you? What cranks up your desires from a buzz to a screaming pitch? If you know the Lord and your desire is to please Him, moving from the central truth of Romans 13:14 out into the various aspects of your life should be clear. Not always easy, but clear.

Five Ways to Deal With Desire

1. Set standards which are beyond compromise.
2. Plan dates that are fun and inexpensive, and offer opportunities for conversation.[10]
3. Talk about the issue with your boyfriend/girlfriend before it becomes a problem.
4. Pray and read the Bible together.
5. Break up.

In the sport in which I used to compete, diet was a primary factor in competition preparation. Starting at least twelve weeks before the season each of us would begin adjusting his diet — no sugar, no bread, no dairy products. Calories were meticulously counted; meals were cautiously weighed, spaced and balanced. Weeks went by with no variation and no cheating, and calories gradually being reduced so the body could adjust progressively to the increased severity. We used to joke about how we would "kill" for a pizza, and there were times I found myself rifling through my wife's magazines cutting out every imaginable cookie recipe!

For sport it is okay to sacrifice, to be tough on yourself, to pay the price for glory, to win. Is it not just as right to sacrifice for holiness? Starving out lust and keeping desire in check is not masochistic. Instead of priming the pump with pornography, fill your eyes, your mind, and your life with activities that do not play off desire. When in competition training, I didn't hang around Baskin Robbins! That's not legalism; it's just common sense.

Helpful Disciplines

Because my physical goals were clear, I experimented with diet in order to achieve a kind of natural state where my body was not screaming for pizza and ice cream all the time. I found that sufficient complex carbohydrates, fruit, and chelated minerals worked wonders in quelling the urge for sweets. Similarly, you can greatly reduce your passion by adjusting your lifestyle. Some things I found that helped me, you may believe to be drastic. Or some things that may work for you were a problem for me. You are free to manage your own life. The question is, are your goals clearly defined? Following are some disciplines that I and others have found helpful.

1. Don't watch television. Howard Hendricks has said, "You can read your Bible every day, pray at every meal, and be in church every time the doors are open, but if you are plugged into the TV, you'll be plugged into the world system every time."

2. Read the Bible daily.

3. Meet for coffee and prayer weekly with at least one friend with whom you can pour your guts out with absolute, total honesty. Every doubt, every fear, every urge . . . everything goes out on the table. This alone will change your life. And he does the same with you.

4. Belong to a group that has a good balance between Bible study and social activities. Hang in there long enough to become comfortable, and be a participant, not just a spec-

tator.

5. Get involved in helping others. This is fulfilling and gets your eyes off yourself. Daniel's admonition to King Nebuchadnezzar is applicable here: "Break away now from your sins by doing righteousness, and from your iniquities by showing mercy to the poor."[11]

Desire is the stirring and pumping in the blood that makes you smile at an attractive person of the opposite sex. It can be the impetus that drives us to want to reach out and give, to sacrifice for another. It is the spring that flings us beyond self and into another's orbit where there is human comfort, uniting with another in love. It is given by God. Rejoice in it—and in the challenge of controlling it.

How Far?

"How far can we go?" is perhaps the question most asked by young people attempting to balance going for the gusto with the goals of God. Like other issues we have touched on, our motives for doing something must move beyond the immediate moment. Drawing from earlier strains in our discussion, we remember that sex is addicting, patterns do develop quickly, and every fiber of our personness becomes enmeshed in any aspect of intimacy.

Robert and Julie were active members of a campus Christian group when they started dating. Soon the intimacy grew. As is usually the case, Julie assumed that increased intimacy meant increased commitment. This common misconception on the female's part rarely has correlation in the man's thinking, however. As Robert later said, "I just assumed that it was part of relating." Unlike Julie, Robert was from a non-Christian background, and he presumed that some sort of sex was a part of dating.

Both Robert and Julie knew clearly that intercourse was wrong, but their increased touching was building up a lot of steam. They spent more and more time alone with each other, and every encounter included more heat and less clothes. It was inevitable that their touching progress, and it was natural that the building pressure would seek release. Their intimacy eventually moved to masturbating each other, then quickly evolved into oral sex.

About this time, somebody new dropped into Robert's life, and off he went. Needless to say, Julie was devastated. Technically she still had her virginity, but just barely, and the scars and the hurt and the emotional rip-off were as devastating to her as what we covered in the first couple of chapters. Future encounters with men became increasingly jaded for Julie and she became cynical. And Robert learned nothing of trusting God and loving others through the experience.

Couples ask, "How far can we go?" because the Bible says nothing about petting. Therefore, they believe they need guidance. Petting is designed to stimulate, not satisfy! Couples go into petting expecting satisfaction and come out frustrated. The Bible talks a lot about sex, but says nothing about petting because petting is not viewed as a separate entity but as a part of sex. It's as simple as that.

Where you are currently in your touching with a boyfriend/girlfriend is incidental. You have only two options: Stop cold, or progress to sexual intimacy. Your body was programmed to go from kiss to copulation, and your will was never designed to play policeman with a whistle against the rumbling steamroller of your hormones. If you are involved in a touching, caressing, petting relationship, your will has no chance against the crushing advance of the inevitable.

To ask the question, "How far can we go?" is to forget the nature of temptation as was covered in "Meanwhile, Back in the Garden." Satan's goal is to get you to act *now,* to take one step. When you have done that, he will prod you to take another. He is the master chessman who knows the game is not won in a whoosh, but move by move. The first step he gets you to take is to focus on self: What can I do *now* that will satisfy my sexual desires, even a little? From this stance we can more clearly answer the question: Is petting moving me toward dependence on the Spirit or away? Is petting an act-now-pay-later proposition? As we have seen from a number of angles, the worldly, Satanic perspective is *do it now and forget later*!

The spiritual perspective is the overall, long-term viewpoint. Everything and everybody is considered, and a decision is made from wisdom, not impulse. This requires Spirit reliance. Jesus said, "Apart from Me you can do nothing" (John 15:5). This is what He was talking about. It can be summed up in the proverb:

> The prudent [cautious, sensible person] sees the evil coming and hides himself, But the naive [ignorant persons] go on and are punished for it (Proverbs 22:3).

Consider this: You are going to marry Ginger. Shortly before you marry, Ginger assembles all the men she has had various degrees of involvement with. Some she has kissed and petted with; a couple have been intense with petting; most she has slept with. You walk in and she lines them up for you to meet. She describes in some detail for you what her involvement was with each guy. How do you feel? Do you pump each one's hand and with a toothy grin say, "Thank you for breaking her in for me"? Or do you throw up? How thick is your philosophical veneer that says, "That's okay . . . it's okay." Or perhaps you are Ginger. Do you want to play "Line 'em Up" for your Prince Charming who is going to give you his ring and his life?

This scenario is not as far-fetched as you might think. In the majority of close, serious relationships, there are questions and discussions on each other's past. The leader of a course in communication I once attended instructed the couples to write down a "sexual history" from birth, in five-year increments, covering every intimate involvement to the present. The counselor heading the class had discovered that a secret sexual past clouds true and pure communication with the spouse.

Therefore, do not think that your involvement with someone special will either end in marriage, which it probably won't (how many people do we marry compared to the number we date?) or be closed out and forgotten. It will come up again and again. You can count on it.

Cheating Your Brother

Lastly, there is one interesting consideration which deserves to be mentioned:

[Let] no man transgress and defraud his brother in the matter [of lustful passion] because the Lord is the avenger in all these things, just as we also told you before and solemnly warned you (1 Thessalonians 4:6).

This weighty passage carries a command and a threat. The threat is that God Himself will retaliate against those who transgress this command. We are not talking about stealing an orange from the local grocer here. This is serious stuff.

And what exactly is the command? It is exactly:

Do not cheat a brother out of rights that belong only to him regarding sex with his woman!

Adultery is primarily in view, but I believe the timelessness of God Himself, combined with the many devastating and detracting factors of premarital sex, allow for an all-time perspective on defrauding. In other words, if I take sexual liberty with a woman, even if she is not married and perhaps has not yet met the man she will marry, I am cheating her *future* husband of rights that are uniquely and solely his. In addition, I am stealing from God, for she is sanctified — set apart — unto Him. Hence, I am a double thief, stealing both from God and from man.

This underscores how crucial it is that one take an overview of all relationships, and all aspects of every relationship. The broadness of this all-time viewpoint is amplified by the broadness of purity in general, not virginity or the lack of it in particular. This can be seen in the following passage:

> For God has not called us for the purpose of impurity, but in sanctification. Consequently, he who rejects this is not rejecting man but the God who gives His Holy Spirit to you (1 Thessalonians 4:7,8).

Impurity versus sanctification is broader than fornication versus virginity. Petting is in the arena of purity versus impurity, and the reference to God having given us His Holy Spirit in this context certainly hearkens back to our discussion in chapter 2 on 1 Corinthians 6 and the body being the worship site of God and the dwelling place of His Spirit. Believers are sanctified to God, which means set apart. There is no place for philosophical game playing as we attempt to circumvent the letter of the law while we fill up our own greed.

Asking "How far can I go?" is essentially asking, "What can I get away with and not have God ticked off at me?" This is totally missing the point of both sex and godliness. Sex is not merely a toy to enjoy a little bit now and a lot after marriage. It is the gift of the key to the door of the inner self. It is the mystery that opens one's personness down to the core. It is the loom that weaves a bonding oneness with a life-mate from the altar to beyond the veil of time.

Peer Pressure

It is exhilarating to be on a winning team! In both sports and business I have had the privilege of being on stage to collect "The Big One." The heat of the lights and the cheering of the crowds is an euphoric high unlike any other. Often the difference between winning and losing is the coach. A player will kill for a coach who knows the player personally, cares about him, and expects the best from him. An athlete will submit to curfew, diet, training regimentation, anything, when he knows he is loved and counted on.

As the coach of this really big game called Life, God has told us just that: He loves us, cares for us, knows us, has a purpose for us, and believes in us.[12] The question is, are we listening?

When we do not know how God feels about us, or do not accept how He feels, then how we feel about ourselves is open to other influences, and a lack of inner confidence can result. A vacuum of confidence can produce low self-esteem and a poor self-image. The lower one's self-esteem, the more susceptible he is to outside influences in order to fulfill a basic human need for approval. It is simply human nature to need affirmation from beyond ourselves. If our brain and heart are soaked in the approval of God, what others think we should do or say is immaterial. The stronger your spiritual core, the less responsive you are to negative peer pressure. That peer pressure is what Solomon had in mind when he wrote, "A [person] of many friends comes to ruin." [13]

Lowered confidence, poor self-image, and low self-esteem result in what sociologist David Reisman calls an "other-directed personality."[14] This is like a sixth sense one develops to discern what others expect of him and to act accordingly. This approach to life invariably requires compromising whatever personal identity one has.

Poor self-image results in fear as well. Relationships are patched together in the desperate hope of not offending anyone, an improbable achievement at best. This person fears that if he does not have the approval of others, he is reduced to nothingness. Fear finds its home in the same vacuum as low self-esteem, where God's commitment to us is absent. When His love is present, it displaces fear:

> There is no fear in love; but perfect love casts out fear because fear involves punishment [i.e., rejection by others!], and the one who fears is not perfected in love (1 John 4:18).

Moses exemplified how one's inner spiritual condition can inspire a person to want to do what is right, what God says to do, regardless of who does not agree:

> By faith [Moses] left Egypt, not fearing the wrath of the king; for

he endured, as seeing Him who is unseen (Hebrews 11:27).

In addition to other-directedness and fear, the absence of God's affirming support results in a distorted sense of self-consciousness. Fearing rejection, and being hypersensitive to the expectations of others, one's overriding impulse is to blend in and avoid standing up for what he believes in.

Most people actually do not want to conform to the negative influences of others. They want to stand on their own, but they lack the internal integrity to resist the flow of the group. The solution, as it was with Moses, is spiritual. No other power on earth can deliver what it takes to withstand the pressure of peers. Even the person of elevated status, who has an achievement-rich self-esteem, may lack the strength to say NO to the most obvious harm when everybody else is saying YES.

One drug-related death among the American royalty of sports celebrities is a tragic case in point,[15] Len Bias. Two days after being drafted by the world-champion Boston Celtics, Len died from cocaine. Just eight days later, the day before his wedding, Don Rogers, a member of the 1984 NFL All Rookie Team of the Year, died from a cocaine overdose. Three players of the University of Virginia football team — responsible for 56 percent of their team's points the previous season — were charged by federal prosecutors in a Virginia drug distribution ring. Steve Howe, once a dazzling pitcher for the LA Dodgers, was fired from the Dodgers and is now ineligible even for minor league teams, due to his drug problems.

The list goes on and on. We can be blessed with a sparkling personality that may get us elected, or with superstar abilities that lift us head and shoulders above the crowd, but power confidence and power self-esteem come only from the Spirit, the inner core of the self.

Nancy Reagan's "Just Say NO" campaign is commendable for its position and its fervor, but we must recognize the gripping force of peer pressure, and the need of the spiritual source of power to resisting that pressure. The power to resist comes from the Spirit:

> God has not given us a spirit of timidity, but of power and love and discipline (2 Timothy 1:7).

Recently at the gym someone was passing around photos

taken of a *Playboy* "Playmate" at a recent car show. Perched on the hood of a truck was this shapely, attractive girl in a skimpy outfit, but what struck me were her eyes. She looked as if she had not slept in a week, but I doubt if lack of sleep was her problem. Her eyes were vacuous. No depth. The saying "What you see is what you get" occurred to me as I looked at her, because what you saw was all there was. She had nothing else to give. She was a floater, flowing with the current, and it showed.

What a contrast is Ricky, up from the dregs of Dallas, a kid Dr. Hendricks talks about as an example of this very point. Ricky was a macho honcho from a Dallas street gang. By some fluke of divine intervention, Ricky got invited to a weekend camp by one of the churches. Not real clear on what the program was, Ricky came prepared to party—whiskey, pot, et al. What Ricky was not prepared for was encountering the power of God.

Ricky got saved. But not like some people get saved. Ricky got changed! As he had in everything else, he jumped in with both feet. Returning to Dallas Sunday night, Ricky took off for his neighborhood to tell his friends about Jesus Christ.

Tuesday morning the police found Ricky in the gutter of a downtown street, barely alive. He had been beaten literally to within an inch of his life. Ricky recovered and eventually won many of his former gang members to Christ, and he went on to make a difference in his community. In the process, he learned that resisting peer pressure can also carry a price.

The pressure of our peers is normal and unavoidable. Standing up for convictions will result in conflict, not conformity, and we all have to accept that. But like storybook heroes from Ivanhoe to Dirty Harry, the exciting people in life are those who make a difference under fire. From uncompromising convictions come self-respect, maturity, and a sense of purpose—something worth living for, and worth dying for.

> If I were still trying to please men, I would not be a bond-servant of Christ (Galatians 1:10).

Our Need for Others

One of the tenets of our American heritage is rugged individualism. From Davy Crockett to Rambo, the image of the strong, silent powerhouse, a need-nobody, need-nothing lone ranger has become an ingrained part of our national identity and has carried over into the church. Dirty Harry has his .44, Rambo has his knife, and the Christian has his Bible. Verses like "I can do all things through [Christ] who strengthens me" (Philippians 4:13) become a code of the road as he rides into the heat of battle like Johnny Pilgrim to conquer sin, the devil, and the world—alone. In this not-uncommon approach, Christian "fellowship" is to the Christian life what exercise is to health: a nice pastime for those who have time to pass, but hardly a requirement.

This is a murderous misunderstanding, on both accounts. Exercise is not just necessary for optimum health; it is essential for any kind of health. Interdependence with other believers is not just icing on the cake of Christianity; it is as essential as any other ingredient in the legacy left us in the New Testament.

The truth of this can be seen in the lives of the apostles. They are rarely alone. Aloneness is never advocated either in lifestyle or doctrine. Paul, for instance, as a choleric in temperament,[16] was a driver, a leader, a loner. A choleric does not need people the way a sanguine needs people in order to be happy or fulfilled. Yet Paul had a spiritual need for his brothers. In his writings he reveals this camaraderie:

> Paul . . . and all the brethren who are with me, to the churches of Galatia . . . (Galatians 1:2).

> Paul and Timothy, bond-servants of Christ Jesus, to all the saints in Christ Jesus who are in Philippi . . . (Philippians 1:1).

> Paul and Silvanus and Timothy to the church . . . (1 Thessalonians 1:1).

The only circumstance that cut Paul off from his friends was jail, and even then he had visitors all the time. In his teaching, Paul stresses the critical nature of togetherness, not in theory but in actuality: "So we, who are many, are one body in Christ, and individually members one of another."[17]

That we are all gifted for the body with differing gifts underscores our interdependence.[18] Our being together isn't just nice. Fellowship is not merely a social activity that we engage in because we are social creatures, and because it is fun to be together. The fact is, I am *incomplete* as an individual Christian: "We are members of one another."[19]

"The eye cannot say to the hand, 'I have no need of you'; or again the head to the feet, 'I have no need of you.' "[20] Even God is not alone, not singular. He is three!

Does that mean that God in me is insufficient to achieve purity and sustain celibacy? Sorry, that's a go-nowhere question, like "Can God make a rock so big He can't lift it?" Remember what was said earlier about God's intelligence being far above ours? That means there will be gaps in our reasonings and holes in our understandings. We will never be able to lock up every question with complete answers from every angle. It would seem reasonable that God's Spirit would be sufficient for what an individual needs. Reasonable, but erroneous. He simply did not design us that way. God tells us what we need, and we need other believers in order to walk in holiness. Bottom line:

If you attempt celibacy without the dynamic, continual support of caring Christian friends, you will fail.

Paul tells Timothy:

Flee from youthful lusts, and pursue righteousness, faith, love and peace, with those who call on the Lord from a pure heart (2 Timothy 2:22).

If you try to flee youthful lusts and pursue righteousness, faith, love and peace on your own, with little or no contact with others who call on the Lord from a pure heart, you will not succeed.

Dating Non-Christians

Obviously, this touches on the question of dating non-Christians. I am not going to say yes or no to that, for the Lord calls us to freedom and there are a lot of considerations involved in every situation. If your primary social input is your non-Christian boyfriend/girlfriend, though, you are laying odds heavily against yourself. Dating is not a reasonable evangelism field, though I have known a number of people who have become Christians through the witness of a special friend. Put yourself in the company of a rich environment of friends who love the Lord, get your head into the spirit of 2 Timothy 2:22, and go from there. Make your decisions from wisdom and power, not from heat and loneliness. If you are clear on the issues covered in chapter 6, "What God Says," then walk circumspectly, and if you see yourself losing ground, do whatever is necessary to get right.

Safeguarded

In the secular '60s, drugs and sex were draped with many

reasonable sounding rationales. They served as a sign of rebellion against both an unjust government and acquiescent parents who were too caught up in dead materialism to care about the morality of life, or war, or any other heavy issue. Sex and drugs became the flag-waving symbols of staunch resistance to a relentless and sightless world gone mad with killing and vain political filibustering. What could a 21-year-old student do to make a personal statement against noxious materialism, vicious competitiveness, and mindless murder in a hopeless cause half a world away? He could let his hair grow (and grow!), look like a vagabond, and blow up the Bank of America. They did all three at my campus, the University of California at Santa Barbara. But the most pervasive personal statement was summed up in the popular slogan, "Make love, not war." That said it all, because sexual license had taken on causal, political import. It was not just hedonistic ballyhooing. Immorality became a moral stand against an immoral society (if that isn't the quintessence of irony!). At least that was the gist of the jive at the time.

In the midst of this, our little band of believers traversed the years and the culture like a boat paddling across mine-infested waters. We met weekly for Bible study, prayer, and socials. We lived together in apartments, thereby avoiding the press of worldliness rampant in the dorms and the Greek houses. We spent our vacations at Christian conferences. We were totally enmeshed with each other in a culture within a culture. Is there some other way?

A person's teen years and early twenties comprise the age of greatest sexual compulsion. Many times I yearned for the bondage of sin, cried for the freedom to let my seemingly indomitable lust reach out for satiation, even if it meant being dashed on the rocks while the sirens sang. But because my life was intertwined with many others, I was safeguarded. So were they. And the answer is no, there is no other way.

> Abhor what is evil; cling to what is good. Be devoted to one another in brotherly love . . . fervent in spirit, serving the Lord; rejoicing in hope, persevering in tribulation, devoted to prayer, contributing to the needs of the saints, practicing hospitality (Romans 12:9-13).

Marrying an Unbeliever

Even though one could probably piece together from the

Scriptures in general the conclusion that a Christian should marry only another Christian, God finds that situation so serious that He lays it out with crackling clarity:

> Do not be bound together with unbelievers; for what partnership has righteousness with lawlessness, or what fellowship has light with darkness? Or what harmony has Christ with Belial [Satan], or what has a believer in common with an unbeliever? Or what agreement has the temple of God with idols? For we are the temple of the living God; just as God said, "I will dwell in them . . . Therefore, come out from their midst and be separate," says the Lord, "and do not touch what is unclean" (2 Corinthians 6:14-17).

Paul uses here five contrasting parallels to convey the point without equivocation:

Do not get hooked up with an unbeliever.

This can seem inconsequential in the exciting developmental stages of courting, but in the mundaneness of an on-going marriage relationship, sharing in this crucial aspect of life is essential for any depth of communion. If the spiritual is central for one person, then it is doubly true when two are united.

Dr. James Dobson says that the overwhelming marital problem expressed by women is lack of spiritual leadership by the husband. Isn't that amazing? Usually the spiritual focus is rarely an issue of attention when dating, but then it evolves into prominence in the permanent and godly state of marriage. That being the case, it would seem wise to make it a focal point while dating, wouldn't it? To marry an unbeliever is to torpedo any chance of maximum happiness in marriage. Oh sure, he might suddenly get turned on to God somewhere down the road, but that is a long shot. Be aware of this fact: Those things which are important in dating and those of insignificance seem to flip-flop after the wedding. Whom we date is a matter of choice, but whom we fall in love with usually isn't. Don't play a game where the odds of losing are guaranteed.

Marrying an unbeliever is setting yourself up for a lifetime of grief. And when children come, that grief can evolve into deep despair as the priorities of the two of you continue to grow further apart. Living by faith means taking God at His Word and learning from the mistakes of others. Being a Christian means being a "slave of Christ, doing the will of God from the heart."[21]

A Concluding Hope

We must always keep in balance the fact that God's primary business is that of redeeming. Many of these pages may cause you to reflect, or even cry, "Had I only known that sooner!" But don't despair. Jesus did not come to save the righteous, but sinners. The closer we can conform our lives to truth, the fewer mistakes we make, the happier we will be and the fewer problems we will have. But in all instances, today is the beginning of the rest of your life.

△△△

Here's What You Can Do

1. List date activities that appeal to you, those that major on communication and minor on entertainment. One young lady recalled that one of the most memorable dates she had was wandering through a graveyard reading epitaphs.

2. Ask yourself: *Am I separate from the world? Am I willing to take the narrow, hard stand of Jesus Christ, regardless of the cost? If not, when will I deal with that?*

3. Accept your singleness as if it were a permanent state, and your dependancy on the all-sufficient Christ. Now, look for ways to be of service within the body of Christ.

4. Pray daily for your future spouse (marriage is the "normal" state for most people), for his or her purity (sexual and otherwise), and singleness of devotion to Christ.

5. Resolve to marry only a believer, one who has already been walking in the Spirit. Granted, this narrows the prospects considerably, but it is the will of God for you.

Upping the Ante
I

Venereal Diseases and Homosexuality

> The truth can walk around naked; only lies must be
> clothed in euphemisms.
>
> Yiddish Proverb

There are in our society two major issues relevant to our
topic. They are as political as they are spiritual and as human as
they are theological. Consequently, it is difficult to touch on them
dispassionately. Both issues are intense, and they inspire intense
feelings. They are the physical consequences of "free love": venereal diseases (also called sexually transmitted diseases or STDs)
and unwanted pregnancies. We will look at venereal diseases,
especially AIDS, in this chapter, "Upping the Ante I," and pregnancy and abortion in the next chapter, "Upping the Ante II."

Please do not think that what has come before is lessened by
the weightiness of these life-and-death matters. In fact, Paul says
the things that are not seen are the things that are eternal; the
things which are seen are temporal. Yet, because truth, whether
eternal or temporal, is serious business, when it finally hits on the
physical plane it is blood and guts, anguish and death.

AIDS

Seemingly everyone in America, perhaps even most of the
world, has become familiar with AIDS, and the fact that it is a
lethal, communicable disease. But few people are aware of the extent of its spread, or the magnitude of its implications, or the

conspiracy to prevent its solution.

As we have noted, the psychological, emotional and spiritual fallout of nonmarital sex hits everyone, every time, who engages in it. And those consequences are just as debilitating as the physical consequences can be. So it is unfortunate when we disregard these deep, nonphysical repercussions of sexual lawlessness, and are moved to abstinence only by the specter of pain, humiliation, and possible death that accompanies venereal diseases.

AIDS, the most frightening of the STDs, is the Russian Roulette of "free love." It may just go "click" this time, and maybe the next, but the odds against you increase with each encounter. When the "bang" does come it literally can blow you away.

The perversity of the human heart is like a monster that changes its shape, color and size in its attempt to evade the light of truth. It is not surprising, therefore, that some people speculate about AIDS being a direct judgment from God. Actually, it doesn't matter whether or not God is behind this disease. He has booby-trapped the path of sin with trip wires designed to thwart the evil and to persuade us to return to sanity and to His ways. Failing to do so could bring moral, physical and financial ruin to America, and the cessation of our role as a world power.

The Extent of Its Spread

36 thousand people have died from full-blown AIDS at a medical cost averaging $147,000 per victim[1] and another 64 thousand are in the final death-throe stages. Unfortunately, this is just the beginning. In his testimony before Congress, July 22, 1985, Dr. Dani Bolognesi of Duke University Medical Center, stated that 2 million Americans were already permanently infected with AIDS, and that number is expected to double each year.[2]

As we shall see from other medical sources, the prognosis for eventual death from the disease is 100 percent. It is estimated that there are currently 40 million people infected worldwide.

Dr. W. Hazeltine, a leading AIDS researcher, says, "We must be prepared to anticipate that the vast majority of those now infected will ultimately, over a period of five to ten years, develop life-threatening illnesses."[3]

According to one missionary in Zaire, every family within her area had at least one member dying of AIDS. Experts estimate that within the next few years, 25 percent of the population of

Africa will be dead of AIDS.

85 percent of the nation's urban drug users have AIDS.[4] Many within this group support their habit through prostitution. This implies that many men outside the drug sub-culture are contracting the disease and transmitting it to present and/or future girlfriends and wives. It is also common for drug users to pick up extra money by donating blood.

It has only been since September of 1987 that the U. S. Centers for Disease Control (CDC) has expanded its definition of AIDS beyond those in the third stage (see the section in this chapter on page 146 entitled, "Stages of AIDS"). In the years right after the disease was discovered in 1976 (it was identified and labeled as AIDS in 1981), there was only one case of a female with AIDS in the third stage. All other cases in the entire country were male homosexuals.[5]

Currently, the disease is spreading primarily through homosexual and bisexual males, who comprise 75 percent of all persons with AIDS (PWA), through the sharing of contaminated needles, and through prostitution. Studies estimate that 50 to 80 percent of prostitutes in America and other Western countries are AIDS carriers, and therefore, are infectious.[6]

A single virus, introduced directly into the blood by any means (including a minor needle prick), will regularly transmit infection.[7] Hence, 9 thousand hemophiliacs are infected with the virus and another 20 thousand have been given AIDS-contaminated blood in America alone.

AIDS is transmitted by the blood because it is in the blood. It also has been isolated from saliva, tears, urine, cerebrospinal fluid, brain tissue and vaginal secretions.[8] Dr. Jefferey Laurence, AIDS researcher at New York Hospital-Cornell Medical Center, has said that cells outside the blood, such as skin and related tissues, also serve as reservoirs for the virus.[9] These factors portend ominously for possible so-called casual means of transmission. On January 11, 1985, Dr. James Slaff, Medical Investigator at the National Institute of Health stated, "There is risk of infecting others by exposure through oral-genital contact or intimate kissing." Dr. Slaff continues:

> Because the AIDS virus has been cultured from the saliva of infected individuals, the FDA currently recommends that infected individuals refrain from "French" kissing. Dr. Zake Salahuddin has

provided an example in which the only possible vector [means] of transmission in an elderly infected woman, was kissing her AIDS husband, an impotent transfusion recipient.[10]

It is apparent that AIDS is broadening its impact, a fact that has been suppressed in the media. Dr. R. Restak has said in the *Washington Post:*

> This disease is only partially understood, is presently untreatable, and invariably fatal. For these reasons alone, caution would seem to be in order when it comes to exposing the public to those suffering from this illness. In addition, the incubation period is sufficiently lengthy to cast doubt on any proclamations no matter how seemingly authoritative in regard to the transmissionability of this illness.[11]

Casual Transmission

One of the main reasons casual transmission is a factor to reckon with is highlighted by Dr. Montagnier of the Pasteur Institute:

> The potential for genetic variation is perhaps the greatest danger in the future of the AIDS epidemic . . . A further change of the virus in its tropism [ability to infect different types of cells] and ways of transmission cannot be excluded.[12]

After the infection occurs, the body begins "shedding" the AIDS virus, excreting it through various bodily secretions. This is why infected people who have not yet developed symptoms are able to transmit the AIDS virus to others. Today the disease is transmitted primarily through sex, intravenous use of needles, and blood transfusion. Tomorrow the means of transmission may change in unpredictable ways. Indicative of this change is a report from the CDC that three health care workers were infected with AIDS through the skin. One may have gotten it through the mouth or eyes when blood splattered in a medical procedure; the other two perhaps through chapped or inflamed areas of the skin. But none contracted the disease through needle puncture or other common vectors.[13]

Once infected, there is no way of becoming dis-infected. One remains permanently capable of passing the deadly agent on to others. Quite simply, he or she can never engage in intimate sexual activity, including kissing, without endangering the life of another person.[14]

Condoms

Also, surprising to some, the efficacy of condoms in preventing AIDS transmission is unproven.[15] Condoms have a 10 percent failure rate in vaginal intercourse and a 50 percent failure rate with anal intercourse. Like any product, condoms are subject to quality control problems. Three American condom manufacturers have recently recalled several lots of their anti-disease contraceptive rubber products because they failed the leak tests. Bill Grigg, FDA spokesman, said that 100 thousand condoms were involved in the domestic recall. And consider this: If safe sex is safe, why does the Council on Scientific Affairs of the American Medical Association still say, "Sexual contact should be avoided with persons known to have or suspected of having AIDS"?

"Safe sex" is a shallow wish for hedonistic pleasure with impunity. The propaganda continues, but with never a mention of abstinence as an alternative. Concluded one *Time* magazine article: "For now, at least, the . . . call for an informed populace and safe sexual practices seems to be the best preventative medicine around."[16]

Other STDs

Whether or not people will use condoms is also a significant question, especially in light of the fact that, although condoms have been around for decades, we nevertheless have five other STDs of epidemic proportions: chlamydia, herpes II, venereal warts, penicillin-resistant gonorrhea, and candida.[17]

Chlamydia is the most common disease among these, infecting 1,300,000 people annually; 15 to 25 percent of American women have it. No symptoms are shown in 60 to 80 percent of the victims, but it can cause tubal pregnancy (in the Fallopian tube instead of the uterus), sterility, and pelvic inflammatory disease (PID). PID hospitalizes 200 thousand women annually and has caused more than 250 thousand known deaths.

25 percent of American adults have **herpes simplex II.** In men it can cause prostatic, penile, and testicular cancer. Women increase their risk of cervical cancer, and pregnant women with herpes may have miscarriage, stillbirths, or offspring with brain damage.

Venereal warts may cause sterility.

Between 1985 and 1986, the spread of penicillin-resistant **gonorrhea** increased 90 percent. Of these victims, 20 percent of the men and 80 percent of the women show no symptoms, yet, untreated, this disease can lead to sterility, arthritis, and blindness. The path of sin is indeed booby-trapped.

Apparently, selling the populace on the virtues of condoms to avoid these diseases has not been successful. Human nature assumes "it will never happen to me."

Hard Facts

Because the incubation period for AIDS is slow (5 to 30 years), it is reasonable to conclude that all infected individuals will eventually succumb.[18] That means millions of Americans will be languishing with debilitating diseases, incapable in many instances of caring for themselves, running up horrendous medical bills . . . yet there are only about 360 thousand hospital beds currently not occupied. Where will these people go? Who will pay the billions of dollars in costs? As one writer put it, "Refusing to make plans to cope with the actual scale of the AIDS epidemic would be criminally stupid. There is no question that the world is going to experience an enduring tragedy."[19]

In the 1300s one of the greatest horrors of human suffering was the Bubonic Plague, or "Black Death," so called because splotches of blood would form under the skin and turn black. The disease came from bites of fleas from diseased rats. Not understanding the relevance of hygiene and pest control, the populace was ignorant as to how to stop the inexorable steamroller of death, and it crushed 30 million people—approximately 25 percent of Europe. Surgeon General C. Everett Koop has said that AIDS will make the Black Death look like a Sunday school picnic!

With the plague, symptoms were immediate and death was swift. Victims were isolated, but millions still died. With herpes, sores appear in three to five days giving early warning, and they recur throughout a lifetime, yet 500 thousand new cases are reported annually in the United States. The AIDS victim, however, may show no symptoms for several years and still be a fully infectious carrier. At present no restrictive measures are put on him by the law, and he can infect many people in a variety of ways before he becomes too debilitated to function. Combine these factors with a "value-free" society, which glorifies sexual adventure,

144 THE HIGH COST OF FREE LOVE

and the situation is set for the maximum number of people becoming infected—and dying.

These are some of the facts pertaining to this new disease. It is going to get much worse. According to Dr. Halfdan Mahler, director of the World Health Organization:

> We are running scared. We cannot imagine a worse health problem in this century. We stand nakedly in front of a very serious pandemic as mortal as there has ever been. I don't know of any greater killer than AIDS, not to speak of its psychological, social and economic maiming . . . Everything is getting worse and worse in AIDS and all of us have been underestimating it. As many as 100 million people could be infected with the AIDS virus in five years.[20]

The Nature of the AIDS Virus

> The AIDS virus shows every sign of being just as deadly as the plague during the Middle Ages. We are on a crash course with reality. This is not a practice run. There is no second chance . . . The alarm must be sounded, loudly and persuasively. If it is not, the conclusion is inescapable: Millions may die.[21]

In December of 1982, there were 711 cases of full-blown AIDS reported from sixteen countries to the World Health Organization. Five years later, there were 42 thousand cases in ninety-one countries . . . and even this is a fraction because, to save face, countries are reticent to report. Some are ill-equipped to recognize AIDS every time, and some are pressured from authorities to keep quiet.[22] Some countries in Africa are 30 percent infected and escalating; in Africa, 90 percent of the prostitutes and 10 percent of the pregnant women have AIDS.[23] From 1986 to 1991 the projected numbers with AIDS worldwide are estimated to jump from 40 million to 200 million. In America, the estimated jump will be from 3 million to 15 million.

Understanding the incredible complexity of the virus explains how such an explosion is possible.

Once in the blood, the HTLV III, or AIDS virus, hunts with a determined single-mindedness for the master coordinator of the immune system, the helper T cell. These cells have receptor sites designed like parts of a jigsaw puzzle, and the virus fits right into the slot like a key in a lock.

Having thus entered the cell, the virus sheds its protective outer protein coating, releasing an RNA strand and an enzyme.

This deadly duo then do a magical conversion, changing the RNA strand into double-stranded deoxyribonucleic acid (DNA), the computer program of each cell that determines its reproduction. This deceptive invader then penetrates the cell nucleus, usurping the command center, and reprograms the cellular machinery to produce multiple AIDS viruses. These multiple offspring burst out of the cell, killing the host T cell in the process. In this fashion, it is only a matter of time before the immune system is overcome, literally beyond repair.

Avoiding Detection

Hiding inside the cell's DNA is the **first** way the virus can avoid antibody detection. By analogy, if the CIA were looking for a Caucasian in China, but the Caucasian had transformed himself into a spirit and entered the body of a Chinese, what would be the chances of the CIA locating him? About the same as an immune antibody locating the invading culprit hiding within the DNA of a host cell. The consuming action of the virus in overpowering the immune system is relentless and inevitable.

The **second** way of avoiding antibody detection is the virus's ability to transfer from cell to cell without entering the blood stream. This unique capability can render the detection process so mathematically improbable as to be virtually impossible. Microbiologist Ashley Haase of the University of Minnesota says, "Even if you have antibodies to the virus circulating in the blood, they won't be able to destroy the infection."[24]

Third, this virus duplicates and mutates at such a blinding speed that it becomes unrecognizable to the antibodies that had just figured out what they were looking for. Says Dr. W. Hazeltine, prominent investigator at Harvard's Dana Farber Cancer Institute, "Nobody would have thought this level of [gene activity] was possible before we did this study. We were shocked. It is about 1000 times faster than the genes we know about."[25] Adds Dr. Luc Montagnier, the eminent French AIDS researcher who, concurrently with Dr. Robert Gallo, discovered the HTLV-III retrovirus as the AIDS agent:

> The potential for genetic variation is perhaps the greatest danger in the future of the AIDS epidemic. It will make it difficult to design efficient vaccines protective against all strains, and further change of the virus in its [ability to infect different types of cells] and its ways of transmission cannot be excluded.[26]

Any one of these three detection-avoidance methods would

render the success of utilizing an effective cure highly unlikely. Combined, they make the progress of the virus unstoppable.

Stages of AIDS

There are three stages to the AIDS virus:

1. HIV positive. This person is infected and infectious. He has antibodies which are 90 percent traceable by blood testing, using the ELISA blood test. There are a few people who are positive but for inexplicable reasons do not reveal antibodies in the test. There are no medical complications or symptoms during this stage. Not until September of 1987 did the CDC consider this person a PWA. They considered only stage-three carriers PWA. This has been highly curious, because no other disease has been compartmentalized this way. For instance, if one tests positive for syphilis, he is said to have syphilis, and the medical testers are obligated by law to instigate a tracing activity to alert former sexual partners of the infected person. Such tracing is not required for HIV positive patients, which is also curious. As we shall see, many mysterious attitudes surround the specter of AIDS.

2. ARC—AIDS Related Complex. This stage is deadly: weight loss, swollen lymph glands, chronic diarrhea, drenching night sweats, perpetual fatigue and/or psychogenic disturbances. This is sometimes referred to as "pre-AIDS," which is ridiculous; the person has AIDS. Dr. Slaff states that there are over fifty clinical manifestations for ARC.[27]

3. Full-blown AIDS. This is the stage when the infected person is overcome with opportunistic infections to the extent that he cannot function alone. The immune system is so devastated that infections and diseases that would ordinarily be fought back by the immune system simply move in and take over. Typically, these include:

   (a) pneumocystis carinii pneumonia: infiltrates and damages the lungs;

   (b) Kaposi sarcoma: an invasive form of skin cancer that affects internal organs;

   (c) candidiasis: fungal infection also known as thrush; infects the esophagus and eventually the central nervous system;

   (d) cytomegalovirus: viral infection which also attacks

the lungs, spreads throughout the body and can cause blindness;

(e) herpes simplex (HSV): in AIDS patients, can be fatal;

(f) toxoplasmosis: a small parasite found in cat feces; though normally a mild asymptomatic infection in persons with an intact immune system, in AIDS patients it can cause headaches, severe lethargy, seizures, vomiting, fever and psychological disturbances;

(g) cryptosporidiosis: intestinal disease causing cholera-like diarrhea (10-30 bloody quarts every day!), dehydration, malnutrition and severe weight loss;

(h) cryptococcosis: fungal infection that can cause diffuse meningitis, stupor, mental disturbances and personality changes, severe headaches and double vision;

(i) tuberculosis: making a dramatic comeback according to federal and local officials; as is commonly known, tuberculosis is highly contagious and can easily have the potential to strike beyond AIDS victims.[28]

Over half of those people who have full-blown AIDS are dead in 18 months; 70 percent are dead inside two years. None are alive five years later.

One of the most significant factors which impacts every facet of the AIDS problem is that it is a visne virus belonging to the family of lentiviruses (meaning slow, as in a lengthy incubation period before symptoms develop). There are only three lentiviruses known: one in sheep, one in horses, and one in goats. A report in *Science*, January 1985, showed that the HTLV-III was related to the visne lentivirus causing chronic degenerative brain disease in sheep.[29]

The significance of the slow nature of the virus means that the difference between stage one and stage three is simply a matter of time, not kind. It had been hoped, and in some circles believed, that stage one infection did not mean death. 36 thousand people dead from a virus is bad, but to say that every infected person (3 million in the U.S., 20 million in the world) is eventually going to die of AIDS may sound drastic. Nevertheless, Dr. Jay Levy of the Cancer Research Institute, University of California School of Medicine, San Francisco, has concluded:

> The initial description in 1954 of these slow virus or lentivirus infections by Sigurdsson defined the acquired immunodeficiency syndrome: a long but predictable incubation period of months to years; an infectious agent that produces inapparent but progressive pathologic damage; and a protracted course, generally ending in serious disease or death.[30]

AIDS also kills directly, not just indirectly through suppressing the immune system. In sheep, with no immune deficiency, and no symptoms for 1 to 6 years, the brain infection with the lentivirus results in death in 100 percent of the animals.[31] Dr. Slaff reports the case of a medical school teacher who developed dementia without any manifestation of ARC or full-blown AIDS. Viral replication of the HTLV-III within the brain and cerebrospinal fluid was cited as the cause of death.[32]

The dementia that occurs from AIDS is becoming more prevalent as the virus spreads. Combined with the immune suppression syndrome, this two-pronged killer is rapidly becoming the crisis of the hour and has been named the number one priority of the Public Health Service.

The Case for a Cure

It can appear absurd to say that there is not now nor will there ever be a cure for AIDS. Americans have come to expect control and success in any field of endeavor whenever they have poured in enough ingenuity and money. It was said that sound would never travel through wire, light could never blaze from a glass bulb, and man would never fly. And scientists have conquered polio and syphilis, and significant gains are being made toward a cure of cancer.

In AIDS, however, there exist complexities so incredible and complications so overwhelming that even if a cure could be designed, millions between the ages of 25 and 49 in our country alone would already be dead, the health care industry would be in shambles, the federal government Medicaid/Medicare programs and the insurance companies would be bankrupt, and the very security of our country would be in severe jeopardy. The World Health Organization has said:

> The combined impact of the HIV pandemic of AIDS upon health care, insurance, legal systems, economic and social development, and indeed entire cultures and populations is already extraordinary

and will become increasingly onerous.[33]

In other words, by the time a cure is found, it will be too late in every sense of the word.

The three tricky detection-avoidance methods used by the AIDS virus have already been indicated as serious reasons for a forthcoming cure to be doubtful at best. There are additional reasons the hope of a cure or vaccine is, as Dr. Slaff has said, "a bad bet."

No vaccine has ever been developed against an RNA virus. Never. If the natural immune system is absolutely powerless against this invader, what can man do? Most other vaccines, like polio, or flu, inject small parts of the actual disease into the person, and the immune system develops antibodies against the stranger. Then if an actual polio virus or flu bacteria attempts to attack the body, antibodies are already in place. AIDS, however, is the first virus to attack the immune system itself. Says researcher Opendra Narayan of Johns Hopkins: "The chance of going into the lab and creating something nature has not done yet is slim."[34]

Lentiviruses are extremely virulent and complex, further diminishing the hopes of developing a cure or a vaccine. The few in animals have proved so completely resistant to any type of treatment that slaughtering the infected animals has become the universal means of control.

The virus changes surface characteristics as it is transmitted from one individual to another. The five or six genes are unstable within each person and there is not even a single virus entity isolated from a given person! The same person can harbor multiple forms of the virus.[35] By 1985 there were around two hundred isolates (i.e., identities) of the virus.[36] By the time you are reading this, there are undoubtedly more.

Combating the direct AIDS attack on the brain is even more unfathomable. The virus invades and reproduces within the central nervous system, crossing over what is known as the "blood-brain barrier." This by itself creates virtually insurmountable obstacles in treatment. The virus hides within the genetic material, and therefore the only way to kill it would be to kill masses of brain tissue. Hardly a reasonable approach. Dr. Seale catches the conclusive nature of this catastrophe and the apparent hopelessness of curing AIDS:

The almost unlimited varieties of antigenic strains of lentiviruses produced by antigenic drift (i.e., change) combined with the inability of antibodies produced by the host to eliminate the virus from circulation, have rendered ineffective all attempts to produce vaccines to prevent lentivirus diseases in animals. Effective protection against infection with the AIDS virus using existing vaccination techniques would seem to be theoretically impossible.[37]

The Homosexual Connection

"I have contracted a virus called AIDS. This is a medical problem, not a moral problem." This statement was made by Randy Giddings at a symposium for social workers in New Orleans, August 1987. It was apparent from the reaction of the audience and the statements of subsequent speakers that ostensibly no one missed a beat at Giddings' denial of morality being at the heart of the AIDS issue.

Since our culture has been awash in a sea devoid of absolutes for some time, morality has become whatever is the consensus of the masses, or whatever is determined in courts, or whatever one merely decides for himself. In 1973 homosexuality was removed from the list of mental disorders—through the lobbying efforts of the National Gay Task Force—in the *Diagnostic and Statistical Manual of Mental Disorders*. Therefore, homosexuality is okay.

Passage of a so-called "homosexual rights" act in New York City (March 20, 1986) prohibited discrimination based on sexual orientation in housing, employment or public accommodation. And such laws currently exist in every major American city except Chicago. Therefore, homosexuality is okay.

If homosexuality is okay, it is not a moral problem. If homosexuality is not a moral problem, then AIDS is not a moral problem. The ignorant acceptance of homosexuality as a viable, harmless alternate lifestyle has put our society into a double bind, effectively blocking any definitive move against the AIDS encroachment.

This is the first confusion that has put us off balance in dealing conclusively with the AIDS phenomena.

The second confusion, designed to evaporate any condemnation associated with AIDS, is a blurring of the distinction between the guilty victims and the innocent victims. Indicative of this current propaganda is the sales pitch of a "value-free" video, which, according to a Concerned Women of America newsletter, is being shown to New York City students:

> You know, it is not their fault they have AIDS. AIDS isn't anybody's fault. Maybe you're feeling angry or frustrated because you're going to have to deal with this from now on. Well, there's no one to blame except the virus.

Recently in *Time* magazine there was a picture of Pope John Paul II, tears in his eyes, holding tightly a four-year-old boy with AIDS. No, it is not that child's fault that he has AIDS, and for him it is not a moral problem. But to infer, as is the intent of the New York City school sex-education video, that AIDS is nobody's fault and it is not a moral problem does heinous violence to the truth. Indeed, that little boy will never see his tenth birthday because our country has said that homosexuality "is not a moral problem."

Sodomy

It would not be accurate to say that sodomy—the anal intercourse commonly practiced among homosexuals—causes AIDS, or that the virus somehow has a magnetic attraction for homosexuals. However, the health factors endemic to the homosexual, the unimaginable promiscuity rampant within the homosexual community, and the valueless atmosphere of our pluralistic society have caused the AIDS epidemic. Look at these statistics of who has AIDS:

73% homosexual and bisexual men

17% intravenous drug users

3% blood recipients

1% heterosexuals who have had sexual contact with someone with AIDS

1% infants born to infected mothers

5% individuals outside any of the above groups (i.e., a health care individual who pricks his finger with a needle from an AIDS patient)

To call homosexuality a moral problem means it is a spiritual aberration. It is contrary to truth, and truth is central to humanity. Therefore, it is a human problem because it cuts across the basic fiber of true humanness. We are not animals evolved from the primordial slime of the ocean who can choose any course with approval from God as if He were some dimwitted Santa Claus. God's parameters are absolutes. To cross them is to be broken by them. They are breaking us now. And the homosexual is the first and continuing primary cause of the spread of this disease within our culture.

"The enormous prevalence of AIDS, along with several other grave communicable diseases endemic to homosexuals, is not mere inexplicable chance. There are a number of biological and social factors which have been distinctly linked with their spread."[38]

When sodomy is performed, the peculiar forced inward expansion of the anal canal results in a tearing of the lining as well as bleeding of the anal fissures.[39] Colitis, a severe inflammation of the mucous membrane of the colon, often develops from repeated sodomy, as well as mucosal ulceration of the rectal area, and inflammatory psoriasis. The trauma of sodomy produces this unique psoriasis from the rectum to the pubic area, penis, and scrotum. This is known as Kobner's phenomenon.[40] During sexual activity, the area becomes raw, bleeding, and exposed to infection. States one national case study, before AIDS was identified:

Blood from rectal mucosal lesions, [which] are known to be common in homosexual males who engage in rectal intercourse, could contain the infectious agent responsible for this epidemic.[41]

Although this study and numerous others correlate the relationship between homosexual behavior/disease and the susceptibility of AIDS, the correlation is continually downplayed in the media. Recently on television two sitcoms dealt with AIDS and how people handled it; in neither case was the one with AIDS a homosexual.

The damage to the rectal wall facilitates access to the bloodstream of AIDS-infected sperm and other disease-causing organisms. And sodomy has proven debilitating to the immune system even without AIDS.[42]

Sodomy often injures the rectum, and sperm, being aggressive, invariably enter the bloodstream where they are perceived as a foreign substance. The immune system then works to develop antibodies against the sperm. Human seminal fluid apparently contains components that can suppress the immune system,[43] so this process does just that.[44] An impaired immune system is susceptible to diseases whether or not the person has AIDS, but this, of course, creates an especially receptive environment to the AIDS virus.

Studies show that three-fourths of homosexual males manifest sperm-induced immune dysregulation. Therefore, the homosexual male is considerably more predisposed to severe opportunistic infections and Kaposi's sarcoma.

It is not difficult to conclude from these studies, therefore, that homosexual behavior is not harmless; it is not simply another alternate lifestyle of equal normalcy. Rather, it is a dangerous, destructive practice that amplifies the development and spread of disease. This is in addition to the severe spiritual ramifications of an activity constantly denounced by God (cf. Romans 1:18-32; 1 Corinthians 6; 1 Timothy 1:3-11). But realizing that many people are unimpressed with spiritual realities and truth, it is relevant to know that there are medical and physiological grounds for ridding our society of homosexuality apart from so-called "religious" reasons.

The damaging practice of sodomy can itself be classified as sadomasochistic. Few people outside the homosexual community, however, are aware of the degree to which severe bodily abuse and degradation are a part of the homosexual "alternate lifestyle." In some cities, like San Francisco, where a certain percentage of the murders are reportedly linked to homosexual sadomasochism, workshops are offered on how to engage in homosexual sex torture without killing each other.[45]

Susceptibility

Homosexuals often contend that AIDS among heterosexuals in other cultures, especially in Africa, discredits the homosexual connection. This point is pushed repeatedly by value-free protagonists who want to indicate that the high rate of AIDS among homosexuals is just happenstance.

It is not:

In light of the fact that 90 percent of homosexually active men demonstrate chronic or recurrent viral infections of herpes virus, cytomegalovirus, and hepatitis B, it is possible that these recurrent or chronic infections may themselves be triggering factors for the development of acquired immunodeficiency.[46]

In addition to the homosexual's body being more susceptible to disease due to sodomy, the fact is that diseases and infections common among African patients with AIDS—where poverty, inadequate sanitation, and generally unhealthy living conditions exist—are also common among Western homosexuals but not heterosexuals. The range of viral and protozoal infections among homosexuals is identical to that among African villagers.[47] This is undoubtedly because of the unhygienic sexual practices which facilitate the spread of infectious agents. And when diseases already are present, the destructive effect of AIDS is turned into a landslide catastrophe.

Bathhouses

In the book *Homosexualities*, authors Bell and Weinberg, both advocates of homosexual liberation, state that the average homosexual male has scores of sexual partners in a year. Over a few years that's hundreds. Thousands over a lifetime is not unusual.[48] To facilitate inexpensive, frequent, anonymous sexual activity, bathhouses and clubs have sprung up, especially in the larger cities, as gathering places for homosexuals to gratify their rapacious hunger for perversion. In a single afternoon or evening a patron might have nearly a dozen sexual encounters.[49] Says Enrique Rueda in his documented exposé, *The Homosexual Network, Private Lives and Public Policy*:

> The degree of promiscuity in the baths defies the imagination of those not familiar with homosexuality. From the point of view of traditional values, they are probably some of the most destructive and degrading institutions in America today . . . From the medical point of view, the baths constitute a major focus for transmission of disease. Psychologically, they constitute the antithesis of mental health. Ethically, it is difficult to justify the impersonality and degradation they institutionalize.[50]

One study showed that homosexual men in the last stages of AIDS had 50 percent of their previous sexual encounters in bathhouses.[51] It is no wonder that 70 to 90 percent of practicing homosexuals in San Francisco and New York City are infected with AIDS.[52] Nor is it surprising that one study of 6,875 homosexual men in San Francisco saw an increase of those with AIDS from 4.5 percent in 1978 to 74.5 percent in 1985.

Aids and the Law

This homosexual connection with AIDS has been discussed here not only because homosexuality is itself a moral issue, but because, for the first time, we have a killer disease which is behaviorally condoned, protected by law, and civil-rights related. The result of viewing homosexuality as a political and civil rights issue instead of a serious health problem has led many cities to pass legislation protecting the behavioral rights of those who are predominantly responsible, by that very behavior, for passing the deadly disease on to virtually millions, both guilty (by act) and innocent (by accident). Says Dr. Harold Voth, Chief of Staff at Topeka VA Medical Hospital:

> It is our belief that the increasing acceptance and protection of sexual deviancy may ultimately lead to the destruction of our civilization.[53]

Here are some ways political pressure has stepped in to protect rights of homosexuals, thus insuring the spread of AIDS:

1. In California, and perhaps in other states, it is illegal for a doctor to reveal to his nurse that a given patient has AIDS.

2. There are no laws prohibiting AIDS carriers or homosexuals from giving blood. Such a law would be considered discriminatory, defaming the integrity of that person based on his so-called unrelated sexual preference.[54]

   These days blood is screened after it is given, but the people themselves are not screened. Catch the difference? It would be a violation of civil rights to prevent a person from donating blood or from participating in any other medically risky activity.

3. There have been homosexual rights laws passed in more than 50 cities and in many states, thereby disqualifying any legislation that would even hint at discrimination. Through political pressure, homosexual activist groups have put the clamps on any form of AIDS discrimination — such as blood testing, segregation in hospitals, etc., because the chances that the AIDS patient is homosexual are 3 to 1. Of course, the image they project is a humanitarian concern for the sick, which is of quite minor value to them compared with protecting their own.

4. Because segregating an AIDS patient would violate his rights, AIDS patients are placed in hospital rooms with non-AIDS patients whose immune systems are low due to cancer, chemotherapy, organ transplant, open heart surgery, etc. The non-AIDS person does not have the right to be informed of the proximity of this deadly, communicable disease, whereas the AIDS patient is protected from ostracism by his civil rights. This is typical of the cross purposes of civil rights and medical propriety. The Council on Scientific Affairs of the American Medical Association says: "The patient with AIDS . . . should not be in contact with other immunocompromised persons."[55] Would

that be said if sex and blood transfusions were the only means of transmission?

5. When Mervyn Silverman was the health administrator in San Francisco, he attempted to halt the spread of AIDS by shutting down fourteen gay bathhouses, bookstores and clubs. In December of 1984 he was pressured into resigning. Apparently, he was made an offer he couldn't refuse. In a similar situation, when the issue of closing Club Dallas Bathhouse, with a patronage of more than 30 thousand, was brought to the attention of authorities, it was said that to do so would be "purely political."

6. Dan Bradley, an admitted homosexual, is the former head of Legal Services Corporation (LSC) for the Federal Government. Under Bradley's leadership, the powerful LSC distributed $300 million a year to fund various leftist and pro-homosexual activities. He is currently on the board of directors of the Gay Rights National Lobby.[56]

7. The AIDS crisis has become a financial bonanza for homosexual groups seeking federal funds to "educate" their constituency and public school children in the virtues of "safe sex."

8. Anti-sodomy laws have been repealed throughout the United States due to the activist efforts of many gay groups. Indicative of this, the highest court in New York decided the anti-sodomy law was unconstitutional and irrational, stating that "no showing has been made . . . that physical injury is a common or even occasional consequence of the prohibited conduct."[57] The bulk of medical studies refute this allegation; the following excerpt from one study is indicative:

> Anal intercourse presents physicians with surgical as well as medical problems, ranging from anal fissures and impaction of foreign bodies in the rectum to major diagnostic dilemmas. Infection in traumatized rectal mucose and in amoebic or herpetic ulcers above the level of the anal ring may produce formations that mimic rectal carcinoma (i.e., cancer).[58]

9. Through the lobbying efforts of the National Gay Task Force, the board of trustees of the American Psychiatric Association (APA) agreed to remove homosexuality from the list of mental disorders. Said Dr. Charles Socarides, member of the APA, in his book, *Beyond Sexual Freedom*:

> Moving swiftly, a small band of well-intentioned but misguided psychiatrists, disregarding a large body of scientific

evidence to the contrary, accomplished what every other society with rare exception would have trembled to attempt—the revision of a basic concept of life and biology: that men and women normally mate with the opposite, not the same, sex.

10. Congressman Henry Waxman of Colorado, a long-time supporter of homosexual causes, has worked closely with the Gay Rights National Lobby and its "AIDS Project" to get millions of dollars allocated for AIDS research.

11. The media is also used to distort the reality of AIDS by focusing the light away from the homosexual community where the brunt of the responsibility lies. And the media's approach is not surprising, since 80 percent of television broadcasters do not regard homosexuality as wrong.[59] Consequently the situation has been distorted. Major studies revealing the potential of casual transmission have gone completely unreported, while wild hopes of a cure and groundless optimism about a vaccine have received clamorous display. Why? To deflect the heat from the causes which are going unattended.

While it seems a groundswell of alarmed citizens requesting change is developing, at this writing these things are all still true. Pending legislation may bring positive results as time goes on, but up to now, this stamp of acceptability gives the homosexual activists a fulcrum to leverage their positions throughout the media and the government. They posture themselves as simply another persecuted minority in our otherwise free society, demanding their rights. Steadily gaining politically, they have emerged as a power-wielding alliance that can, with chilling results, determine political and employment success for an individual.

The conflict between what is medically proper and what is politically expedient for this fractured minority will continue to build. Who wins this struggle will depend largely on who screams the loudest in our society—the innocent sick and dying, the healthy uninfected and the heretofore silent moral majority, or the homosexuals and their political sycophants who want to protect their libertine lifestyle at any cost. Militant homosexuals, allied with pro-homosexual mayors, health officials, state and federal government agencies, key persons and congressmen, will compound the AIDS crisis and make it difficult to dismantle.

The Search for a Solution

Dr. J. L. Fletcher says in *Homosexuality: Kick and Kickback:*

> If we act as empirical scientists, can we not see the implications of the data before us? If homosexuality, or even just male homosexuality, is "okay," then why the high prevalence of associated complications in general, and especially in regard to AIDS? Might not these "complications" be consequences? Might it not be that our society's approval of homosexuality is an error and that the unsubtle words of the Bible are frightfully correct?
>
> From an empirical medical standpoint alone, current scientific observation seems to require the conclusion that homosexuality is a pathological condition . . . Certain cause and effect data are convincing—so convincing that health care providers in this age of unbridled enthusiasms for preventive medicine would do well to seek reversal treatment for their homosexual patients just as vigorously as they would for alcoholics or heavy cigarette smokers.[60]

The invention of the pill, the cure for syphilis and gonorrhea, and a heavy dash of Bacchanalian philosophy inflamed the sexual revolution in the late '60s and throughout the '70s. Although other complications—like pregnancy and herpes—multiplied at alarming rates, the threat of death from syphilis was evaporated. Now we are back with a death threat inestimably worse. The result: The sexual revolution is dead.[61] Marriage is more popular; the number of teen pregnancies is down; abortions are down [but only by a mere 5 thousand—they still run 1.3 million a year!]; the divorce rate is declining; and there is a new baby boom.[62] In a poll by *People* magazine, 73 percent of the respondents concurred that the threat of disease has stopped unfaithfulness.[63]

Of course we all want a cure, especially for assisting the helpless and the innocent who have and will have this death-dealing disease because of someone else's perversion. But a result of equal horror from such a cure is inescapable: Homosexuality will be given the license to escalate to new heights and promiscuity will again accelerate apace with a renewed glee. A cure may be desirable at any cost, but there is cause to reflect thankfully on the current situation and direct our attention toward another goal: a solution. A solution that is both personal and political.

Abstinence is such an obviously preferable choice, for safety's sake if for no other, that it hardly needs to be defended beyond the substantial medical evidence we have looked at. To abstain sexually in all romantic ventures, to include an ELISA test [the test to determine if AIDS antibodies are present] with the other premarital blood tests, then to remain monogamous throughout marriage is the winning course to get from birth to old age without being sabotaged along the way.

The power of God gives us the clarity of thought to put reason and righteousness above glands, and it allows our sexuality to seek its own natural level of importance. Sin, culture, and that same old adversary with his same old tricks are what stir up lust so outrageously that we would willingly risk life itself in the vain attempt to quench its all-consuming fire.

Apart from divine intervention or finding a cure, we are without hope unless we realize that we must get involved in political activism to press back the amazing inroads homosexuality has made. We must match and exceed the efforts of the homosexual community and alert the majority to the death-dealing realities of "gay liberation." We must lobby, vote, send money, picket and pursue every legal means available to thwart the public manifestation of homosexual acceptance in every form. To fight malaria, health officials don't just sit in a chemistry lab looking for a cure; they spray the swamps to kill the source.

Up to this time, any suggestion that legal measures—such as closing the bathhouses or preventing homosexuals and PWAs from giving blood—should be instituted have been stonewalled by so-called civil libertarians claiming that morality cannot be legislated. Legally and politically we have yet to wake up from the stupor of such sophistry. There is legislation against drunk driving based on the moral conviction that the welfare of the majority supersedes the right of the drunk to drive recklessly. Similarly, we need to recognize that preventing the spread of AIDS will mean stepping on people's toes and offending a vocal minority which has made significant strides in getting the populace to call black white, but such offense is simply unavoidable.

For our country to survive, the homosexual activist movement must be shoved back and buried politically. Dr. Restak says:

> Only sentimentalists refuse to make any distinction between the victims of a scourge and those not presently infected . . . The threat of AIDS demands from us all a discrimination based on our instinct for survival against a peril, that if not somehow controlled, can destroy this society . . . This is not a civil rights issue—this is a medical issue. To take a position that the AIDS virus must be eradicated is not to make judgments on morals or lifestyles. It is to

say the AIDS virus has no "civil rights."[64]

The best possible scenario would be to sell society on the biblical perspective of homosexuality (thus creating an irrefutable, lasting basis for physical and mental health in the country, because the spiritual *is* central). Short of that hoped-for eventuality, we must at least make every conceivable move to block AIDS, and that means moving against homosexuality as a health threat. As it currently stands, the civil rights of homosexuality and the worsening AIDS crises have blurred together. The latter cannot be successfully attacked because it is inextricably tied in with the former. Both must be denounced and eradicated for the same reason—the health and preservation of this nation.

We must lock onto our constitutional rights and not sit idly by while our country gets flushed by default. Indeed, we are commanded to be the salt of the earth, to *preserve* our society. Our great country has provided the means to be heard and heeded, but to this time and in this arena only the homosexuals have grasped the significance and power of such availability. This fight against AIDS and its perpetrators will be an uphill battle. We are fighting darkness in the courts, in the media, and in the murky morality of the masses. Thomas Paine's stirring words must move us again to gain the ground we have lost:

> These are the times that try men's souls. The summer soldier and the sunshine patriot will, in this crisis, shrink from the service of their country . . . Tyranny, like hell, is not easily conquered.

While we hope for a cure we must move on a solution: personal abstinence and political activism. There is time to win this war, but that time must be now!

△△△

Here's What You Can Do

Rather than enumerate further plans of action at this point, I would simply like to refer you to the last two pages of this chapter and the two moves we all can make toward finding a solution:

1. Maintain personal abstinence if single and strict monogamy if married.
2. Get actively involved politically in any way we can.

    We also can encourage others to do the same.

10

Upping the Ante II

Pregnancy and Abortion

> The most important issue facing this generation is the devaluation of human life. With over 1,500,000 abortions annually, and the recurring problem of infanticide, we have reached a crises point in America. We face, most imminently, the death of our culture.
>
> John Whitehead
> Founder of the Rutherford Institute

The promiscuity of our culture, even in an age of multiple birth control methods, has resulted in a tremendous, growing surge of unwanted pregnancies during the last fifteen years. In an atmosphere almost devoid of moral standards, it is not surprising that abortion on demand has emerged as an attempted solution to an embarrassing consequence of "free love." Reciprocally, promiscuity has continued to spiral upward during this same time because abortion is now offered as a means of controlling birth and avoiding consequences. Unless change intervenes, this madness (combined with the AIDS epidemic) will bury America.

For a while the age-old Christian ethic of moral integrity and absolute values in a God-centered society coexisted with the increasingly pervasive time-plus-chance view of man. Then as the Christian ethic seemed to coast to a halt, the secular viewpoint picked up speed. In the secular view, man is not really unique— he is merely the product of unconscious evolutionary processes. Consequently, for most people, the view of self as well as the worth of others has been free-falling rapidly. Supreme Court Justice Oliver Wendell Holmes reflected the relativism of this consensus when he said, "Truth is the majority vote of that nation that can lick all others."[1]

Though unfounded and unproven, the concept of man as merely a mechanistic jumble of molecules has allowed today's distressing evils to mushroom. Pornography, promiscuity, abortion, infanticide, euthenasia, child abuse, wife beating, drug abuse, street crime and white-collar crime all proliferate in a vacuum of godly, intractible absolutes based on the nature of man and the existence of God. Nothing is considered wrong because everything is relative and laws are arbitrary. People are for using and abusing; life is what we say it is; death is right for someone else when we say it will be; and pleasure and affluence are everything. Is it possible to reduce the worth of a person beyond this?

On the other hand, if man is made in the image of God, that adds inestimable worth to every individual in spite of any declaration to the contrary. And if it can be demonstrated, biblically, medically or philosophically, that the unborn is an alive human being, with worth equal to any other person, then the option to take its life is out of our hands. Abortion is murder. All other considerations would flow from this premise and be evaluated in light of this truth.

Irresponsible pregnancy is a humiliating result of lawless intimacy. It happens to more than a million singles every year, and, increasingly, abortion is chosen as a final solution. I hope that these pages will so horrify, alarm, and alert you to the dispicable heinousness of this crime that you, regardless of your situation, will never consider it as an out.

A Scriptural Position

Then God said, "Let Us make man in Our image" (Genesis 1:26).

This does not refer to physical form, for God has no body. It is figurative: Man shares in God's nature, though finitely. His communicable attributes (i.e., life, personality, truth, wisdom, love, holiness, justice) equip man for fellowship with God Himself.

The impact here is the intrinsic, eternal value of life. It is designed after God's own life. Therefore, an attack against innocent life is an attack against God.

Let the day perish on which I was to be born, and the night which said, "A boy is conceived" (Job 3:3).

This is a distressful passage at the beginning of Job's long ordeal, but from this verse we can see that Job was a living, human boy from the point of conception.

> Thy hands fashioned and made me altogether; And wouldst Thou destroy me? Remember now, that Thou hast made me as clay; And wouldst Thou turn me into dust again? Didst Thou not pour me out like milk, And curdle me like cheese; Clothe me with skin and flesh, And knit me together with bones and sinew? Thou hast granted me life and lovingkindness; And Thy care has preserved my spirit (Job 10:8-10).

Job is reminding God that to destroy him would be inconsistent with His own integrity, because He had previously created Job in his mother's womb with His own hands. The image of milk to cheese is depicting an intricate embryonic development, a process in which he was given skin and flesh and knit together with bone and muscle. In that procedure he was given life and a spirit, and God was watching over him. Job was Job in that fetal state, not some glob of cells that became Job upon birth.

> If men struggle with each other and strike a woman with child, so that she has a miscarriage [lit., her child comes out], yet there is no further injury, he shall surely be fined as the woman's husband may demand of him; and he shall pay as the judges decide. But if there is any further injury, then you shall appoint as a penalty life for life (Exodus 21:22,23).

The situation is this: Two men are arguing vehemently, and in the scuffle one accidentally strikes another man's wife. The result is a premature birth, not a miscarriage. The word is *yalad*, translated "child," not miscarriage, and the phrase "comes out" or "departs from her" is *yatsa*, the same word used in Genesis 25:25,26 to describe the birth of Esau and Jacob. If, then, the woman is struck so as to cause her to go into labor and deliver her child prematurely, but no permanent harm comes to mother or child, then a fine is imposed on the assailant. But if the result is the death of the child or the mother, then the law of retribution would apply: a life for a life.

God gave the law to Moses and the nation of Israel. This is part of that law. It is clear, therefore, that God considered the unborn a person, and the assailant could forfeit his life for having caused the death of the fetus or the mother.

> For the life [lit., soul] of the flesh is in the blood, and I have given

it to you on the altar to make atonement for your souls (Leviticus
17:11).

This is an extremely powerful argument for the life of the
embryo and developing fetus. Because the life of an animal is in
the blood, God says its blood is a temporary covering for man's sin
until the prefect covering, the Lord Jesus Christ, would come
(Hebrews 9:11-14). Then the covering would be the life of Jesus,
His blood, that would release us from our sins (Revelation 1:5).

The life of an animal, or the Son of God, or a man, is in the
blood, **not** in the air! On January 22, 1973, the Supreme Court
ruled in Roe v. Wade that a fetus became a living human being
when it was breathing outside the womb. This is an arbitrary and
ultimately innacurate assessment of life.

Dr. Jerome Le Jeune, Professor of Fundamental Genetics,
Medical College, Paris, France, puts it this way:

> If a fertilized egg is not by itself a full human being, it could
> never become a man, because something would have to be added to
> it, and we know that does not happen.

During open heart surgery the patient's lungs are artificially ventilated to avoid collapse, but they do not oxygenate the blood.
Rather, a cardiopulmonary bypass is performed, oxygenating the
bloodstream directly. This is exactly how the fetus is fed oxygen —
directly into the blood.

If the fetus is not human and not viable because he is not
breathing, what is true of the heart patient? The Supreme Court
claimed that the fetus was not legally a person for this very reason
and therefore had no protection by the state. If the process of
oxygenating the blood reduces the legal standing of the fetus as a
human being, is the heart patient's legal standing equally dimin-
ished? If the doctor chooses to sabotage the operation and kill the
patient, or if the patient's wife comes into the operating room and
puts a bullet through his head, will there be no reprisals because
the patient's blood was being oxygenated directly, and therefore
he was a non-person and devoid of legal protection? Well, you say,
hang around a few hours. The operation will be over and he will
be breathing. Ah, so! Hang around a little longer. The baby will
be born and he will be breathing, too!

Ridiculous, isn't it? How much easier to go with God's definition of life. As long as the blood is flowing and the systems are
being fed with nutrients and oxygen, that blood is alive and that

being is living, regardless of how the blood is being oxygenated.

> For Thou didst form my inward parts; Thou didst weave me in my mother's womb; I will give thanks to Thee, for I am fearfully and wonderfully made; Wonderful are Thy works, And my soul knows it very well. My frame was not hidden from Thee, When I was made in secret, And skillfully wrought in the depths of the earth. Thine eyes have seen my unformed substance; And in Thy book they were all written, The days that were ordained for me, When as yet there was not one of them (Psalm 139:13-16).

Who was involved in putting together our insides? God. Hence, the psalmist says in another place:

> Know that the LORD Himself is God; It is He who has made us, and not we ourselves (Psalm 100:3).

Famed feminist, Margaret Sanger, has said, "No woman can call herself free until she can choose consciously whether she will or will not be a mother." Of course, she is referring to the right to abort. Unfortunately, that choice to be or not to be a mother should have been made before she decided to have sex, not after conception, because now she is dealing with God's work in which He is directly involved:

> Cursed is he who strikes his neighbor [i.e., any innocent person] in secret (Deuteronomy 27:24).

> Now the word of the LORD came to me saying, "Before I formed you in the womb I knew you, And before you were born I consecrated you; I have appointed you a prophet to the nations" (Jeremiah 1:4,5).

If this passage were the only one to comment on the situation preceding birth, a case might be made that this refers only to Jeremiah, who had a unique calling and an unusual and demanding ministry. But the many additional passages revealing God's intimate involvement in creating the unborn preclude such a narrow interpretation. God knew each of us; He formed each of us. And He seeks us now because He knew us then! (Cf. also Isaiah 49:1,5.)

> And it came about that when Elizabeth heard Mary's greeting, the baby leaped in her womb; and Elizabeth was filled with the Holy Spirit . . . "For behold, when the sound of your greeting reached my ears, the baby leaped in my womb for joy" (Luke 1:41,44).

Again, this passage conceivably could be set aside as irrelevant because of the highly unusual nature of the principals.

And it is an unusual circumstance, to be sure. Mary, bearing the Son of God just conceived by the Holy Spirit, goes to visit her relative, Elizabeth, six months pregnant with John the Baptist, who was later declared by Jesus to be the greatest person in the kingdom of God! Truly unusual circumstances.

What we can glean from this unique get-together is greatly instructive. The word used for the baby is *brephos*, Greek for embryo, fetus, babe, infant, or young child. Here it is used of an unborn; in 1 Peter 2:2, Acts 7:19 and 2 Timothy 3:15 it is used of an infant or young child. When in other instances the Greek language is known for its accuracy in delineating specifics (i.e., as in three different kinds of love), the Holy Spirit, as the author of the Bible, takes advantage of the fact that all phases of young life, born or unborn, are recognized as alive human children. No further delineation is required because any differentiation would be inconsistent and untrue.

These passages provide a clear biblical base for making a godly decision on abortion. This is no technicality, no theoretical debate about metaphysical ethics. This is life and death.

The number of people killed in America since 1973 by abortion is twenty times the number of American soldiers killed in every war we have ever been in.[2] In 1980, abortions outnumbered live births in thirteen U. S. cities.[3] In 98 percent of the cases, abortions are done for "social" reasons, having nothing to do with rape, incest, possible deformity of the newborn, or the health of the mother. Four hundred to five hundred abortions annually are "live."[4] These living children, although they are breathing and have reasonable viability, are nevertheless discarded, killed by suffocation or morphine injection, or simply left to die because they were the "product of abortion" and therefore had no rights. What medicine could do to save the child, the law prevents, or makes no provision for. By definition, because the child is the product of an abortion, he is considered nothing more than garbage to be thrown out . . . mere tissue.

Mere tissue? Twenty-one days after conception the baby's heart is beating through a closed circulatory system. At forty-three days, its brain waves become detectable. At ten weeks, almost seven months before normal delivery time, the fetus is not appreciably different from 20 weeks or 30 weeks; it is only a matter of maturation. All systems and organs are functioning. The question has been raised: If the mother's stomach were transparent and this work of God could be seen as it developed, how many abortions would there be?

A Philosophical Position

What is the most dangerous place in the United States? Your car on New Year's Eve? The bottom of a coal mine? Shark-infested waters? The front lines of a battlefield? No. It is your mother's womb. Since 1973 less than 50 percent of all children conceived have made it out alive. Until the laws change, that warm, cozy womb is the most dangerous place to be. Apparently you beat the odds. Congratulations!

The Roe v. Wade decision stated that only "viable human beings who have the capacity of a meaningful life" may, but need not, be protected by the state. The unborn child is not legally human. Furthermore, abortion is considered an "act of privacy" which belongs solely to the mother. She alone may choose to kill the child anytime between conception and birth. Consequently, an unborn child is killed in the U. S. every 20 seconds. That is 4,400 a day: 1,500,000 a year in the U. S. and 60,000,000 worldwide. We have seen how God is involved in the work of the developing prenatal child; here we will strive to realize more fully that abortion is not a religious issue; it is a human issue.

A woman is said to have the right over her own body. But the fetus is not a part of her body, and it did not originate solely from her. When the egg and sperm get together in the Fallopian tube, it is called a zygote. It then floats down into the uterus and attaches itself to the mushy interior wall. Here it develops its own separate blood supply, separate circulatory system, separate heartbeat, and separate brain waves. It may be a different sex and it probably has a different blood type. That human embryo is antigenetically foreign tissue to its mother. If one were to attempt to graft the skin of the baby onto the mother, it would be rejected. The embryo, and subsequent developing fetus, takes total control over its residence. If the mother fails to ingest sufficient nutrients for herself and the baby, the baby will pull nutrients out of the mother's body: calcium from her bones and teeth, vitamin B from her liver, etc.

The act of birth is thought to be triggered by a complexity of processes. A unilateral decision is made by the mature fetus and communicated electro-chemically from his brain to the aging placenta, which is also changing hormonally, and which in turn notifies the uterus. Contractions and labor begin.

Absolute rights over another person are very rare, if they exist at all. A parent does not have absolute rights over his born children—he cannot mistreat them, keep them from being educated, or kill them. If a person has a communicable disease, the government has the right to quarantine him and take other measures that otherwise impose on his individual rights. Explicit First Amendment rights to religious liberty are put aside in medical/legal disputes, such as a blood transfusion for an underaged Jehovah's Witness or a medical procedure for children of Christian Scientists.[5] No one's rights are absolute in the real world.

To say that the unborn is the mother's body, her property over which she has total and exclusive right, is to say she has the right of life and death over a person who rents out a room in her house. That the fetus is her property is scientifically unsound; that the fetus is not a living person is scientifically unsound; and that the unborn has no rights is purely arbitrary.

The issue obviously rests on whether or not the fetus is a living human being. Years ago a beating heart determined if someone was alive. The heart of the embryo begins palpitations on the eighteenth day and is in full swing within another two weeks. Since medicine has become more advanced and life more complicated, brain death has been used to determine legal life or death. If an EEG shows signs of life, that person is considered alive. A fuller diagnosis of life and death was developed in 1968 and is called the "Harvard Criteria."[6] Established by a committee at the Harvard Medical School and largely used by medical schools and hospitals, it decrees four criteria for determining death: lack of response to external stimuli, lack of deep reflex action, lack of spontaneous movement and respiratory effort, and lack of brain activity. Anybody familiar with prenatal realities knows that all four of these factors are well in place before the conclusion of the first 12 weeks. Psychiatrist and fetalogist Dr. Thomas Verney had this to say about the Harvard Criteria:

> These physiological guidelines are the best we can devise, since ego, spirit, self, soul—whatever name one chooses to define human life—lie well beyond our measurement tools. The fact that the unborn tests "alive" by all four criteria raises significant questions about our current attitude toward abortion.[7]

Concerning the arbitrary assessment of viability outside the womb, this criteria is progressively losing ground as science continues to strive ahead. An eight-month-old fetus used to be considered a preemie, and sent everyone on the hospital staff scurrying. Not long ago, seven-month-old babies were pulling through with regularity. Today, five- and six-month-old premature deliveries are living while six-month-old babies across the hall are being killed in or out of the womb, because the woman is aborting. This reduces the issue of viability to an absurdity.

Scientists now can fertilize an egg outside the womb. Nourishing and maintaining the fetus through the gestation process may be merely around the corner. Currently there is an artificial womb, a "constellation of devices," that can assume some heart, lung, kidney, and digestive functions for full-term babies born with certain problems. The necessary use of anticoagulants preclude use of this for preemies, but what if technology leaps this hurdle? It could reduce the viability standard even further. Asks David Rothman, professor of social medicine at the Columbia College of Physicians and Surgeons: "Are we then going to say to women, 'Either you keep the fetus inside you, or we will take it out and keep it alive ourselves'?"[8]

As we can see, biblically, medically, and legally (i.e., according to the Harvard Criteria for determining death), the fetus is a living person deemed otherwise only by the U. S. Supreme Court. Roe v. Wade overturned and abrogated anti-abortion laws in all 50 states. Laws created by elected officials across the country were swept away in a moment of time by seven unelected judges.

It was not so very long ago that the esteemed U. S. Supreme Court declared blacks non-persons, in the Dred Scott decision of 1857. As a non-person, he had no rights and could be bought, sold, raped, beaten and killed. And the simplistic line given then, "If you think slavery is wrong, nobody is forcing you to own slaves. But don't impose your morality on someone else," is not much different from what we hear now.

Some people, though, especially Abraham Lincoln, fought for the fact that slavery was not a personal, private issue. It was a human issue. We admire that decision and conviction, not recognizing how contrary it is to our do-your-own-thing, don't-impose-your-morality-on-me philosophy predominating in present-day society. If we fail to get Roe v. Wade reversed because it is wrong, we would never be able to abolish slavery if it were an issue today. We have allowed our culture to become overwhelmingly relativistic, lacking ethical, moral and spiritual absolutes from which to make definitive judgments about anything important.

On the basis of what ethical framework does an abortionist doctor, who may feel it is unethical to kill a newborn for any reason, kill the unborn? If it is only because it is legal, as of Roe v. Wade, that indicates the relativity of morals. That is the same court that said blacks were not human! Are they "not human" when the court says they are not, and then "human" when the court says they are? Or are they human regardless of what the court says? Similarly, was it unethical and immoral to kill unborn children before Roe v. Wade, but now it's okay since they are "not human" because seven judges say so? Does that make sense?

Is it ethical to kill a baby one minute after it is born? How about one minute before it is born? Or one minute before that? At what point is life worthless, the next minute precious and worth saving? Or consider this: Is it accurate to say that you came from a human baby, or that you **were** a human baby? Likewise, did you come from a fetus, or **were** you a fetus? Did you come from a fertilized ovum or **were** you a fertilized ovum? That fertilized ovum had all 46 chromosomes that make up you. At that point you were individually structured into an entity that will never be repeated. So, at what point were you not you but something else?

Is this a complicated issue or is it just the Supreme Court that has clouded our minds? Is abortion murder or isn't it? That is the issue. If it is murder, this unhinges all the arguments from rape and incest to deformity. Society does not kill the rapist — why kill the innocent product of the crime? Does mental anguish justify killing another human being?

If a pregnant woman contracts German measles, the risk of fetal deformity is increased, and she is usually encouraged to have an abortion. But what if a child is born under normal circumstances and he is defective? Do we kill him? He would be just as dead six months before birth (if the mother had German measles and got an abortion) as six minutes after. Or, if an eight-year-old has an accident or contracts a disease that leaves him mentally or physically handicapped, do we kill him, too?

Helen Keller became sick with brain fever before she was two years old, leaving her blind and deaf. With the help of the remarkable Anne Sullivan, she learned, graduated from college with honors, lectured on five continents, wrote books that are translated into fifty languages, and is one of the most famous, inspiring, productive individuals in the history of the world. Should she have been killed because she had obstacles to overcome?

Infanticide (killing the infant) is not something of the distant past of Nazi Germany. It has evolved as a natural result of dehumanizing the fetus through the legalization of abortion. What typically happens is that an extreme case is put forth with pressure on the public and on the legislatures to accept a lower view of human life in an unusual situation. In this way, sympathy for ideas and practices are gained which then are not limited to extreme cases. This can be called "sociological law," something which fluctuates with the spirit of the times.

Here are some pinions in the infanticide movement:

- In 1973, 14% of infant deaths at Yale-New Haven Hospital were caused deliberately.[9]

- In 1976, 17 of 28 eminent bioethicists said in a medical journal article that killing the handicapped child is sometimes acceptable.[10]

- In 1977, three-fourths of the pediatric surgeons said they would not act to save a mentally retarded child.[11]

A survey in 1979 showed that about half the physicians contacted felt it was all right not to perform corrective surgery on an infant with Down's Syndrome. They also would deny food to these retarded children, which would subject the children to a very inhumane death by starvation.[12]

In another interview, the majority of doctors said it would be all right to directly intervene to kill a self-sustaining infant.[13]

Commented Dr. R. T. F. Schmidt of Cincinnati, then president of the American College of Obstetrics and Gynecology:

> The fact that 17 of 20 expert panelists believe that some severely defective infants should be killed under certain conditions is deeply disturbing. This position is not only deeply disturbing to our traditional concept of the inherent value of human life, but is potentially shattering to the foundation of Western civilization.[14]

Unfortunately, not everyone concurs with Dr. Schmidt. The Nobel Prize laureate, James D. Watson, who discovered the double helix of DNA, had this to say:

If a child were not declared alive until three days after birth, then all parents could be allowed the choice only a few are given under the present system. The doctor could allow the child to die if the parents so choose and save a lot of misery and suffering. I believe this view is the only rational, compassionate attitude to have.[15]

Comments another Nobel laureate, Francis Crick, as quoted in the Pacific News Service:

No newborn infant should be declared human until it has passed certain tests regarding its genetic endowment and that if it fails these tests it forfeits the right to live.[16]

This is the current state of much of intellectual thought since our society has drifted from its biblical and ethical foundation. In contrast, Dr. C. Everett Koop comments about a child under his care, Chris Walls, who received 15 different operations over the first 1,100 days of his life:

The surgeon is accountable for the way he uses the gifts that God has given him. He is also accountable for the life entrusted to his care. It is a question of moral principle. But even if we were pragmatists, we would still believe that doctors should work to save the Chris Wallses of this world. For when a hospital is geared to save lives at any cost, this attitude affects health care down to the most mundane level. On the other hand, when one set of patients can be eliminated at will, the whole spirit of struggling to save lives is lost, and it is not long before a doctor or nurse will say, "Why try so hard on anybody? After all, we deliberately fail to treat some patients and we kill others." Even if it were not expressed this blatantly, an erosion would take place, which over a number of years would undermine the care of all patients in any institution that kills any patient placed in its care.[17]

Abortion itself is an unspeakable crime, but it is only the beginning. Says Professor Joseph Fletcher, writing in *The Humanist* (July/August 1974): "To speak of living and dying, therefore ⁒ . . . encompasses the abortion issue along with the euthanasia issue. They are ethically inseparable." When there is no solid foundation for the right to life, crumbling values fall on one another like dominoes.

You may think it will stop here—with the killing of the unborn, the non-perfect newborn, the non-contributing elderly, but upon what do you base that hope? In the past it has gone from these beginnings to killing quite a variety of people for a variety of reasons. In Auschwitz, one of the Nazi death camps, 17,000 people were killed every day, according to Dr. Olga Lenzyel, who was there as an inmate.

The whole concept of defining the quality of life by setting up tests that must be passed is an arrogant characteristic of man's darkest hours. Helmut Thielicke, German pastor during World War II, says that the unimaginable horror of those times can be reduced to one theological/philosophical point: Personhood was redefined.

It is therefore not surprising that our society is moving from legalizing abortion to condoning infanticide and euthanasia. It springs from the same source it did four decades ago: Somebody is redefining humanness for somebody else—and that somebody else is getting killed as a result. As the blacks were when the Supreme Court defined them as un-human in 1857. As the unborn are now, because the Supreme Court has defined away their humanness.

A Concluding Position

The man of the family could not hold a job, was a problem drinker, and did little to lead his family. His wife lost their first son when he was only six days old. Less than two years later, the depressed, poor, sick woman was pregnant again. In addition, she had tuberculosis, which she eventually died of, and four of her seven children never made it to adulthood.

Would you recommend abortion in this despondent situation? If so, you would have just killed Beethoven.

With 4,400 abortions every day in America, one wonders how many Beethovens of various fields have been killed. The Supreme Court said they did not know when life began, so they opted for "viability." So people are killed one at a time.

They could have asked the theologians or the scientists, or they could have asked the American people, because they would have gotten it right, too:

- 86 percent of Americans disagreed with the court's ruling that life begins at birth.[18]
- 65 percent of Americans believe abortion is morally wrong.[19]
- 77 percent oppose abortion on demand for social, non-medical reasons.

There is **no** majority assent for abortion under any circumstances after 12 weeks except where the mother's life is in danger.[20] That is practically an impossible occurrence, as much as that exception is proffered. C. Everett Koop says that in his thirty-six years of pediatric care and surgery he had never once seen a mother's life in danger that could not be solved by inducing labor or by Caesarean section. Killing the fetus to save the mother was never an alternative that required consideration.

It was Christians who stood against the permissive attitude toward abortion in Roman society. The Apostolic Constitution, an eight-volume set of early Christian literature dating from the 4th century, reflected the thought of Christian theologians from former centuries. It stated:

> You shall not slay your child by causing abortion, nor kill that which is begotten, for something that has been shaped and has received a soul from God, if it be slain, shall be avenged as being unjustly destroyed.[21]

We are not talking about removal of fetal tissue, or retrospective methods of fertility control, or medical procedures, or interrupting a pregnancy.

We are talking about murder.

And we need to get angry about murder. There are supposedly 40 million professing evangelical Christians in America. That is a massive voting bloc that could make a massive impression in any political campaign. If Christians registered and voted every time along pro-life convictions, there would not remain an elected official at any level of government at any time who would be pro-abortion. And that could sway the Supreme Court.

We are not lacking in the means to change our country, we just have not been roused enough to act. Voting is cost free and takes little time, yet only 54 percent of these who could voted in the 1980 presidential election. Only 52 percent of those calling themselves Christian were even registered. The decisions in this country are not made by the majority, but by the majority of those who vote!

When the rights of some are extinguished, the rights of all are in jeopardy. Murder portends ominously for the future of us all. With callousness toward the value of any human life comes the increasing likelihood of mass slavery or death based on some elitist's definition of a life not worthy to be lived. This attitude has a downhill momentum of its own that is gaining speed. Times of monstrous inhumanity are not jumped into suddenly; they are slipped into gradually.

Let us stop being apathetic and start being salt, start being light, and start making a difference. And this difference must begin with the plight of the unborn.

**All that is necessary for the triumph of evil
is for good men to do nothing.**
                                        —Edmond Burke

ΔΔΔ

Here's What You Can Do

1. Reread the scriptural and rational arguments against abortion until you **know** them. You probably know someone, or undoubtedly will, who is pregnant and contemplating this course of action. Share these truths with that person. Be salt and light in your world. Remember: It is not dying that causes scars—it is killing.

2. If you have had an abortion, repent. This, as other sins, needs to be dealt with in the light of God's righteousness (His immutable justice), His mercy (His choice to not give us what we deserve), and His grace (His choice to give us what we don't deserve, not only His love, but also His righteousness itself). He not only forgives—He also forgets! You can do the same.

3. Be sure you are registered to vote. Be informed on the issues when elections come around. Then be sure you **do** vote. Encourage others to vote, too.

4. Don't be swayed by the many good and just positions of any political party. Vote along spiritual lines: Vote for the candidate who is pro-life and anti-homosexual.

11

Suffering Without Sorrow

> For any life to be great, or even effective, it must be focused, dedicated, and disciplined.
>
> H. Emerson Fosdick

Happiness and fulfillment are not to be found by doing what we want. Living successfully is a constant juggle of needs, desires, musts, oughts, and sensitivities, balancing life with God, life with self, and life with others. Life is simply not a straight line where one decides what to do and then does it with no thought thereafter. There is a continuous bombardment of questions, doubts, temptations and fears and a multitude of voices all attempting to influence every step of the course.

For instance, let's say I am a runner. I like to run and I want to run as well and as fast as I can. This is as far as the "want to" goes. Discipline must assert itself here because if I am to achieve these goals and fulfill my potential as a runner, I cannot always eat what I want, when I want. I must determine a diet best for me and for my aims, and stick to it. I must establish a training schedule and adhere to it, regardless of whether I "feel" like training or not. I must even sleep regularly, and monitor all other activities in my life as well. Discipline means saying no to the impulse to do that which would detract from my goal.

The Joy of Self-denial

Those who do what they want, when they want, are lousy runners, if they run at all. Those in serious training cannot avail themselves of the multiple pleasures available at every turn and whim. There is both joy and sorrow in that self-denial. The joy is in the results; the sorrow is in the agony of denying the appetites that cry out for gratification. Anyone who has ever attempted to diet knows the agony of self-denial. Just by looking around you can see that the agony of denying food must be intense indeed, since so few people are willing to do it.

But these two aspects must be stressed: (1) The joy is in the results of self-denial, not the process; and (2) you can learn to like what you have to do. Those who are lean and in shape have learned to like carrot sticks and exercise. And you can learn to like celibacy, even though it is a course in suffering, because the benefits are so rich. Paul says:

> Everyone who competes in the games exercises self-control in all things. They then do it to receive a perishable wreath, but we [do it to receive] an imperishable [one]. Therefore I run in such a way, as not without aim . . . but I buffet my body and make it my slave (1 Corinthians 9:25-27).

Those groups who push sexual activity as obvious and inevitable, such as Planned Parenthood and television producers, do so as if self-denial is not a part of anybody's life in any area. "Abstain?" And they look at you as if you had on your grubbies and were headed for a presidential dinner. The fact is, everybody who starts a diet or trains for an athletic competition, or goes to war for his country, is probably doing some things he would rather not do in order to attain or keep something he wants rather badly. It is done every day, and it is really as simple as that.

But "simple" and "easy" are two different concepts. Consequently, there are many who claim they are willing to die for Jesus Christ, yet they appear to be unwilling to live for Him because living for Jesus Christ means living sacrificially. And living sacrificially means being celibate. And being celibate means suffering.

When we talk about "suffering for Jesus," however, it must always be in light of suffering outside of Jesus. Suffering for Jesus is not the only way people suffer. Those outside of Jesus, those who are unwilling to suffer the pain of denying sex, also suffer. We must always remember that. The celibate single tends to focus on self and say, "Woe is me!" as if, were he to indulge his sexual appetite, he would have no more woe. This is a deception.

We can never tell from a person's outward appearance what is going on inside, and it would be a mistake to think that the pain of self-denial in celibacy is greater than the pain others endure because of their lack of celibacy. Writes one respondent to a popular sex survey in "New Woman":

> I am 35 years old and have only recently come to terms with the fact that my free attitude about sex has been destructive. After many lovers, three serious affairs with married men, two marriages, one abortion, and herpes, I wish someone had suggested that my casual attitude was wrong.[1]

A more sweeping statement on the suffering fallout of free love is a *Time* editorial of the fast-lane Baby Boomer generation as it clamored out of free-wheeling adolescence into adulthood:

> Long absorbed in themselves, the Baby Boomers are a generation that has avoided or postponed commitment to others. Many have little loyalty to employers and less to political leaders or ideas. They get married later, have children later, divorce more than their parents, and quite a few, it seems, are destined for an awfully lonely old age.[2]

Choosing

Those who go their own way also suffer. The difference is in the choice. Continuing our analogy, if you choose to be lean or compete athletically, that means there are certain things you must do and not do—no choice about that. If you choose to eat what you want and train if and when you want, then you get what you don't want—fat, and out of shape. No choice about that, either. You must choose to suffer self-denial in the process, or choose painful results in the end. The bottom line is, you cannot have both pleasurable, unrestrained, undisciplined means and end up with pleasing results in any area of life. That is against the laws of the universe. As the saying goes:

> No pain, no gain; No thorns, no throne;
> No gall, no glory; No cross, no crown.
>
> William Penn

Suffering: God's Road to Revolution

God is not a sadist, though Job reflected on that curious possibility. He neither enjoys suffering nor enjoys seeing us suffer, yet He created a world in which suffering plays a part and has a purpose. Life turns a corner with new hope and meaning when we accept that suffering brings insight, meaning, and growth that cannot come any other way. In this we must submit to the nature of life and the purpose of God.

One cannot fulfill his potential apart from suffering. As life and time continuously unfold across the stage of our planet, each person plays a role in the intricate drama of God's intentions. We can see from the life of Jesus that His role and destiny included suffering. He was perfected by it, and He learned obedience from it.[3] In addition, He suffered for us and left us an example to do likewise.[4] If His role included suffering, ours will, too.

If there is a post-salvation experience which brings about a life-changing, deeper walk with Jesus Christ, demanding our all and filling us to overflowing, it is realizing the connection between suffering and spiritual growth. This theme is found throughout the Scriptures, and is central to the walk of faith:

> That I may know Him, and the power of His resurrection and the fellowship of His sufferings, being conformed to His death; in order that I may attain to the resurrection from the dead (Philippians 3:10,11).

Not only are we to submit to suffering, but we are also to embrace it with the attitude Jesus Christ had—an unswerving resolve to do God's will regardless of the cost.[5] That is, the cost up front. It really helps when we keep this certainty clearly in focus: The issue is not the cost of self-denial vs. no cost. This issue is the high cost of following Jesus Christ vs. the high cost of free love.

If we choose to back away from the severity of celibacy, we will pay a severe price another time, in another way, as life stumbles along a dark and frightening path through a wilderness of chaos.

As we evolve out of childhood, through puberty and on into adulthood, one of the greatest challenges we encounter is our sexuality. Dealing with tumbling, screaming hormones and with pounding peer pressure is perhaps our first chance to grab life by the throat and choose our own course, painful as it may be, toward a predictable goal with definable gains. Most of the years leading up to puberty are dominated by the impulse to lock down happiness *now* and gratify needs *now*. Faced with this new sexual need we must choose deferred gratification in order to find the deeper joy beyond superficial happiness and satisfaction. Saying no to immorality may be the first big step in saying no to self. And saying no to self is a significant turning-point in ascribing purpose to our lives and in following Jesus Christ.

> If anyone wishes to come after Me, let him deny himself, and take

up his cross, and follow Me. For whoever wishes to save his life
shall lose it; but whoever loses his life for My sake shall find it
(Matthew 16:24,25).

What makes celibacy painful is primarily the feeling of being
out of step with everyone else. The music is about love/sex, the
films incorporate sex as a natural aspect of relating, friends can
think you are "out of it," unsophisticated and strange, and the opposite sex can think you are a bore. Nobody likes the feeling of
being shunned. That is suffering.

All who desire to live godly in Christ Jesus will be persecuted (2
Timothy 3:12).

If you are used to being sexually active, reverting to just
shaking hands goodnight can be a real come-down. There is nothing in the world like the tingling excitement of skin on skin, and
when you have to deny the addiction and cut off the patterning,
it is all very tough. Denying self, picking up your cross, and following the lordship of Jesus Christ can seem like bearing the
unbearable, pursuing the impossible. Nevertheless, this is where
it's at. This is what Jesus was talking about.

These experiences are supposed to hurt. It teaches us to find
peace and joy outside of circumstances, and outside of physical
gratification. Always giving in to the senses of the body by eating,
looking or feeling, is to miss the core of New Testament teaching:
Satisfaction is in knowing God and walking with Him.

To the degree that you share the sufferings of Christ, keep on
rejoicing; so that also at the revelation of His glory, you may
rejoice with exultation. If you are reviled for the name of Christ,
you are blessed, because the spirit of glory and of God rests upon
you (1 Peter 4:13,14).

The nature of God and the rudiments of His life as it is lived
out in His people is contrary to the flow of culture. It always has
been that way and it always will be that way. That is not to say
that Jesus is "counterculture," for that is its own culture just as
definable as the "system." Jesus could be a businessman in a corporation or He could be a drop-out hippie farming the land
somewhere. Where you are vocationally or economically matters
little. Who you are is what must cut across the culture. And that
cut can create resentment in others and alienation in yourself.

An example would be this: A person living with a boyfriend
or girlfriend decides to take the above-quoted verse seriously, take

Jesus at His word, and move out. Result: resentment and alienation. Jesus said, "If the world hates you, you know that it has hated
Me before it hated you."[6] Paraphrase: "If a person hates you for
following Me and My ways, you know that he has hated Me first."
If, as a single person, you take the position that your body is not
your own, that the deity of gratification is not your master, and
that sex has the mystical power to destroy you, your stand may be
lonely and painful. You will suffer.

Suffering: The Poignant Pain of Waiting

A small boy sat watching a chrysalis as the butterfly struggled to free itself. It struggled, then rested. Struggled, then rested.
This went on for quite a while until finally the butterfly was free.
It hung onto the shell, slowly flapping its large, colorful wings, and
eventually flew away into the bright spring sunshine.

The boy thought how sad it was that the butterfly had to
struggle so hard to be free. An adjacent chrysalis began to quiver
and crack, as the next butterfly began its fight for freedom. The
boy resolved to help this one, and gently ripped open the crack to
make the escape much easier. To his dismay, the unfolded butterfly emerged from the cocoon, fell to the ground, and died.

Many of us are as unfamiliar with the ways of God as the boy
was of the ways of the butterfly. God designed the struggle of the
butterfly to force his circulation throughout his body and into his
large wings. By the time the effort was complete, his circulation
was in full swing, his blood had reached his extremities, and his
life was assured. Preventing the battle for emergence for the other
butterfly short-circuited his circulation and resulted in death.

> For to you it has been granted for Christ's sake, not only to believe
> in Him, but also to suffer for His sake (Philippians 1:29).

God has designed for us times of struggle. Not unlike the butterfly, there can be no fullness in our life without it. Wrestling
with our sexuality is certainly not our only struggle, but it is a significant and continual one. God has ordained that we wait for
sexual fulfillment. Waiting takes time. Waiting is suffering.

The media says, "Add water and stir." The problems served
up in TV commercials are solved in 60 seconds or less. Uncle Ben
can deliver ready rice in one minute. The world's idea of waiting
is typically summed up in this recounting of Valerie Bertinelli and
Eddie Van Halen: "When she saw Eddie, she said, 'My heart

melted and I knew I didn't want to be without him.' Valerie admits she wanted to sleep with Eddie immediately. He made her wait a month, [so they could] get to know each other better."[7]

All this and more conspires to constrict our thinking into short, touchable, seeable time frames. God's waiting is open-ended and invariably longer than we would choose. It is as if time does not matter to God. Or, perhaps it is more accurate to say that His methods of preparing us for a given task require more time than we would ever dream imaginable.

You are probably familiar with the fact that Moses' preparation for leading God's people out of Egypt was forty exciting years of herding sheep on the back side of the moon! But did you know that Joseph, after repudiating the sexual advances of his employer's wife, was thrown into the slammer—not for a few months but for almost three years? The man God would use to bring about the salvation of two nations—Egypt and his own people—was rotting away with the rats and the losers in some dungeon, year after stinking, despairing year. That was his preparation.

We hear a lot about how David's youth was spent tending sheep, and that prepared him for shepherding God's people. What we don't hear much about is how he spent eight to ten years running from cave to cave with his band of outlaws, a price on his head, and no foreseeable future but the desperate death of a fugitive. What happened to his anointing by Samuel as a young boy in his father's house? No doubt David asked that question thousands of times, staring up at the star-filled heavens, seeking the God who was silent. God was hiding and David was waiting.

Paul also spent precious years languishing away in prisons at the whim of a capricious governor who had no idea what was up. Paul had churches to establish, people to witness to, Spain to conquer for Christ! Didn't God know that? Instead, Paul sat under the crushing agony of waiting as if suspended in airless space.

These illustrations have to do with waiting. Whom you marry is one of the three most significant decisions of your life (the other two: accepting Jesus Christ as your Savior, and choosing a vocation). Just like every blow of Michelangelo's hammer on the chisel cut another chip off the block of marble, contributing to the gradual shaping of his magnificent Pietà, so every day of your life, every experience, every pain contributes to who you are and to your preparation as a marriage partner. If you sign up for

God's program, you must realize that the process will encompass the poignant pain of waiting for sexual fulfillment.

Waiting teaches lessons that can be learned in no other way. It teaches valuing what God values, and prioritizing life from God's perspective. Without suffering and waiting, we are hopelessly mired in bland worthlessness. But by waiting, your mind and heart become clear to learn other things God wants to instill in you. David says:

> How long, O LORD? Wilt Thou forget me forever?
> How long wilt Thou hide Thy face from me?
> How long shall I take counsel in my soul,
> Having sorrow in my heart all the day?
> How long will my enemy be exalted over me?
>
> Consider and answer me, O LORD, my God;
> Enlighten my eyes, lest I sleep the sleep of death,
> Lest my enemy say, "I have overcome him,"
> Lest my adversaries rejoice when I am shaken.
>
> But I have trusted in Thy lovingkindness;
> My heart shall rejoice in Thy salvation.
> I will sing to the LORD,
> Because He has dealt bountifully with me (Psalm 13).

David became a man after God's own heart because he learned the lessons God had for him through waiting. When you impatiently give in to your passion, you lose the core of true passion—your God-called, God-inspired, God-sent personal destiny.

Suffering: The Price of Glory

Celibacy is but a pebble in the quarry of the difficult dealings you encounter from one end of your personal life to the other. Yet, how many of us stumble over that pebble? As we saw in chapter 9, seemingly most people would rather gamble with incurable diseases and even death than surrender to celibacy.

Suffering through celibacy pays off, though. Over and over in the Scriptures you will find a solid connection between suffering and reward, for the Lord promises to "give to each man according to his ways, according to the results of his deeds."[8] The payoff is glory and the kingdom of God, which may be a little like saying the reward is a question mark. How much do we know about the kingdom of God, or about glory?

But, you may ask, don't we receive the kingdom of God as part of the package deal in salvation? Ah, yes, "If indeed you continue in the faith firmly established and steadfast, and not moved away from the hope of the gospel that you have heard."[9] And how often does continuing steadfast call for suffering? Every time. Often the suffering is in muted style, as in celibacy, rather than something notable, like being locked in irons and beaten.

> That you may be considered worthy of the Kingdom of God, for which indeed you are suffering (2 Thessalonians 1:5).

Speculation aside, Jesus Christ considered glory and the kingdom of God worth becoming a man for, worth dying for, worth being separated from the Father for, and worth sharing with us.

> If [we are] children, [we are] heirs also, heirs of God and fellow heirs with Christ, if indeed we suffer with Him in order that we may also be glorified with Him (Romans 8:17).

Whatever glory is, it is the opposite of premarital sexual gratification. That may sound far-reaching, but look at it this way: The TV commercial for Crystal Lite Lemonade illustrates the issue when the aerobic nymph pauses for a swig and declares, "I believe in me!" That could be a beacon for the sexual quest—essentially self-seeking and God-ignoring. Self-serving and self-glorifying. Hence, the self becomes the god of self, because only what self desires is of importance and is surrendered to.

Whereas indulgence focuses our eyes on self, suffering effectively diverts our eyes off self and opens the eyes of the heart to empathize with others. It also opens us up to being directed by God, and puts us on the path to a great eternity.

> For momentary, light affliction is producing for us an eternal weight of glory far beyond all comparison (2 Corinthians 4:17).

A Summary

We must recognize that the Lord created the situations of life as well as life itself. Your passions and drives were put in you to control, not to indulge indiscriminately. In an earlier chapter, we examined this as a point of testing and explored the purpose of testing. Here we are examining the result of the test: suffering and the purpose of suffering.

It is easy to feel like the proverbial maiden all dressed up with no place to go. You have the hormones to drive you, you have the body that is so eager to slip into high gear, and you have the world on its feet screaming "Go for it!" Instead, you cap it. You suffer. The pain of self-denial in celibacy is the will of God and it is the only avenue of growth, both personally and spiritually.

If we suffer, we shall also reign with Him (2 Timothy 2:12, KJV).

When we recognize that suffering is inevitable, regardless of the route chosen in life, and when we understand the purpose of pain in the plan of the eternal Provider, then we can enter suffering more boldly, knowing it is the arena where character is forged, shaped, tempered and polished. Furthermore, we will see through the phony front trumped up by anti-Christian media hype that depicts Christians as pencil-necked wimps, who are enduring life in religious drudgery, motivated by self-righteous prudity.

Life is a crucible that can cleanse and strengthen you like steel, or shatter you. Imbued with the power of God, you can draw on your inner resources to wrestle with life, and you can win. That is your destiny in Christ.

Do not be ashamed of the testimony of our Lord, or of me His prisoner; but join with me in suffering for the gospel according to the power of God (2 Timothy 1:8).

△△△

Here's What You Can Do

1. List the people and places that cause you to desire worldliness and lawlessness. Determine to avoid them. How will you bring about the avoidance?

2. Make a list of pains and stresses you are *avoiding* by being celibate. There are many! Review this list often, and add to it whenever another one occurs to you.

3. Many people around you are suffering either the temptation of sexual lawlessness, or its consequences. Learn some of the verses in this chapter and look for opportunities to share. Be salt and light!

12

Hitting the Wall

> Were we in our own strength to confide,
> Our striving would be losing.
>
> Martin Luther

Hitting the wall" is a phenomenon experienced only by long-distance runners. It usually takes place approximately fifteen to twenty miles into a marathon when the body has totally exhausted the supply of energy-producing carbohydrates, the muscle fuel called glycogen. Glycogen is first depleted in each muscle cell, then it is drawn from the liver. Every gram of fuel is gone with six to ten miles to go in the race. Then, with the body fighting for its life, the organism does something which takes only seconds for some but agonizing minutes for others. It does a complicated chemical shift from burning glycogen to burning body fat. The runner feels like he just hit a wall!

The mind becomes disoriented, angry, and beyond fatigue. All systems are crying to stop, and he wants to tie his shoe, but his shoe is not untied! Then he is panic-stricken: "Where am I? What am I doing here?" he screams inside his head.

Many runners have a partner who talks them through this period of pain and bewilderment as they shuffle down the course. Once the shift is in place and the body is through the wall—ah, that is exhilaration! Running becomes effortless and euphoric, skimming the ground, boundless in energy. The feeling of power and endurance is unmatched even by the enthusiasm of the first few miles.

In the foregoing chapters we have covered many reasons for celibacy and for choosing God's ways. We have witnessed the emptiness and destruction of free love from many angles. This chapter offers an explanation as to how to drop sin and walk away. Or, if you are a virgin, this chapter can help you keep from getting sucked into the maelstrom of sexual intimacy before you realize the ruthlessness of the demon you are dealing with.

Our store of human effort, like muscle glycogen, has limits. Making the shift to the power of God can be disorienting and perplexing. Life can be a breeze for you, and you think it always will be, when suddenly you hit the wall and are slammed against the reality of your own limited resources. What to do? How do you depend on the power of the Spirit and not in personal strength of will? How does one steer a course through the quagmire and win against an enemy more cunning than Medusa?

This chapter, "Hitting the Wall," is an attempt to answer these questions. In your mind, the truth of this concept must permeate the concepts in every other chapter with its influence. If the reality of the power of God is not brought forcefully into your life, then celibacy will not bring the freedom, insight and strength that it potentially can. Instead, it will become a captor binding the struggling lust screeching within you, and eventually you will rid yourself of its restraints. You will allow desire to catapult you into failure and emptiness.

But Jesus said His yoke was easy, His load light.[1] Let's examine how this can be.

Living

Walk by the Spirit, and you will not carry out the desire of the flesh (Galatians 5:16).

In chapter 2, "Sex as Worship," the phenomenon of spiritual death was seen to result from the unleashing of immoral spiritual forces through the place and article of worship, the body. In Jesus Christ is discovered the opposite of spiritual death: life.

Jesus said, "The thief comes only to steal, and kill, and destroy; I came that they might have life, and might have it abundantly."[2]

Our thinking usually runs like this: *I am alive, and when I become a Christian, Jesus makes my life abundant—I have joy, peace, and the blessing of God.* This is not accurate. We were dead.

Jesus does not add abundance to our life; rather, He **replaces** death with an abundant life, a life we did not possess before. Jesus said, "He who believes [in Me] has eternal life."[3] A new and different quality of life is coursing through our spiritual veins.

Furthermore, to have eternal life does not say merely that our life will not end, for "life" in that sense does not end for the unbeliever, either. His consciousness continues on into hell. Rather, our eternal life is the life of eternity which is in us here and now. God's life is eternal. The nature of that life is glory and holiness, and Jesus Christ is the embodiment of that life. Paul says the greatest mystery of the ages is that this life, namely Jesus Christ, has been put into us, thereby assuring us of sharing God's glory with Him.[4] We catch a flavor of this in John 6:57: "As the living Father sent Me, and I live because of the Father, so he who eats Me, he also shall live because of Me." Just as we must eat to live physically, we must take Jesus Christ to live spiritually.

I may summon up all my strength of will and dedication, yet I cannot win a battle against a tireless, shrewd enemy, plus a world that bombards me with its sensuality, plus my own inner sin nature that incessantly conspires to pull me down to degeneracy. I am ill-equipped to win against any one of those foes, much less a war on all three fronts! How do I attain and maintain sexual purity? God lives His life in me and through me. Again, as Jesus said, "[Without] Me, you can do nothing."[5]

The Lord Jesus Christ has not left us to fight any battles on our own. Neither is it a case where, out of devotion or debt for what He has done for us, we offer to Him our efforts. Yes, we offer our body as a living sacrifice,[6] but He is not saying, "I died for you, therefore you do this for Me." That is pointless. We cannot do it. Paul says Christ is our life.[7]

Feel too weak in yourself to be holy? Welcome to the human race! Paul felt that way, too. Jesus did not tell him, "If you love Me, you would try harder." Rather, He says, "*My* strength is made perfect in [your] weakness."[8] Paul concludes, "Most gladly, therefore, I will rather boast about my weaknesses, that the power of Christ might dwell in me" (NASB).

Jesus Christ resides in us; He is the power of God.[9] We live for God not by the motivation of love but by the empowerment of life. We "walk in newness of life."[10] The life of God living a godly life through us is what Paul means when he says, "For to me, to live is Christ."[11]

We now have a tug-of-war going on inside which was not there before, because the old life remains plus we have the new life of the Spirit of God within us. When we do not depend on the power of God in us, the old life can still run us around:

> The wishing is present in me, but the doing of the good is not. For the good that I wish, I do not do; but I practice the very evil that I do not wish . . . I joyfully concur with the law of God in the inner man, but I see a different law in the members of my body, *waging war* against the law of my mind (Romans 7:18,19,22,23).

Many Christians who attempt celibacy are defeated because:

1. They are working at it under their own power, their new life being in neutral; and
2. they get frightened orweary in the battle with the flesh.

The beginning of the win is to recognize that

1. God is in you to live His life out through you, not to play coach by the sidelines; and
2. life is a battle, but it is a glorious battle because we already know the outcome!

Not just that He is coming back in triumph, but that He has *already* defeated our enemy, Satan, the prince of darkness:

> He himself likewise also partook [of flesh and blood] that through death He might render powerless him who had the power of death, that is, the devil (Hebrews 2:14).

A Christian walking by the Spirit of God will have his teeth in a tornado at least half the time, but frankly, it is exciting! God has called each of us for a purpose, and that purpose includes neither tranquility nor boredom. A battle it is, but at least we are no longer slaves of sin:

> Now that we are reconciled, we shall be [daily delivered from sin's dominion] through His [resurrection] *life!* (Romans 5:10, Amplified).

Resting

> Not that we are adequate in ourselves . . . but our adequacy is from God (2 Corinthians 3:5).

Once you hit the wall, coming to the end of your own resources of will and strength, you either fall back in exhaustion or break on through to the other side. On the other side is rest.

We enter God's rest when we combine the will and Word of God with faith. In Psalm 95:9-11 and in Hebrews 3 and 4, a thousand years later, the same warning is given: "Your fore-fathers exasperated Me and tested My patience; after seeing Me work for forty years they still went astray in their heart and did not understand My ways. Therefore, they did not enter My rest" (paraphrased).

Pictorially, the promised land was the rest they were headed for, and Egypt the picture of bondage to sin they had escaped. But Canaan could not really provide what God was promising,[12] and ultimately the eternal rest has an eternal fulfillment.[13] But the spiritual counterpart in time is a goal God has for His people. It will not, however, be reached automatically, as the writer of Hebrews makes fearfully clear:

> Take care, brethren, lest there should be in any one of you an evil, unbelieving heart, in falling away from the living God. But en-courage one another . . . lest any one of you be hardened by the deceitfulness of sin . . . Therefore, let us fear lest, while a promise remains of entering His rest, any one of you should seem to have come short of it (Hebrews 3:12,13; 4:1).

Unfortunately many Christians miss God's rest because they expect maximum results from a minimum of truth and study. They get saved, then stumble around in self-effort, a kind of "God helps those who help themselves" mentality, never quite locking in on the humbling reality that "apart from Me you can do noth-ing." If we really believed that, we would spend more time and effort pursuing the God who is our life—and we would discover that when His life is flowing through us we are resting.

The battle with temptation and sexuality is pervasive and perennial. The time and mental effort spent in that embroilment could be spent better in pursuing an involving relationship with the Lord Jesus Christ. That would direct our time and energy into something productive, resulting in growth in knowledge and in power. Because resting in His strength is new and unnatural, however, it requires some diligent attention.

Proverbs 2 speaks directly to this, where the wise father ad-monishes his son to pursue wisdom with the result that . . .

1. discretion will guard you (verse 11);
2. it will deliver you from the way of evil (verse 12);
3. it will protect you from people who want to divert

your way from the path of truth (verse 13); and

4. and it will deliver you from illicit sexual involvement (verses 16-19).

As the writer of Hebrews counsels us against the grief of never really knowing the God of our salvation, the writer of Proverbs instructs us as to how to pursue Him:

> If you will receive my sayings, And treasure my commandments within you, Make your ear attentive to wisdom, Incline your heart to understanding; For if you cry for discernment, Lift your voice for understanding; If you seek her [wisdom and understanding] as silver, And search for her as for hidden treasure; Then you will discern the fear of the LORD And discover the knowledge of God (Proverbs 2:1-5).

Receive, cry for, and seek—then you will know God. In order to rest in Jesus Christ and watch His life flow through you and change you, you must know Him intimately.

Mark Jordan, a friend of mine, explains the change this perception, this dependence, made in him:

> I began to realize that the reason my life didn't change much after I got saved was that I didn't change my habits. I was still flipping through the same porno magazines at the store; I was still hanging out at the same places; and I was still moving on the chicks as part of the same ego trip. The only real difference was, now I felt guilty.
>
> I became fed up with it and cried out to God to help me. He showed me I had to start with the habits, and He gave me the desire to make the needed changes. When I face temptation and similar situations now, I play a game with myself. I thrust my hands down in my pockets, breathe deep, smile, and quote 2 Corinthians 12:10: "When I am weak, then I am strong." The smile reminds me that Satan is defeated and I am dead to sin. Breathing deep reminds me that the breath of the Spirit is in me. The hands in my pockets remind me that I am powerless without His power. It may sound corny, but for the first time in my life I am excited about being holy, and *that* is a miracle!

To determine if you or someone you know is resting in the power of God and not just toughing it out in super-effort, look at the results. His life in ours will accomplish holiness and growth and service without physical, mental or spiritual breakdown. Such breakdown mercilessly rips the mask off one's efforts and reveals a life that may be enamored with goodness but does not know God.

Coach Tom Landry of the Dallas Cowboys says there are two

kinds of football players: the pretenders and the contenders. The pretenders can play as long as things are going their way; the contenders can make it happen regardless. "You know," he says, "I've been coaching thirty years, and I can't tell them apart in the preseason. With their helmets and pads on they all look alike. But after a few exhibition games I can pick them out blindfolded. The pretenders are the ones who don't get up."

I sat with young Jim, another friend, over lunch one day, discussing life in broad strokes. He said, "I just couldn't take it any more. I thought I could, but God would throw something at me and I'd say, 'Okay, I can handle that.' Then something else— 'Okay, I can handle that.' Finally I'd say, 'I've had it,' and walk away." Jim wasn't getting up.

I do not know if it was God hurling things at Jim or if it was someone else, but the game of life definitely is played in the arena of conflict. The apostle Paul was overflowing with joy in his affliction, not in spite of it, but in a sense, because of it[14] To the degree that we are joyful in our burdens, that is the degree we are walking in newness of life.[15]

Resting in the power of God provides endless energy for the battle.

We will be able to get up continually and get back at it. As the prophet said, "The joy of the LORD is your strength."[16]

Near the end of the film, "The Empire Strikes Back," in the saber battle between Luke Skywalker and Darth Vader, Luke's strength wanes and Vader's is sustained. Then Vader stands still, and through the sheer power of the Force hurls pipes and furniture at Luke, who is immediately knocked off balance, becomes bruised and bewildered, and is in pain. That is a picture of the hapless Christian blinded in his own confusion, who cannot even fathom the enemy's strategy, much less defend himself against it.

John said, "His commandments are not burdensome."[17] There were times I was sure John was dead wrong because I was breaking under the pressure, not sure I could maintain my sanity through to the morning! If Jesus' yoke is easy and His load light, it is not because there is nothing to it, but because Jesus Christ, the power of God, is carrying the load. That is the big difference. That is resting.

Knowing God is our high calling. Increased righteousness of

lifestyle will grow as our dependence on Him increases: "That the requirement of the law might be fulfilled in us, who do not walk according to the flesh, but according to the Spirit."[18]

> Seeing that His divine power has granted to us everything pertaining to life and godliness, through the true knowledge of Him who called us by His own glory and excellence . . . (2 Peter 1:3).

Balancing

In a classroom lecture a while back I heard Dr. Charles C. Ryrie say, "David trusted God, but he threw the rock."

We have established that the Christian life is God's life in us (just as the sap of the vine flows through the branches), and it is us resting in the power of God. Now the question is: Practically speaking, what does that look like? When I resist temptation, am I doing it in my own strength or God's strength? If I flee fornication, is the flesh just trying to conform to the law of God, or is God's life working through me? Does resting mean no effort? How can I avoid hitting the wall of self-effort if I am the one in the ring with Satan, the flesh, and the world?

The answer is not easy. The fact is, we are quietly being trained by the Spirit through failure. There does not seem to be much in the way of alternatives. This does not mean we must be fornicators and adulterers in order to learn God's ways; it does mean that an inevitable amount of shifting back and forth from self-reliance to Spirit-reliance will take place "until Christ is formed in you."[19] Being changed by the Spirit of the Lord from one degree of glory to another degree of glory[20] is a process.

And that process is often maddening, quizzical, indefinable, and illusive. Meanwhile, the ways of God and His expectations are unavoidably clear and unmoving. The first step in deciphering the process, therefore, is this understanding:

> What God says, He commands; What He commands, He expects; What He expects, He empowers to fulfill.   — Robert Andrews

Balance, then, is: You obey the commands, and in your heart you focus on an attitude of dependence — "Without You, Lord, I'm not going to make this."

When we look at the Scriptures to find examples, this is the balance we see:

> I labor, striving according to His power, which mightily works within me (Colossians 1:29).

> If by the Spirit you are putting to death the deeds of the body, you will live (Romans 8:13).

> [They were] speaking boldly with reliance upon the Lord, who was bearing witness to the word of His grace (Acts 14:3).

> Work out your salvation with fear and trembling; for it is God who is at work in you, both to will and to work for His good pleasure (Philippians 2:12,13).

This is as clear as it gets. These verses capture the essence of Dr. Ryrie's insightful comment about David. Trusting God did not mean waiting around for God to act **apart from human involvement.** In the four passages above we see Paul laboring and God's power flowing through him. **You** are putting to death the deeds of the body, but it is by the Spirit within you. The apostles spoke boldly while concurrently relying on the Lord. **You** are working out your salvation, yet it is God working it out in you.

This co-workmanship, or blending of the efforts of God and man is difficult to describe without emphasizing one aspect of it and thereby misstating it. It is a mystery which is similar to the production of the Scriptures themselves: Man sat down and wrote, but the product was divine, not human, even though man applied the ink to the page.

The dimension of this convoluted mystery that is most characteristic of God is its requirement for faith. People of no faith would see nothing miraculous in the 66 books of the Bible, yet the person of faith is rocked off his fenders every time he is confronted by the piercing words of truth on every page.

David believed God would see him through in his fight with Goliath, so he acted on that belief. One stone felling the giant was considered an act of God by men of faith observing it, but merely a lucky shot by men of no faith who also were standing by.

Similarly, my friend Mark shared how God had enlightened and empowered him to clean up his life, and to him the new desire for holiness was a miracle, an obvious working of God. To others, though, who were not of faith, his change was not proof of anything but a redirection of life. "People do that every day."

The point is this: Faith is what ignites the power of God in the inner man. And faith is what is required of every person to see God.[21] Therefore, resting in Him has nothing to do with effort or no effort. Action, effort and doing are all on the physical plane; resting, faith, and the flow of God's life are all on the spiritual plane. When Peter says, "As long as you practice these things [i.e., moral excellence, knowledge, self-control, godliness, etc., verses 5-7 of 2 Peter 1], you will never stumble,"[22] he is fully aware that their production in one's life flows from resting in God's life, and not from sheer willfulness. We are to "put no confidence in the flesh,"[23] because God will supply all our needs according to His riches in glory in Christ Jesus.[24]

To obey the word of God is not just obedience; it is faith. In Hebrews 3:18, the writer says the people who did not enter God's rest were those who were disobedient. In the next verse he says, "And so we see that they were not able to enter because of unbelief." When we believe, we obey; outward obedience is simply the manifestation of inward belief, the two being woven together like strands in a rope. If you will believe that and adhere to that, the grief you will avoid is beyond your imagination!

I am pushing this point hard because I, myself, have run the whole gamut—from para-church fellowships to lunatic fringe groups where the truth of this basic issue fluctuated between obscurity and unabashed error. It has been said, "God will change your desires, therefore you essentially only need to do what you want to do." It has been said, "Conforming to the letter of the law [i.e., the Bible] is dead legalism and worse than useless."

I learned that in the midst of the changes God is working in me, the desires of the flesh can return suddenly, and that defeating them (resisting Satan) takes effort and discipline as I rely on the power of God. I cannot sit back and expect God to eradicate these "impulses." I cannot think that because I have them means they are okay with God, or He wouldn't allow them. I cannot think that because I have these impulses they must be fulfilled or I will have no peace. It takes much effort, discipline and reliance on God. He has given me the overriding want-to to be pleasing to Him and the power to exercise the discipline.

Conversely, the rules have been preached, written up and rammed down unreceptive throats without the slightest enlightenment as to *how* to mix truth and faith and come up with the explosive New Testament power needed to live the Christian life.

In the midst of this confusion over faith and effort, our sexuality is doing a non-stop jig on the periphery of our consciousness. The slightest push and lust is slam-bang onto center stage, pulling you off into the darkness. Confusion can cause you to jettison your Bible as a useless legal code that cannot be attained. Result: defeat.

I believe it is extremely critical, therefore, that the how-to of celibacy be explained so as not to leave the reader with murky misconceptions or garbled guesses. Celibacy is not a suggestion—it is a command, a command which God expects us to obey, and which He empowers us to fulfill. If we misread that empowerment, it will meet a suffocating death, as a noble idea does when smothered by impossibility.

Holiness is not an achievement. It is an attitude of dependence that grows into a lifestyle. Faith is never passive, for Paul says, "Be careful to engage in good deeds."[25] Am I, therefore, the one who is expected to be good? Of course not. Jude ascribes glory only to "Him who is able to keep you from stumbling."[26] He transforms me, for I am not able to be good in and of myself.

Contradictory concepts? No, actually complementary truths. Paul strikes the balance:

> By the grace of God I am what I am, and His grace toward me did not prove vain; but I labored even more than all of them, yet not I, but the grace of God with me (1 Corinthians 15:10).

Yeah, that's the ticket!

△△△

Here's What You Can Do

1. It is possible to fit comfortably into a Christian context without reaching for spiritual excellence. Whether it's the busyness of work, the demands of studies, or the everyday hassles of life and the "need" for relaxation, we often coast without reaching. Examine your life to see if that has been happening to you, and if so, determine what you will do to change it.

2. Read your Bible.

3. Be exercising your spiritual gift. If you don't know what it is, find out. If you still don't know, guess. Do something. Get involved, and get your eyes off of self.

13

A New Breed

A Call to Righteousness

> The quality of a person's life is in direct proportion to his commitment to excellence regardless of his chosen field of endeavor.
>
> Vince Lombardi

The basketball game was nearly over. The ancient rivals were deadlocked in a tie score: Virginia Tech, 77; Florida State, 77. The tension and the sweat were thick as the second hand began its last sweep around the clock. The fans were on their feet. Florida State had the ball, then missed the shot. 6-foot, 5-inch forward Les Henson grabbed the rebound with one second to go. He turned and threw the ball the entire length of the court—89 feet, 3 inches! The net rippled slightly as the ball passed cleanly through the hoop.

The horn sounded. The scoreboard flashed the final score: Virginia Tech, 79; Florida State, 77. Pandemonium erupted! Florida State fans stood frozen, mouths open, incredulous at having witnessed the impossible. Virginia Tech fans were delirious, jumping and screaming in euphoric amazement! Virginia's coach was incoherent, the players ecstatic at their good fortune. Reporters were everywhere, all jamming microphones in Les's face: "Les, that's a collegiate record! The longest field goal in the history of college basketball! How did you do it? How did you do it?"

Replied Les calmly, "I made the shot 'cause that's what I was aimin' to do."

The challenge of Les Henson is having the guts to aim at the impossible and do it. And what could be more impossible in our sex-drenched culture than to aim at maintaining purity and do it? This is no simplistic assignment for spiritual nerds. The power to do it comes from God, and the will to do it must be charged with vision. That vision must be infused with the clarity of living, day to day, by eternal values which mesh with everyday activities. It does not matter what you do—what matters is who you are. It does not matter where you are—what matters is your lifestyle in that place. As God works in and through you, life takes on great purpose. And that purpose can transform you, and your surroundings.

The great metaphysical questions have always been: Who am I? Where did I come from? and, Where am I going? The Christian has these sewn up. The answers are the milk of the truth. The great question each of us must now ask himself is: So what? Now that I know where I've come from, who I am, and where I'm going, how is my life different and what am I doing about it?

Beyond the fact that, as a believer, your name is recorded in heaven, the greatest cause for rejoicing in this life is that the Lord God has cut a niche in life just for you. There is a purpose and an impact every person can have by design when he follows Christ as He progressively reveals His life and will.

Paul wrote of King David, "After he had served the purpose of God in his own generation, he fell asleep."[1] What an epitaph! Achieving the purpose God has designed for each of us is the quintessence of personal fulfillment; it is completing the plan for our existence; and it glorifies God. It takes a lot of time, a lot of waiting, and a lot of learning to arrive at a sense of that destiny, and part of the realization of it is recognizing that the time, waiting, and learning were unavoidable in achieving the plan and purpose of God for us. As we have seen, personal purity in the sexual realm is the dawning of that destiny, because it is a first step toward denial of self and focusing on God and His ways. Without that, nothing makes sense and nothing moves forward.

Death

For most of us death comes out of nowhere like a speeding bullet and catches us unaware. Even in sickness and old age it is impossible to believe that "this is the moment . . . here we go!"

Though 4,690 people die every hour, our ability to rationalize is so powerful that we are totally convinced that we will not be in that number this hour, or the next hour, or among the 112,560 people who will die tomorrow.

This attitude is typified by the majority of people on airplane flights. As the plane rolls out from the gate, the young stewardess explains some essentials like where to get oxygen when there isn't any and where to exit the plane before it sinks. It is rather comical, because nobody pays any attention.

A forceful example of this mindset was Salvador Sanchez, 23, World Boxing Council Featherweight Champion and one of the sport's best fighters. Said Sanchez on one occasion, "I'd like to step down undefeated. I'm only 23, and I have all the time in the world."[2] Two weeks later, just north of Queretaro, Mexico, his Porsche 928 collided with two trucks. Sanchez was dead wrong. He did not have all the time in the world. He had two weeks.

Death is like the convergence of two parallel lines out on the horizon. The closer the so-called point of convergence appears, the more distant it becomes. It never really gets near. I will live today, and I will live tomorrow, and I will see you next week. No problem.

That is how we look at it.

But there is a problem. I am going to die. And I am going to be judged. And so are you. The Scripture says, "It is appointed for [every person] to die once and after this comes judgment."[3] No reprisals, no plea-bargaining, no acquittals, no avoidance on technicalities, and no chance of parole. Death is sure.

Death changes things. It can, it should, affect the way we live now. Not the act of death, per se, but the consequences of death. Death is the quiet arbiter of life. It highlights one's values and priorities. Those who are not changed by it are cowed by it.

Toward the end of a magazine interview with Brigett Bardot some years back, her thoughts turned morbidly moralistic. In a husky whisper, the legacy of a lifetime of Gauloises cigarettes, she confessed she thinks of death every day. "It must be our punishment. And we deserve it. It is the decomposition that gets me. You spend your whole life looking after your body, and then you rot away. Like that."

When death takes us, the things we had thought were so important are suddenly shamed as laughable as we enter into the blinding presence of His eternal light. In that day, there will be no place to run to, no place to hide. That which one convinces himself he cannot live without—like fulfilling his sexual needs *now*—will hold neither sense nor value.

This scenario can be heard in Jesus' telling about Lazarus and the rich man. (See Luke 16:19-31.) Once in hades, the rich man was stabbed awake by the awful recognition of two frightening facts: (1) He realized his previous carefree life was bereft of eternal values and eternal perspectives, and he mourned over it. (2) He knew his family was headed in the same direction, and he wanted someone to go and tell them so they would live differently and avoid such a fate—but he was powerless to help them.[4]

Will we be surprised and regretful at our own foolishness?

Life is a long, long destiny that extends far beyond death. The true believer lives a life that reflects that destiny daily, recognizing that this life is, after all, only a fleeting breath in the boundless expanse of eternity. While in this time frame, however, he walks in the ways of God, fleshing out the words on the pages of Scripture, modeling for the world a life of purpose, and enticing others to Jesus by the quality of his life.

Yes, the life of faith and obedience is tough. When the writer of Hebrews says to "lay aside every encumbrance, and the sin which so easily entangles us, and run with endurance the race [of life] that is set before us," the word for race is "agony."[5] Though this life with God is no walk in the park, anything else is a downward slide on cut glass. Sin has not delivered what you thought it would, and it never will. It can't.

We have reviewed how the cost of free love has both a psychological and emotional price tag. Also, that certain spiritual forces can be unleashed with mighty, destructive force because sex is one of God's primary symbols and because the body is the article of worship and the site of worship. Sex out of God-given context is an unwieldy power that bludgeons us repeatedly in its misuse until our soul is a dried husk and the strength to love and commit deeply are distant memories in the desert of our inner life. And the inescapable reality of incurable venereal disease that can even kill has reduced the intimacy of uncommitted love to a mocking caricature. Finally, the specter of certain death, wherein we face the one who made the rules, kicks the cost of free love into the stratosphere.

Do you want your life to make a difference? Do you want a life now that will pay off when it is time to turn in your chips? Do you want to get more spiritual impact out of every day? Then get a glimpse of eternity. Reach out and grasp the brilliant sapphire of forever and don't let it go. Be dazzled by that which lasts. Only by that which lasts!

Pick a Passion

The Brookings Institution, the largest and perhaps most distinguished liberal research and study organization ("think tank") in America, has concluded that the future of our democracy depends on the strength of the nation's religious institutions. Breaking with past positions characteristic of secular organizations, the report entitled "Religion in American Public Life," says,

> Human rights are rooted in the moral worth with which a loving creator has endowed each human soul, and social authority is legitimized by making it answerable to transcendent moral law.

The Brookings Institute is acknowledging by observation that the spiritual is central to life. This has been the thrust of these entire thirteen chapters. The exigencies and activities that dominate the majority of our time and thought do not give power, purpose or direction to life. The spiritual does.

We all have passions that run our lives: our job, our children, a hobby, or even partying. My challenge to you is to bring the spiritual to the surface and make it your passion — not necessarily making the spiritual your job or making it a hobby, but making it your passion in everything!

When did Jesus say, "I was watching Satan fall from heaven like lightning"?[6] Was it when He fed the five thousand? Was it when He raised the dead or made the blind see? Was it when He was raised from the dead Himself? No. It was when He sent His disciples out in twos to bring the message to the people:

> The one who listens to you listens to Me, and the one who rejects you rejects Me; and he who rejects Me rejects the one who sent Me (Luke 10:16).

When we walk and talk the life of God, the power of Satan is continually broken. Each of us can be a light, a witness, a testimony in a world gone mad. Not preaching on a hill somewhere to thousands, but speaking the truth to a friend, to a child, to a stranger, in a class, anywhere. Every time we do, Satan falls again, and his power is broken there, in that moment of time, in that place.

In the 1950s, the Oklahoma football team cherished an unprecedented record of 47 straight wins. Season after season they loomed larger than life and were literally unbeatable. Upon inspection, it became evident that there was more than pride and talent at work there. Coach Bud Wilkinson was able to create in every player a fierce loyalty which knew no bounds.

Each week the team watched films of the previous game and each player's personal performance was scrutinized and graded by the coaching staff. Each one was disciplined to correct errors and praised for spirit and winning technique. The following week they were better than the week before. Out on the field the Sooners ignored the screaming fans, frenzied cheerleaders, blaring bands, bad calls, and the red-hot determination of the opposing team. They weren't playing for any of these. They were playing for the audience that mattered: a coach who loved them and who would be evaluating their performance the next day. That was all that counted!

There is a need for a new generation of men and women who are wholly dedicated to purity, to godliness, and to the kingdom of God above all else, and who put everything else in a distant second place. The great preachers in our land, the great teachers, great men and women of God, cannot last forever, and they cannot reach everyone you know. A new wave of committed heralds of God's life must be willing to make a difference where they are, willing to play the game of life only for the coach who bought them with His blood, and not for the fickle, screaming fans.

In our time immorality is a vampire sucking the blood out of the rising generation, Christians included. Vast masses of people are weakened and made vulnerable, already addicted to the next tumble in a loveless bed of cultural conformity. Only a clear voice, ringing with the power of God, can break their chains of slavery to the cold heat of dead passion.

Serve the purpose of God in your generation. Be a revolutionary! Live and die for a cause that not only is bigger than yourself, but one that also reaches beyond death and time. Dream big dreams of singleminded dedication to whatever God gives you to do. As your character is forged in the fires of nonconformity, you will rise to your destiny and you will play a meaningful part on a stage grander than any you could imagine! Paul says that no eye has seen, nor has any ear heard the magnificent things God has planned for those who love Him (see 1 Corinthians 2:9). Rise to the fullness of the calling of God within you!

Do it now!

▲▲▲

Here's What You Can Do

1. There is no action without first a vision. See yourself as a revolutionary, as outlined by the precepts, attitudes and demeanor set forth in the New Testament. If you set out to be a revolutionary outlined by the imaginations of your own mind, you'll just end up wierd. The world already has its fill of wierdos.

2. Share your vision with other believers.

3. Make a list of your spiritual successes. Keep it current. The future is based on factual history; the present needs constant encouragement.

4. LIVE! Schedule time with those of like-minded convictions for fellowship, prayer, and/or Bible study. Stimulating togetherness has a sling-shot effect on maturity and consistent holiness.

Epilog

If you are over 18 years of age and have grown up in America where the bulk of the aforementioned statistics are based, then the odds are that you are not a virgin.[1] Somewhere along the time line you got involved sexually. Again, statistically speaking, you probably aren't with that person (or persons, if you have had a number of intimate relationships through the years), you probably have experienced some of the consequences covered in the preceding thirteen chapters, and you would probably like to play the rest of the game of life as cleanly as possible and avoid as many traps as possible. Hopefully, the "how to avoid" and the "what to do" questions have been answered somewhat satisfactorily.

Now, how do you get started?

It was my intention in writing *The High Cost of Free Love* to present a case for abstinence that was so powerful that not only would the virgin avoid lawless sexual entanglements, but also that others, regardless of their past or present, would be so struck with the biblical and rational arguments that such involvement would be immediately considered anathema. I hope the case for celibacy hits so hard it solidifies the rational processes, sinks deep into the feelings of the soul—for it is our emotions that fire up our rational convictions—and crystallizes and clarifies light and life in the human spirit.

Though it was in no way intended, it may be that all this power I'm striving to impact you with is leaving a heavy residue of guilt. It is to this possibility that I wish to direct my final comments.

First, if you are not absolutely certain that if you were to die today you would go to heaven, make certain. You will find a good guideline in the appendix, "Would You Like to Know God Personally?" This will walk you through the steps to make sure your relationship with God is what it needs to be.

You have probably heard this in terms of the word *saved*. From time to time I have occasionally considered substituting some other word since a lot of people don't like to use it in this day. However, I have yet to come up with a reasonable, much less a biblical, alternate. Although it is an archaic term, quite removed conceptually from the flow of thought and communication in our modern world, it does have an ongoing value. Every translation of the Bible, no matter how current or far-reaching in its attempt at modern usage, employs the term. And I dare say, when we are in eternity, and you roll over and glance out over the edge into the abyss of outer darkness that will be hell, the word *saved* will have a profound meaning for you.

So get saved. Accept God's gift of Christ's sacrifice on your behalf; turn from your sin (this is *not* an optional part of salvation!) and walk in truth.

You do not have to read your Bible to get saved, but you do have to read it to know the truth. Knowledge itself is not a guarantee of spiritual renewal, but it is an essential foundation that must be laid if we are to see a reformation in our lives. A biblically illiterate person will neither grow spiritually nor impact his culture for Jesus Christ.

To walk in truth means to do the truth. James says that the one who does not do the truth but only hears the truth is deluding himself (James 1:22). It may be that the narrow gate Jesus talked of is a bit narrower than some of us think.

Moving beyond salvation, you need to know that God is not an accuser; Satan is the accuser of the brethren (Revelation 12:10). At this time, the throne room of heaven is like the Mad Hatter's court scene. Satan tempts and cajoles you into sin, then, when you jump into it, loudly defames you before God. He yells, "Yeah, yeah, yeah!" to entice you into the trap, then he turns on you, pointing and stomping and yelling at God, "You see the worthless one over here? Yeah, the dolt with the foul mouth! The one who knows only how to blow it!"

Then he turns the heat of his insults directly on you, and it is so loud you swear your eardrums are going to burst, "You're useless. Not only can't you serve God, you miserable piece of camel dung, but you also just proved you don't really want to! You're just a hypocrite—and you know how much you hate hypocrites! I know, I know, it would have been nice to be holy, but give me a break! You? The Billy Grahams and Martin Luthers of this world are made different from you.

"Look, just put this impossible program on hold and get out from under all this pressure. And in case you get any future ideas, just remember, you're nothin'; maybe you can get some sense of fulfillment somewhere else—as a matter of fact, I'm sure you can—but not in this spiritual field. It's just for cornballs with no brains and no hormones, anyway. So forget it. It isn't going to work."

After you've been knocked around a few times by this insidious craziness of his, you can become immobilized by guilt and quite literally be shuffled off to the sidelines, out of the battle, the spiritual warfare, and you can remain there indefinitely.

Chapter 12 dealt with soliciting the power of the Holy Spirit to fight the war. Here I want to clarify the tactics of Satan and focus on some recovery truths.

Satan is the accuser. You must always remind yourself of that. Jesus Christ is the defense attorney, the Advocate (1 John 2:1). He is before the Father offering His blood for your sins—that blood that has released you from your sins (Revelation 1:5). God is not holding anything against you, and Jesus Christ is not accusing you. You have to take that by faith because in the beginning it is difficult to distinguish all the voices inside your head.

A recent magazine article for Rain Soft Water Conditioning shows a young girl about five years old looking into a large mirror. She is wearing a blue dress, a red and white sash, and her mother's shoes, which are twice as big as her feet. In the mirror, however, is a full-grown woman in a similar blue dress, and the sash says "Mrs. America." The little girl is seeing what she imagines herself to be.

That is what God does to us: We look into the mirror of our soul and see the perfection God has transformed us into, and we move from glory to glory as we are conformed to that exalted image (2 Corinthians 3:18). We are holy and blameless before Him (Ephesians 1:4). That is not myth and it is not future. It is now!

We are totally forgiven of everything, past, present and future (Ephesians 1:7; Hebrews 10:15-18). We are enriched in everything because of our identity with Him (1 Corinthians 1:5), and He will make us to stand in the presence of His glory, blameless and with great joy at the judgment (Jude 24,25).

If and when you sin again, none of that changes. That is grace.

Truth also precludes using grace to sinful advantage—that is, to see what you can get away with. Paul says:

> What shall we say then [to this grace]? Are we to continue in sin that grace might increase? May it never be! How shall we who died to sin still live in it? (Romans 6:1,2)

God will not be manipulated by His own principles and forced into a corner. If our attitude is, "What can I get away with?" the issue is not sin; the issue is the heart. It is salvation and repentance.

God not only loves you, but He also believes in you. He is not holding anything in reserve, waiting for you to prove yourself. His forgiveness of you and commitment to you is absolute. Total.

> He has not dealt with us according to our sins,
> Nor rewarded us according to our iniquities.
> For as high as the heavens are above the earth,
> So great is His lovingkindness toward those who fear Him.
> As far as the east is from the west,
> So far has He removed our transgressions from us.
> Just as a father has compassion on his children,
> So the LORD has compassion on those who fear Him.
> For He Himself knows our frame;
> He is mindful that we are but dust (Psalm 103:10-14).

For some, another step is necessary in addition to accepting God's forgiveness. Although some people can receive forgiveness from God, they have difficulty forgiving themselves. In essence, such people indicate that their standard of forgiveness is higher than God's, and that the blood of Jesus Christ is insufficient for their sin—two obviously absurd ideas. I think those people are not accustomed to forgiving, either themselves or others. This needs to be a step of faith. God said that all my sins are forgiven and forgotten, and therefore what I feel is true is irrelevant. Only what God says is relevant.

Nobody said it better than Corrie Ten Boom: "He buries our sins in the deepest ocean and puts a sign up: NO FISHING!" If

Satan cannot drag you into sin today, He will attempt to drag you down to defeat by focusing your mind (yes, he can do that if you allow him to) on your past, and the litany begins again: "See! You're rotten, you're despicable, you're not worthy. YOU ARE NOT FORGIVEN!"

The way you deal with this tactic is not by wrestling with him, and certainly not by getting depressed over the whole thing, and not by trying *not* to think about whatever it is. By faith, displace the thought with another. Simply turn from thinking about your past and attend to something else. "Resist the devil and he will run away."

Also, the Holy Spirit does not bring guilt: Guilt deflates us and alienates us from God. He does convict: Conviction draws us to the loving Father. It encourages us to acknowledge that what we did was sin and that it was out of character for what we have become in Christ. And it urges us on in the excitement of growing in the destiny for which He created us. To sin is to forget the image of blameless glory which we see in the mirror of our souls (2 Peter 1:9). God has made us sinless—in Christ—and He has delivered us from the mesmerizing power of sin's grasp.

In regard to the temptation of sexual lust, Mark 8:33 has provided for me significant insight that has translated into spiritual power. Jesus is explaining to His disciples that He must suffer and die. "Peter took Him aside and began to rebuke Him." (Can you believe that!) Jesus looked him straight in the eye and said, "Get behind Me, Satan; for you are not setting your mind on God's interests, but man's."

The point is this: Peter loved Jesus and Jesus loved Peter. But in that moment of time, Peter was an unwitting dupe for Satan's strategies. So it is with people today. They often are used as lures in the sexual gavotte to entice us to sin, plunging us into guilt, alienation and the often irreparable consequences that follow. Be understanding.

Guys, do not condemn women who dress provocatively, who attempt to entice with their eyes, and who may even confront with the offer of uninhibited sexual pleasure. Resist in strength and compassion, not with sharp words or haughty glares.

Women, do not hate men because they often seem irrepressibly affronting and singleminded in their assault on your bodies. Resist firmly with the consequences clearly in focus. Be clear in your position, but with a compassion born of insight. As Paul so sharply highlighted, our struggle is not against flesh and blood (Ephesians 6:12).

One final thought. Jesus Christ is able to cause flowers to grow from the rubble and dirt of your past. How He does that is the grandest mystery in the universe. The more I contemplate the inexhaustible ways of God, the more convinced I am that creating the vastness of the skies or the intricate complexities of the atom are of no consequence compared to creating something redeemable and eternal from the convoluted evil of the human heart.

Yet the creative brilliance of our God is even more mysterious than that. Not only can He make something beautiful out of the mess of your life, but He also makes that beautiful creation, which is you, and which will show forth His dynamic goodness throughout all the ages to come, to develop into full bloom **because of** the mess of your life.

Here is an example of this that defies the rational: Solomon was David's son, the third king of Israel. He was the wisest king of all, though certainly not sinless. He built the magnificent Temple for Israel to worship in (worship had been observed in a tent up to that time). He was chosen to pen some of God's infallible Word. He was in the chosen line of the Messiah, beginning with Adam, truly an unusual honor. David had many other sons, but it was Solomon who received all this blessing. Yet he was the son of Bathsheba, the offspring of perhaps the most infamous adulterous couple in the history of man.

Obviously, had David not had that adulterous affair with Bathsheba, Solomon would never have been born. Just as obviously, God is not the author of sin. He did not desire David to sin; He did not induce him to sin But had David not sinned, the plan of God would not have come to pass. Indeed, what God pulled out of that sin absolutely defies the imagination! Why did He do that? More to the point, how did He do that? We are at a rational impasse. How the pieces of this puzzle fit is a mystery beyond human comprehension.

In your life, God will work a similar miracle—yes, a miracle that will make the feeding of the five thousand on the shores of the Jordan mere child's play. A miracle of such depth and breadth that the clarity of your perception of both sin and God will develop beyond your dreams, and love and life will grow from a trickle in your heart to a raging torrent.

I believe this is the juncture at which more people are dissuaded from a life of ministry than at any other. They simply feel unworthy.

Amen. They are unworthy.

So are you and so am I.

Now that we have that settled, let's get on with serving God and making a difference in our world. R. C. Sproul, in his book, *The Holiness of God*, put it this way:

> No minister is worthy of his calling. Every preacher is vulnerable to the charge of hypocrisy. In fact, the more faithful a preacher is to the Word of God in his preaching, the more liable he is to the charge of hypocrisy. Why? Because the more faithful a man is to the Word of God, the higher the message is that he will preach. The higher the message, the further he will be from obeying it himself.
>
> I cringe inside when I speak in churches about the holiness of God. I can anticipate the responses of the people. They leave the sanctuary convinced they have just been in the presence of a holy man. Because they hear me preach about holiness they assume I must be as holy as the message I preach. That's when I want to cry, "Woe is me."[2]

Again, this is not an excuse for moral laxness or an undisciplined life. It is just to say that God does not choose to limit Himself to sinless or innocent people. Commit yourself to being available and you will prove this to be true.

Today is the beginning of the rest of your life. Forget your past, and don't let anybody, including Satan and his infernal clamoring inside your head, dig up past sins like exhuming old bones from a grave. As Satan worship increasingly spreads, as nations enter increasingly dark economic tunnels, as the world in which we live lurches and staggers into increasing moral anarchy and ethical nihilism, there is no more exciting time to be alive! Our God will not abandon us. Indeed, even more power will pour forth from His throne of fire to emblazon our spirits and steel our character to meet the challenge.

Be on the team with everything you've got. Believe me, you won't regret it.

Would You Like to Know God Personally?

The following four principles will help you discover how to know God personally and experience the abundant life He promised.

1 GOD **LOVES** YOU AND CREATED YOU TO KNOW HIM PERSONALLY.

(References contained in these pages should be read in context from the Bible whenever possible.)

2 MAN IS **SINFUL** AND **SEPARATED** FROM GOD, SO WE CANNOT KNOW HIM PERSONALLY OR EXPERIENCE HIS LOVE.

God's Love

"For God so loved the world, that He gave His only begotten Son, that whoever believes in Him should not perish, but have eternal life" (John 3:16).

God's Plan

"Now this is eternal life: that they may know you, the only true God, and Jesus Christ, whom you have sent" (John 17:3, NIV).

What prevents us from knowing God personally?

Man Is Sinful

"For all have sinned and fall short of the glory of God" (Romans 3:23).

Man was created to have fellowship with God; but, because of his stubborn self-will, he chose to go his own independent way, and fellowship with God was broken. This self-will, characterized by an attitude of active rebellion or passive indifference, is evidence of what the Bible calls sin.

Man Is Separated

"For the wages of sin is death" (spiritual separation from God) (Romans 6:23).

This diagram illustrates that God is holy and man is sinful. A great gulf separates the two. The arrows illustrate that man is continually trying to reach God and establish a personal relationship with Him through his own efforts, such as a good life, philosophy or religion.

The third principle explains the only way to bridge this gulf . . .

3 JESUS CHRIST IS GOD'S **ONLY** PROVISION FOR MAN'S SIN. THROUGH HIM ALONE WE CAN KNOW GOD PERSONALLY AND EXPERIENCE HIS LOVE.

He Died in Our Place

"But God demonstrates His own love toward us, in that while we were yet sinners, Christ died for us" (Romans 5:8).

He Rose From the Dead

"Christ died for our sins . . . He was buried . . . He was raised on the third day, according to the Scriptures . . . He appeared to Peter, then to the twelve. After that He appeared to more than five hundred" (1 Corinthians 15:3-6).

He Is the Only Way to God

"Jesus said to him, 'I am the way, and the truth, and the life; no one comes to the Father, but through Me' " (John 14:6).

This diagram illustrates that God has bridged the gulf which separates us from Him by sending His Son, Jesus Christ, to die on the cross in our place to pay the penalty for our sins.

It is not enough just to know these truths . . .

4 WE MUST INDIVIDUALLY **RECEIVE** JESUS CHRIST AS SAVIOR AND LORD; THEN WE CAN KNOW GOD PERSONALLY AND EXPERIENCE HIS LOVE.

We Must Receive Christ

"But as many as received Him, to them He gave the right to become children of God, even to those who believe in His name" (John 1:12).

We Receive Christ Through Faith

"For by grace you have been saved through faith; and that not of yourselves, it is the gift of God; not as a result of works, that no one should boast" (Ephesians 2:8,9).

When We Receive Christ, We Experience a New Birth. (Read John 3:1-8.)

We Receive Christ by Personal Invitation

(Christ is speaking): "Behold, I stand at the door and knock; if anyone hears My voice and opens the door, I will come in to him" (Revelation 3:20).

Receiving Christ involves turning to God from self (repentance) and trusting Christ to come into our lives to forgive our sins and to make us the kind of people He wants us to be. Just to agree intellectually that Jesus Christ is the Son of God and that He died on the cross for our sins is not enough. Nor is it enough to have an emotional experience. We receive Jesus Christ by faith, as an act of the will.

These two circles represent two kinds of lives:

SELF-DIRECTED LIFE
S—Self is on the throne
†—Christ is outside the life
●—Interests are directed by self, often resulting in discord and frustration

CHRIST-DIRECTED LIFE
†—Christ is in the life and on the throne
S—Self is yielding to Christ
●—Interests are directed by Christ, resulting in harmony with God's plan

Which circle best represents your life? Which circle would you like to have represent your life?

The following explains how you can invite Jesus Christ into your life:

YOU CAN RECEIVE CHRIST RIGHT NOW BY FAITH THROUGH PRAYER

(Prayer is talking with God)

God knows your heart and is not so concerned with your words as He is with the attitude of your heart. The following is a suggested prayer:

"Lord Jesus, I want to know You personally. Thank You for dying on the cross for my sins. I open the door of my life and receive You as my Savior and Lord. Thank You for forgiving my sins and giving me eternal life. Take control of the throne of my life. Make me the kind of person You want me to be."

Does this prayer express the desire of your heart?

If it does, pray this prayer right now, and Christ will come into your life, as He promised.

How to Know That Christ Is in Your Life

Did you receive Christ into your life? According to His promise in Revelation 3:20, where is Christ right now in relation to you? Christ said that He would come into your life and be your friend so you can know Him personally. Would He mislead you? On what authority do you know that God has answered your prayer? (The trustworthiness of God Himself and His Word.)

The Bible Promises Eternal Life to All Who Receive Christ

"And the witness is this, that God has given us eternal life, and this life is in His Son. He who has the Son has the life; he who does not have the Son of God does not have the life. These things I have written to you who believe in the name of the Son of God, in order that you may know that you have eternal life" (1 John 5:11-13).

Thank God often that Christ is in your life and that He will never leave you (Hebrews 13:5). You can know on the basis of His promise that Christ lives in you and that you have eternal life, from the very moment you invite Him in. He will not deceive you.

An important reminder . . .

DO NOT DEPEND ON FEELINGS

The promise of God's Word, the Bible—not our feelings—is our authority. The Christian lives by faith (trust) in the trustworthiness of God Himself and His Word. This train diagram illustrates the relationship between fact (God and His Word), faith (our trust in God and His Word), and feeling (the result of our faith and obedience) (John 14:21).

The train will run with or without the caboose. However, it would be useless to attempt to pull the train by the caboose. In the same way, we, as Christians, do not depend on feelings or emotions, but we place our faith (trust) in the trustworthiness of God and the promises of His Word.

Fellowship in a Good Church

God's Word admonishes us not to forsake "the assembling of ourselves together" (Hebrews 10:25). Several logs burn brightly together, but put one aside on the cold hearth and the fire goes out. So it is with your relationship with other Christians. If you do not belong to a church, do not wait to be invited. Take the initiative; call the pastor of a nearby church where Christ is honored and His Word is preached. Start this week, and make plans to attend regularly.

Suggestions for Christian Growth

Spiritual growth results from trusting Jesus Christ. "The righteous man shall live by faith" (Galatians 3:11). A life of faith will enable you to trust God increasingly with every detail of your life.

* * * * *

Steven L. Pogue has written an excellent book designed to help you make the most of your new life in Christ. The title is **The First Year of Your Christian Life,** and it is available in Christian bookstores everywhere, or you can call 1-800-854-5659 (714/886-7981 in California) to order from the publisher.

Reference Notes

Author's Comment

1. Letitia Baldrige, *Complete Guide to Executive Manners* (New York: Rawson Associates, 1985), p. xix.

Chapter 1

1. Quoted anonymously in Josh McDowell, *Why Wait?* (San Bernardino, CA: Here's Life Publishers, 1987), p. 115.

2. Sue Mitfenthal, "New Sexual Attitudes," *Glamour* (September 1985), p. 338.

3. Ibid., p. 339.

4. Ibid., p. 425.

5. Jess Lair, *Sex, If I Didn't Laugh I'd Cry* (New York: Fawcett Crest, 1979), p. 8.

6. Ramona Kabotzmih, "Parting Shots," *Ms.* (September 1985), p. 45.

7. Robin Norwood, "TV," *People* (December 1985), p. 47.

8. Don Wildmon, "Monitoring Ratings for 1984," distributed by the publishers of the *National Federation of Decency [NFD] Journal.*

9. Ruth Simpson, *From the Closet to the Courts* (New York: Viking Press, 1976), pp. 56-57.

10. The writings of Philo and Josephus speak of this, and the film "Yentl" is a reasonably accurate reflection of prevailing Jewish attitudes and prejudices at that time.

11. David Givens, "The Casual Zone," *Harper's Bazaar* (February 1985), p. 177.

12. Ingrid Bengis, *Combat in the Erogenous Zone* (New York: Alfred A. Knopf, Inc., 1972), p. 239.

13. Ibid., p. 208.

14. Givens, *Casual Zone*, p. 216.

15. Ibid., p. 216.

16. John 8:34.

17. Dr. Patrick Carnes, *Sexual Addiction* (Minneapolis: Camp Care, 1985), p. 89.

18. Bengis, *Combat*, pp. 218-20.

Chapter 2

1. Ezekiel 16:8.

2. Genesis 12.

3. Ezekiel 16:15.

4. Jeremiah 3:1,2.

5. Psalm 51:4.

6. Genesis 39:9.

7. Genesis 1:27.

8. Ephesians 3:10,11.

9. Revelation 1:5.
10. Titus 1:16.
11. Colossians 3:5,6.
12. Evan Thomas, "Growing Pains at 40," *Time* (May 19, 1986), p. 37.
13. *Food for Fitness*, A World Publication (New York, 1982), p. 47.
14. 1 Peter 2:19.
15. Linda Lovelace, *Ordeal* (New York: Berkley Publishers, Affiliate of G. P. Putnam's Sons, 1984).

Chapter 3

1. 1 Corinthians 11:27-30.
2. Exodus 12.
3. Isaiah 53:7; John 1:29.
4. This was touched on briefly in chapter 2, referring to Ephesians 5 and 1 Corinthians 6.
5. Genesis 45:4.
6. Daniel 5:2.
7. Nebuchadnezzar was actually a grandfather to Belshazzar, but anybody in one's ancestral line could be referred to as a "father."
8. Hebrews 9:23,24.
9. 1 Peter 2:5; 1 Corinthians 6:18.
10. Ingrid Bengis, *Combat in the Erogenous Zone* (New York: Alfred A. Knopf, 1972), pp. 200-201.

Chapter 4

1. See Matthew 19:3-12.
2. Ezekiel 28:12-19.
3. Job 1 and 2.
4. Revelation 12:7-13.
5. Revelation 20:1-3.
6. Genesis 3:1.
7. Matthew 4:3.
8. Job 1; 1 Peter 5:8.
9. Matthew 13:19.
10. 1 Corinthians 7:5.
11. 2 Corinthians 2:11.
12. 2 Corinthians 4:4.
13. 2 Corinthians 11:3.
14. Ephesians 6:12.
15. 1 Thessalonians 3:5; 1 Timothy 3:6; 5:15.
16. Ephesians 2:2.
17. Luke 22:31.
18. 1 Thessalonians 2:18.
19. John 13:2,27.
20. Acts 5:3.
21. Ephesians 6:12.
22. 1 John 5:19.
23. Romans 7:11.
24. Genesis 3:22.
25. Aldous Huxley, *Ends and Means* (Westport, CT: Greenwood, reprint of 1937 edition), p. 270.

26. Many today do the same; they just don't have Huxley's clarity of thought as to putting their lifestyle together with a consistent philosophy of life.

27. Job 1; Matthew 4.

28. Psalm 11:5.

29. Job 13:24.

30. 2 Corinthians 2:11.

Chapter 5

1. Proverbs 1:7.

2. Nehemiah 5:15.

3. Job 28:28.

4. Psalm 25:12.

5. Ephesians 5:15-17.

6. Genesis 4:7.

7. Romans 5:10.

8. From Genesis 3:1-4.

9. Genesis 3:8. See also John 3:20.

10. Dr. Patrick Carnes, *Sex Addiction* (Minneapolis: Camp Care, 1985), p. 31.

11. Genesis 4:8,19,23,24; 6:2,3,5,7,13; 7:21-24.

12. Psalm 51:4.

13. Luke 14:26.

14. Genesis 3:17; Romans 8:20,21.

15. Genesis 2:17.

16. Genesis 3:19.

17. Mark 7:20-23; Proverbs 4:23; 23:7.

18. Genesis 6:5.

19. Genesis 8:21.

20. Psalm 51:5.

21. Romans 8:2; 1 Corinthians 2:14; Matthew 6:2,5,16; Mark 7:6,7; Romans 8:4; Titus 1:15; 3:5.

22. Jeremiah 17:9, KJV.

23. Romans 3:10-12,18, NKJ.

24. See Romans 8:7.

25. Romans 2:14,15.

26. 2 Corinthians 5:17, NASB.

27. John 15:5.

28. Ephesians 2:12; James 3:5,6,8; 1 John 2:29; 3:9; 4:7; 5:1,4,18.

29. 1 Samuel 9:21.

30. 1 Samuel 13:8-14.

31. 1 Samuel 15:3.

32. 1 Samuel 15:15.

33. 1 Samuel 15:24.

34. 1 Samuel 15:13.

35. 1 Samuel 15:22,23.

36. James 4:4.

37. Philippians 3:18,19.

38. Numbers 20:8.

39. Numbers 20:10,11.

40. Numbers 20:12.

41. Hebrews 11:6.

42. Philippians 3:13,14.
43. Judges 16:28.
44. Romans 11:29.
45. Judges 16:30.
46. 2 Samuel 12:10.

Chapter 6

1. Evan Thomas, "America's Crusade," *Time* (September 15, 1986), pp. 61,65.
2. James 1:22.
3. Romans 8:23.
4. Jim Berniere, "Bad Girls of the Sahara," *Film Comment* (October 1985), p. 17.
5. Romans 6:6.
6. Romans 6:12.
7. Romans 6:18,19,22.
8. 1 Peter 1:18,19; Revelation 5:9.
9. 2 Corinthians 5:21.

Chapter 7

1. No, I didn't see it. This summary came from a novel by Joseph Wambaugh, *The Secrets of Harry Bright* (New York: William Morrow & Co., 1985).
2. Dr. Jerry R. Kirk, *The Mind Polluters* (Nashville: Thomas Nelson, 1985), p. 41.
3. Ibid., p. 34.
4. Ibid., p. 32.
5. Ibid., p. 40.
6. Sam Janis, *The Death of Innocence* (New York: William Morrow & Co., 1981), p. 35.
7. "The War Within: An Anatomy of Lust," *Leadership* (Winter, 1988), p. 38.
8. Laura Lederer, *Take Back the Night* (New York: William Morrow & Co., 1980), p. 84.
9. Ibid., pp. 67-68.
10. Ibid., p. 234.
11. Ibid.
12. *National Federation of Decency [NFD] Journal* (January 1986), p. 6.
13. The conscience is a part of the brain, but it is not being included in this brief discussion.
14. Dr. Victor Cline, "Psychologist cites porn's effects," *NFD Journal* (Tupelo, MS: December 1985), p. 7.
15. Kirk, *Mind Polluters,* p. 27.
16. Don Wildmon, "Child Porn Promoted," *NFD Journal* (December 1986), p. 3.
17. Don Wildmon, "Porn Involved in Sexual Abuse," *NFD Journal* (February 1986), p. 9.
18. Ibid., p. 12.
19. Don Wildmon, "Porn Implicated in Victimization," *NFD Journal* (June 1985), p. 4.
20. Don Wildmon, "Rapist Profile," *NFD Journal* (January 1985), pp. 11-12.
21. Don Wildmon, "Over the Edge," *NFD Journal* (May 1985), p. 2.
22. Don Wildmon, "Sex Offenders Cite Porn Influence," *NFD Journal* (February 1985), p. 3.
23. In 1935, American Civil Liberties Union founder Roger Baldwin said, "I'm for socialism, disarmament and ultimately for abolishing the state as an instrument of violence and compulsion. I seek the social ownership of property, the abolition of the propertied class, and sole control of those who produce wealth. Communism is the goal." (Don Wildmon, "ACLU defends child pornography," *NFD Journal* (September 1986), p. 9.)
24. "Nightline," TV Talk Show, June 20, 1986.

25. Ibid.

26. Don Wildmon, "Florida sheriff cracks down on pornographers," *NFD Journal* (August 1986), p. 17.

27. Dr. Reo M. Christianson, "Perversion and the Public," *NFD Journal* (February 1985), p. 11.

28. Dr. Reo M. Christianson, "The Effects of 'Media Morality,' " *NFD Journal* (August 1986), n.p.

29. Ibid.

30. Don Wildmon, "Sweden's Attitude Toward Pornography is Changing," *NFD Journal* (April 1986), p. 5.

31. Andrea Dwarkin, "Pornography and Grief," *Take Back the Night* (New York: G. P. Putnam and Sons, 1986), p. 288.

32. Ibid., p. 204.

33. Ibid., p. 205.

34. Don Wildmon, "Abuse Victim Kills Husband," *NFD Journal* (May 1986), p. 22.

35. Kirk, *Mind Polluters,* p. 23.

Chapter 8

1. "Ava just wanted to be a homebody," *San Bernardino Sun* (December 14, 1982), p. C2.

2. Carol Bowin, "Advice," *New Woman* (September 1986), p. 38.

3. Lois Armstrong, "A Mother's Plea," *People* (September 8, 1986), p. 95.

4. Mike Yorkey, "SBCs on the Move," *Focus on the Family* (n.d.), p. 5.

5. Ibid., p. 6.

6. Ingrid Bengis, *Combat in the Errogenous Zone* (New York: Alfred A. Knopf, Inc., 1972), p. 198.

7. Elisabeth Elliot, *Passion and Purity* (Old Tappan, NJ: Power Books, Fleming H. Revell Co., 1984), p. 129.

8. 1 Samuel 17.

9. Elliot, *Passion,* p. 54.

10. For a comprehensive list of dating suggestions, see Jim Burne, *Handling Your Hormones* (Laguna Hills, CA: Merit Books, 1984), p. 65.

11. Daniel 4:27.

12. See Psalm 139.

13. Proverbs 18:24.

14. Barry St. Clair, "The Power of Peer Pressure," *Parents and Teenagers* (Wheaton, IL: Victor Books, 1984), p. 628.

15. Jacob V. Lamar, Jr., "Scoring off the Field," *Time* (August 9, 1986), p. 53.

16. For illumination on the relevance of the temperaments, see Tim LaHaye, *Spirit-Controlled Temperament* (Wheaton IL: Tyndale House Publishers, 1966).

17. Romans 12:5.

18. 1 Corinthians 12—14; Romans 12.

19. Ephesians 4:25.

20. 1 Corinthians 12:21.

21. Psalm 139, Psalm 51, Genesis 2.

Chapter 9

1. Most recent statistics published by the Center for Disease Control, Atlanta, Georgia.

2. Gene Antonio, *The AIDS Cover Up* (San Francisco, Ignatius Press, 1987), p. xi.

3. P. M. Boffey, "Top Officials and Experts Urge More AIDS Funds," *New York Times* (September 27, 1985), p. 23.

4. J. R. Carlson, et al., "AIDS Serology Testing in Low and High Risk Groups" (Chicago: Journal of American Medical Association [JAMA], 1985), 253:3405-08.

5. "Follow Up on Kaposi's Sarcoma and Pneumocystic Pneumonia," *Morbidity and Mortality Weekly Report* [MMWR] (Washington, D. C.: U. S. Government, August 28, 1981), n.p.

6. Conference Report, Second International Conference on the Acquired Immune Deficiency Syndrome, *Medical Journal of Australia* (November 17, 1986), p. 529.

7. J. Seale, "AIDS Virus Infection: Prognosis and Transmission," *J. Royal Soc. Med.* (1985), 78:613-615.

8. J. A. Levy, et al., "Infection by the Retrovirus Associated With the Acquired Immunodeficiency Syndrome; Clinical, Biological, and Molecular Features," *Annals of Internal Medicine* (London: Annals of Internal Medicine, 1985), 103:694-99. Fujikawax, et al., "Isolation of Human T-Lymphotropic Virus Type III From Tears of a Patient With Acquired Immunodeficiency Syndrome," *Lancet* (London: 1985, British medical periodical), 2:529.

9. J. Lawrence, "The Immune System in AIDS," *Scientific American* (1985), 253:84-93.

10. S. Z. Salahuddin, et al., "HTLV-III in symptom-free seronegative persons" (Lancet, 1984), ii:1418.

11. R. Restak, "Worry About Survival of Society First, Then AIDS Victims' Rights," *Washington Post* (September 8, 1985), n.p.

12. L. Montagnier, "Lymphadenopathy-Associated Virus: From Molecular Biology to Pathogenicity," *Annals of Internal Medicine* (London: Annals of Internal Medicine, 1985), 103:689-93.

13. "Homosexuals and AIDS," *Science* (New York: Cornell Medical Center, Dept. of Obstetrics and Gynecology, April 27, 1984), 131:21:326.

14. Joel L. Nitzkin, M.D., and Mark J. Merkins, M.D., Monroe County Department of Health, Rochester, N.Y., Letter to the Editor, JAMA (1985), 253:3398, citing draft federal regulations in the MMWR (1985), 34:1-5.

15. J. W. Curran, "The Epidemiology and Prevention of the Acquired Immunodeficiency Syndrome," *Ann. of Int. Medicine* (1985), 103:659.

16. Joe Levine, "The Toughest Virus of All," *Time* (November 3, 1986), p. 78.

17. Robert T. Francouer, "The Silent Epidemics Behind the AIDS Epidemic," *The Humanist* (July/August, 1987), p. 25.

18. J. I. Slaff and J. K. Brubaker, *The AIDS Epidemic: How You Can Protect Yourself and Your Family—Why You Must* (New York: Warner Books, 1985), pp. 173-74.

19. Art Myott, "Health Care Economics and AIDS," *The Humanist* (July/August, 1987), pp. 18-20.

20. L. K. Altman, "Global Program Aims to Combat AIDS Disaster," *New York Times* (November 21, 1986), n.p.

21. Slaff and Brubaker, *AIDS Epidemic,* pp. 162-63.

22. Johathan M. Mann, "The Global AIDS Situation," *World Health* (June 1987), pp. 6-8.

23. Ibid., p. 7.

24. Claudia Wells, "Medicine," *Time* (November 3, 1986), p. 73.

25. *Fort Worth Star-Telegram* (July 30, 1985), n.p.

26. Motagnier, "Lymphadenopathy-Associated Virus," 103:689-93.

27. Slaff and Brubaker, *AIDS Epidemic,* p. 142.

28. M. Cinnons, "TB Could Serve as Early Warning Against AIDS," *Dallas Times Herald* (November 28, 1985), n.p.

29. G. M. Shaw, et al., "HTLV-III Infection in Brains of Children and Adults with AIDS Encephalopathy," *Science* (1985), 227:177-82.

30. Antonio, *AIDS Cover Up,* p. 25.

31. Seale, "AIDS Virus Infection, p. 614.

32. Slaff and Brubaker, *AIDS Epidemic,* p. 171.

33. Ibid., p. 8.

34. Levine, "Toughest Virus," p. 78.

35. "AIDS-Associated Virus Yields Data to Intensify Scientific Study," JAMA (November 1985), pp. 2865-66.

36. M. Essex et al., "Antigens of Human T-Lymphotropic Virus Type III Lymphadenopathy-Associated Viruses," *Ann. of Int. Med. (1985), 103:700-703.*

37. Seale, "AIDS Virus Infection," p. 614.

38. Antonio, *AIDS Cover Up,* p. 33.

39. David G. Ostrow, Terri A. Sandholzer and Yehudi M. Felman, *Sexually Transmitted Diseases in Homosexual Men* (New York: Plenum Medical Book Co., 1983), pp. 141-49.

40. Ibid., p. 129.

41. H. W. Jaffe et al., "National Case Control Study of Kaposi's Sarcoma and Pneumocystis Carinii Pneumonia in Homosexual Men: Part 2, Laboratory Results" (London: Annals of Internal Medicine, 1983), 99:145-51.

42. G. M. Marligit et al., "Chronic Immune Stimulation by Sperm Alloantigens; Support for the Hypothesis That Spermatozoa Induce Immune Disregulation in Homosexual Males," JAMA (1984), 251:237-41.

43. *Science* (April 27, 1984). Also S. Hsia et al., "Unregulated Production of Virus and/or Sperm Specific Anti-Idiotypic Antibodies as a Cause of AIDS," *Lancet,* (June 2, 1984), pp. 1212-14.

44. Marligit, "Sperm Alloantigens," p. 241.

45. Enrique T. Rueda, *The Homosexual Network,* p. 89, citing *The Journal* (published in Manitou Springs, Colorado: June 1, 1981), the *Sacramento Bee* (California: March 13, 1981).

46. Ostrow, *Diseases,* p. 204.

47. J. Wever, "Is AIDS an Epidemic Form of African Kaposi's Sarcoma?" Discussion paper, *Journal of the Royal Society of Medicine* [JRSM] (London: JRSM, 1984), pp. 572-75.

48. A. P. Bell and M. S. Weinberg, *Homosexualities: A Study of Diversity Among Men and Women* (New York: Simon & Schuster, Inc., 1978), p. 312.

49. Ibid., p. 239.

50. Rueda, *Homosexual Network,* p. 37.

51. Ibid.

52. Slaff, *AIDS Epidemic,* p. 184.

53. Herald Voth, *Families, the Future of America* (Washington, D. C.: Regnery Gateway Press, 1984), p. 96.

54. M. Chase, "Bad Blood," *Wall Street Journal* (March 12, 1984), n.p.

55. Council on Scientific Affairs of the American Medical Association (JAMA, October 1984), 252:2042.

56. Rueda, *Homosexual Network,* p. 509.

57. Charles Rice, *Legalizing Homosexual Conduct: The Role of the Supreme Court in the Gay Rights Movement* (Cumberland, VA: Center for Judicial Studies, 1984), pp. 19-20.

58. S. K. Ortiz, "Medical Aspects of Homosexuality," *New England Journal of Medicine,* pp. 463-64.

59. Marlin Maddous, *America Betrayed* (Shreveport, LA: Huntington House, 1984), p. 93.

60. Dr. J. L. Fletcher, "Homosexuality: Kick and Kickback," *South Medical Journal* (n.pub., 1984), 77:149-50.

61. New Body Family Services Series, "Safe Sex" (booklet distributed by GCR Pub. Group, Inc., New York, 1986), p. 4.

62. Cheryl Russel, Editor-in-Chief of American Demographics, writing in the *Wall Street Journal* (n.d., n.p.).

63. "Unfaithfully Yours: Adultery in America," *People* (August 18, 1986), p. 89.

64. Restak, "Worry", p. 33.

Chapter 10

1. Francis A. Schaeffer and C. Everett Koop, M.D., *Whatever Happened to the Human Race?* (Old Tappan, NJ: Fleming H. Revell Co., 1979), p. 25.

2. Number of men killed in the Revolutionary War, 23,324; Civil War, 498,332; World War I, 116,708; World War II, 407,316; Korean Conflict, 54,246; Viet Nam, 58,655. Total 1,160,581. Abortions since 1973, more than 20,000,000 (based on statistics from the Center for Disease Control, Atlanta, Georgia).

3. As of 1980, the Natality Division of the National Center for Health Statistics, Washington, D.C., no longer makes these statistics available. The information may be obtainable state by state.

4. "The Dreaded Complication," *Philadelphia Inquirer* (August 2, 1981), p. 13.

5. Bernard N. Nathanson, M.D., *Aborting America* (Toronto, Canada: Life Cycle Books, 1979), p. 192.

6. Landrum B. Shettles, M.D., PhD., *Rites of Life* (Grand Rapids: Zondervan Publishing House, 1983), pp. 56-57.

7. Thomas Verney and John Kelly, *The Secret Life of the Unborn Child* (New York: Human Sciences Press, Inc., 1985), pp. 196-97.

8. Claudia Wallis, "Privacy," *Time* (July 6, 1987), p. 83.

9. Dr. Raymond S. Duff and Dr. A. C. M. Campbell, "Moral and Ethical Dilemmas in the Special Care Nursery," *New England Journal of Medicine* (October 1973), p. 221.

10. "Treating the Defective Newborn," *Hastings Center Report* (April 1976), p. 2.

11. Anthony Shaw et al., "Ethical Issues in Pediatric Surgery: A National Survey of Pediatricians and Pediatric Surgeons," *Pediatrics* (October 1977), vol. 60, 4:2:588-99.

12. C. Everett Koop, "Pro and Con," *U.S. News and World Report* (January 16, 1984), n.p.

13. Schaeffer and Koop, *Whatever Happened*, p. 61.

14. Ibid., p. 62.

15. Ibid., p. 73.

16. Ibid.

17. Ibid., p. 72.

18. Judith Blake, "The Supreme Court's Abortion Decisions and Public Opinion in the United States" (South Bend, IN: Notre Dame Press, 1977), p. 6.

19. Connecticut Mutual Life Report on American Values (Hartford, CT: Connecticut Mutual Life Insurance Co., 1981), p. 1.

20. Human Life Federation Amendment (Washington, D. C.: National Right to Life Educational Trust Fund, 1986), p. 50.

21. Donald Shoemaker, *Abortion, the Bible and the Christian* (Cincinnati, OH: Hays Publishing Co., 1982), p. 51.

Chapter 11

1. Donna Jackson, "Sex Survey," *New Woman* (October 1986), p. 95.

2. Evan Thomas, "Growing Pains at 40," *Time* (May 19, 1986), p. 23.

3. Hebrews 2:10; 5:8.

4. 1 Peter 2:21.

5. 1 Peter 4:1.

6. John 15:18.

7. Fred Bernstein, "Tube," *People* (March 9, 1987), p. 98.

8. Jeremiah 17:10.

9. Colossians 1:23.

Chapter 12

1. Matthew 11:30.

2. John 10:10.
3. John 6:47.
4. Colossians 1:26,27.
5. John 15:5.
6. Romans 12:1.
7. Colossians 3:4.
8. 2 Corinthians 12:9, KJV.
9. 1 Corinthians 1:24.
10. Romans 6:4.
11. Philippians 1:21.
12. Hebrews 4:8,9.
13. Hebrews 11:10.
14. 2 Corinthians 7:4.
15. Romans 6:13.
16. Nehemiah 8:10.
17. 1 John 5:3.
18. Romans 8:4.
19. Galatians 4:19.
20. 2 Corinthians 3:18.
21. Hebrews 11:6.
22. 2 Peter 1:5-10.
23. Philippians 3:3.
24. Philippians 4:19.
25. Titus 3:8.
26. Jude 24.

Chapter 13

1. Acts 13:36.
2. "Milestones," *Time* (August 23, 1982), p. 64.
3. Hebrews 9:27.
4. Luke 16:19-31.
5. Hebrews 12:1.
6. Luke 10:18.

Epilog

1. The loss of virginity is not merely penetration—it is an act of the will. In a culture such as current-day United States, where there is a rape every six minutes and one out of every three or four girls is molested as a child, it has become critical to make this differentiation. If one's only "sexual" experience is this type of aggression, a person should consider himself or herself a virgin. Virginity is not simply a physical issue; it is a moral issue.

2. R. C. Sproul, *The Holiness of God* (Wheaton, IL: Tyndale House Publishers, 1987), pp. 49-50.